# A Practical Guide to Survey Questionnaire Design and Evaluation

*A Practical Guide to Survey Questionnaire Design and Evaluation* summarizes principles, guidelines, and best practices for developing and testing survey questionnaires driven and supported by theoretical and empirical research. It provides a broad overview of literature on questionnaire design, drawing on both theoretical and empirical research.

This book consists of three parts. The first covers the survey response process model, which will serve as the theoretical framework to establish the basic principles of writing different types of survey questions (attitudinal, behavioral, demographic, and knowledge). The second part of this book focuses on special topics such as sensitive questions, developing questionnaires for older adults and children, designing a paper survey, designing a web survey and optimizing for a mobile device, developing questionnaires for a multi-mode survey, and conducting surveys in multiple languages and cultures. The third part of this book describes methods for testing and evaluating survey questions. Topics cover focus groups, cognitive interviewing, expert review, Questionnaire Appraisal System, behavior coding, respondent and interviewer debriefing, randomized experiments, and pilot studies. Given extensive web survey coverage, we also discuss usability testing of web surveys. Finally, we present a brief overview of the use of artificial intelligence and machine learning for questionnaire development and evaluation. Suggestions for further reading, case studies, and discussion questions are included in all chapters.

This book will be of interest to those using survey methodology/questionnaires and graduate courses incorporating survey design across the social and behavioral sciences, including psychology, communication studies, nursing and healthcare research, sociology, anthropology, and education.

**Emilia Peytcheva** is a senior survey methodologist at RTI International and an adjunct assistant professor at the University of North Carolina, Chapel Hill, USA. She holds a Ph.D. in survey methodology from the University of Michigan and has 25 years of experience designing and implementing surveys in different modes.

**Ting Yan** is a Vice President at NORC at the University of Chicago, USA, and an adjunct research associate professor at the University of Maryland and University of Michigan, USA. She holds a Ph.D. in Survey Methodology from the University of Maryland and has more than 25 years of experience in questionnaire design and evaluation. She has published extensively on survey methodology.

# A Practical Guide to Survey Questionnaire Design and Evaluation

Emilia Peytcheva and Ting Yan

LONDON AND NEW YORK

Designed cover image: Getty Images - Andrii Yalanskyi

First published 2025
by Routledge
4 Park Square, Milton Park, Abingdon, Oxon OX14 4RN

and by Routledge
605 Third Avenue, New York, NY 10158

*Routledge is an imprint of the Taylor & Francis Group, an informa business*

© 2025 Emilia Peytcheva and Ting Yan

The right of Emilia Peytcheva and Ting Yan to be identified as authors of this work has been asserted in accordance with sections 77 and 78 of the Copyright, Designs and Patents Act 1988.

All rights reserved. No part of this book may be reprinted or reproduced or utilised in any form or by any electronic, mechanical, or other means, now known or hereafter invented, including photocopying and recording, or in any information storage or retrieval system, without permission in writing from the publishers.

*Trademark notice*: Product or corporate names may be trademarks or registered trademarks, and are used only for identification and explanation without intent to infringe.

*British Library Cataloguing-in-Publication Data*
A catalogue record for this book is available from the British Library

ISBN: 978-1-032-43540-4 (hbk)
ISBN: 978-1-032-43541-1 (pbk)
ISBN: 978-1-003-36782-6 (ebk)

DOI: 10.4324/9781003367826

Typeset in Optima LT Std
by KnowledgeWorks Global Ltd.

# Contents

**PART I**
**Survey Response Model and Questionnaire Design**     1

  1  Introduction     3
  2  Survey Response Model     10
  3  Writing Behavioral Questions     19
  4  Writing Attitudinal Questions     26
  5  Writing Demographic and Knowledge Questions     36

**PART II**
**Specific Considerations**     45

  6  Writing Sensitive Questions and Questions for Sensitive Populations     47
  7  Design of Paper Surveys     59
  8  Design of Web and Mobile Web Surveys     69
  9  Designing Multimode Surveys     85
 10  Design of Multiregion, Multiculture, and Multilanguage Surveys     94

**PART III**
**Questionnaire Evaluation and Testing**     103

 11  Lab-based Methods     105
 12  Expert Methods     113
 13  Field-based Methods     120
 14  Usability Testing     129
 15  Use of Artificial Intelligence (AI) and Generative AI (GAI) for Questionnaire Design and Evaluation     134

    *Bibliography*     *138*
    *Index*     *159*

# Part I
# Survey Response Model and Questionnaire Design

# 1 Introduction

Writing survey questions begins with defining a research objective; that is, what the researchers want to study and measure with the survey. For instance, the goal of the National Crime Victimization Survey (NCVS) is to measure the level of crime victimization in the United States. The next step is to identify constructs (i.e., elements of information) that are sought by the researcher (Groves et al., 2004). In the NCVS, one of the constructs to be measured is nonfatal personal and household property victimizations. Because constructs are theoretical in nature and tend to be broad and multidimensional, question writers need to identify dimensions of a construct (e.g., nonfatal personal crimes include rape or sexual assault, robbery, aggravated and simple assault, and personal larceny) and develop a taxonomy, reflecting the relationships among dimensions and subdimensions (e.g., larceny is a lesser theft than robbery). The goal of this process is to derive a list of single-dimensioned non-overlapping domains that can be operationalized with survey questions. Figure 1.1 presents a simplified example of how we move from a broad theoretical construct to specific indicators (without presenting the actual questions).

The next step is to identify what types of questions will be most appropriate, depending on the constructs or domains – opinions/knowledge about the types of crimes or experiences of crimes. Finally, we gather information on how respondents from our target population talk about these dimensions and subdimensions of the concepts of interest and using their vocabulary, translate the concepts into survey questions with respective response options. For example, focusing on the construct of identity theft, the NCVS asks questions for

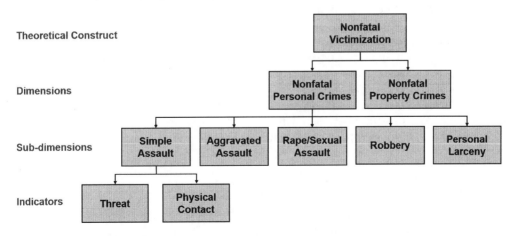

*Figure 1.1* Taxonomy Example of Moving from Constructs to Specific Question Topics.

DOI: 10.4324/9781003367826-2

each of the three dimensions defining identity theft – unauthorized use or attempted use of an existing account, unauthorized use or attempted use of personal information to open a new account, and misuse of personal information for a fraudulent purpose:

> Since [DATE], have you or anyone in your household discovered that someone...
>
> a  Used or attempted to use any existing credit cards or credit card numbers without permission to place charges on an account (Yes, No, Don't Know)
> b  Used or attempted to use any existing accounts other than a credit card account – for example, a wireless telephone account, bank account or debit/check cards – without the account holder's permission to run up charges or to take money from accounts (Yes, No, Don't Know)
> c  Used or attempted to use personal information without permission to obtain NEW credit cards or loans, run up debts, open other accounts, or otherwise commit theft, fraud or some other crime (Yes, No, Don't Know)

In the following sections, we introduce the typology of survey questions, briefly discuss the types of survey error, and focus on mechanisms that induce measurement error, given that this type of error is of most concern for questionnaire designers. The rest of this book discusses how to write various types of survey questions, focusing on design considerations motivated by the survey response model presented in Chapter 2.

**Types of Survey Questions**

We distinguish among four types of survey questions that are discussed in detail in Chapters 3–5:

- **Factual or behavioral questions** typically measure what happened, when it happened, and how often it happened. There is an objective truth associated with such questions even though it is rarely available to researchers. Chapter 3 addresses how to write factual or behavioral questions.
- **Attitudinal questions** measure opinions and perceptions about an attitudinal object. There is no truth associated with such questions because they are subjective in nature. The lack of an objective standard makes it hard to detect measurement error in attitudinal questions. Chapter 4 focuses on developing attitudinal questions.
- **Demographic questions** measure respondents' characteristics that may vary in terms of objective elements (e.g., age) or subjective elements (e.g., ethnicity and gender). Chapter 5 includes guidelines and recommendations for writing demographic questions.
- **Knowledge questions** measure respondents' knowledge on a particular topic. There is an objective truth associated with these questions and it is known to researchers. Such questions are sometimes used to screen out respondents who do not have enough knowledge to answer follow-up attitudinal questions. Guidelines and recommendations on writing knowledge are discussed in Chapter 5.

Another typology divides survey questions by question structure type:

- **Open-ended questions** do not present answer choices; respondents use their own words to provide a response.
- **Closed questions** provide respondents with a list of ordered or unordered answer choices. They can be multiple-choice questions (e.g., offering a frequency scale such

Introduction 5

as *Always, Most of the Time, Half of the Time, Less than Half of the Time, Never*) or simple questions (e.g., offering Yes/No response options).
- **Partially closed questions** provide a list of ordered or unordered answer categories and also include an open-ended option at the end, for example, "*Other (Please Specify).*"
- **Field-coded questions** are administered as open-ended, but interviewers code verbatim responses provided by respondents into one of a set of predefined categories.

Some questions are considered sensitive because they are potentially intrusive, are associated with perceived risk of disclosure to third parties, or invoke social desirability concerns. Chapter 6 offers suggestions on how to write sensitive questions.

**Survey Errors**

Survey researchers are concerned with errors that can occur at each stage of the survey process. We define "error" as any deviation or departure from the desired outcome (Groves et al., 2004). Groves et al. (2004) present the survey lifecycle from a design perspective, demonstrating how a survey moves from the questionnaire design and data collection phases to survey statistics, adding a quality component that indicates where survey errors are likely to occur (Figure 1.2).

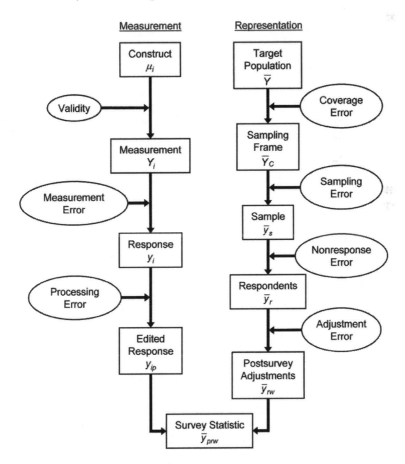

*Figure 1.2* Survey Lifecycle from a Quality Perspective.

Groves et al. (2004) identify six main types of survey errors, classified as either errors of non-observation or errors of observation. The left-hand side of Figure 1.2 presents errors of observation (i.e., we have collected data from the sample member, but there are quality issues with the data collection process); the right-hand side presents errors of non-observation (we have failed to collect data from the sampled member, leading to quality issues). We briefly describe each of the errors below.

*Errors of Non-observation*

- Coverage error occurs because not everyone from the target population is represented on the sampling frame.[1] For instance, an address frame does not include homeless people, resulting in coverage error.
- Sampling error occurs because we are not conducting a census of the target population, but rather estimating a population parameter (such as mean or total) on a sample selected from the sampling frame. If we select a different sample, we would likely get a different estimate; thus, there is a sampling error associated with each survey statistic estimated from a sample.
- Nonresponse error is associated with failure to obtain responses from all eligible sampled units.
- Adjustment error occurs because of weighting or other adjustments to correct for sampling, nonresponse, or coverage errors.

*Errors of Observation*

- Validity reflects the gap between what a survey question intends to measure (i.e., measurement) and the theoretical construct it is supposed to measure.
- Measurement error occurs when answers provided by respondents to survey questions deviate from the truth. Going back to the example in Figure 1.1, we may discover that respondents intentionally misreport their true value on questions related to rape and sexual assault because the questions were too sensitive.
- Processing error is a result of any editing, coding, or imputation during data processing.

Each type of error has its own set of sources. This book is about writing survey questions; thus, our attention will focus on measurement error and the mechanisms that cause it.

**Measurement Error**

Various disciplines have slightly different perspectives on measurement error and potential fixes for it. Survey methodology combines the statistical view and the cognitive perspective. The statistical view on measurement error defines it as the discrepancy between the true and observed values:

$$y_{ij} = X_i + \varepsilon_{ij}$$

where $y_{ij}$ is the actual answer provided by respondent $i$ to question $j$;
$X_i$ is the true value for respondent $i$; and
$\varepsilon_{ij}$ is the measurement error in the actual response provided by respondent $i$ to question $j$.

The goal of statisticians is to measure $\varepsilon_{ij}$ and adjust for it. They are interested in bias (the systematic effect of $\varepsilon_{ij}$) and variance (the variation of $\varepsilon_{ij}$ across respondents) in a survey estimate. When we talk about bias, often we use terms such as *underreporting* when we underestimate the true value and *overreporting* when we overestimate the true value.

The cognitive view on measurement error is mostly concerned with the mechanisms that produce measurement error – for example, question misunderstanding, memory failure, and social desirability – and how to minimize their influences. We will adopt both views in this book, using them to lay the foundations for best practices and recommendations on writing survey questions with minimal measurement error.

Five main sources of measurement error are found in surveys: measurement error can occur because of the interviewer, the respondent, the mode of data collection, the survey questionnaire, or the language in which the questionnaire is administered. Measurement error because of the interviewer can be a result of observable (e.g., race and gender) or unobservable characteristics of interviewers (e.g., rapport with respondents) and interviewing techniques (e.g., pace of the interview). In fact, the survey literature is rich with examples of interviewer effects on survey estimates because of interviewer characteristics (e.g., Bailar et al., 1977; Fellegi, 1964; Rice, 1929; Schnell, 1997) or interviewing techniques (e.g., Hill & Hall, 1963; Mensch & Kandel, 1988; Olson & Peytchev, 2007; Weiss, 1968). For example, African American interviewers obtained lower levels of hostility and fear toward African Americans from white respondents than white interviewers (Schuman & Hatchett, 1976), and in a longitudinal study, Mensch and Kandel (1988) found lower reports of drug use when respondents were familiar with the interviewer. A large body of literature has demonstrated a significant component of variance because of interviewers for both sensitive and nonsensitive survey questions (e.g., Belak & Vehovar, 1995; Collins & Butcher, 1982; Davis & Scott, 1995; Fellegi, 1964; Gray, 1956; Groves, 1989; Groves & Magilavy, 1986; Hansen et al., 1960; Hanson & Marks, 1958; Kish, 1962; O'Muircheartaigh & Campanelli, 1998; O'Muircheartaigh & Wiggins, 1981; Schnell & Kreuter, 2005; Tucker, 1983), including self-administered items, when the interviewer is present in the room (e.g., Collins & Butcher, 1982; Groves & Magilavy, 1986; Mangione et al., 1992; O'Muircheartaigh & Campanelli, 1998).

Measurement error because of the respondent can be a result of respondent limitations or characteristics (e.g., cognitive ability, tendency to acquiesce, or provide socially desirable responses). Three chapters focus on questionnaire characteristics related to measurement error and ways to minimize the potential for it through deliberately manipulating the survey layout, controlling context effects, and minimizing question ambiguity and cognitive burden (Chapters 3–5). Chapter 6 discusses writing survey questions for two sensitive populations – older adults and children under the age of 18.

The mode of data collection has also been found to affect survey reporting, with self-administered modes yielding more accurate reports of sensitive behaviors than interviewer administration (e.g., Bradburn, 1983; Jones & Forrest, 1992; Miller et al., 1990; Schwarz et al., 1991a; Turner et al., 1992). However, there is puzzling evidence of interviewer effects in self-administered modes like audio computer-assisted self-interviewing when an interviewer is present (e.g., Hughes et al., 2002; O'Muircheartaigh & Campanelli, 1998; West & Peytcheva, 2014). We discuss questionnaire design for two self-administered modes (paper surveys in Chapter 7 and web and mobile web surveys in Chapter 8). Chapter 9 discusses designing questionnaires for studies mixing multiple modes of data collection.

Finally, the language in which a survey is administered impacts the survey response process (Peytcheva, 2020; Schwartz et al., 2010). To the extent to which language can cue socially desirable reporting through its link to cultural values and norms, it can induce measurement error. For example, one of the first studies that discovered the effect of language on survey responding was an experiment by Triandis et al. (1965), where Greek-English bilinguals were asked the same questions in both languages. The study found low correlation between responses provided by the same respondents when the questions differed in social desirability in the Greek and American cultures. Subsequent studies have demonstrated that language can be a powerful cue to the cultural frame that respondents adopt; they may provide completely different responses to the same questions, depending on the language used to ask those questions (e.g., Marian & Neisser, 2000; Marin et al., 1983; Peytcheva, 2019; Ross et al., 2002; Schrauf & Rubin, 2000; Trafimow et al., 1997). We discuss questionnaire design considerations for multilanguage surveys in Chapter 10.

**Assessing Measurement Error**

As with any type of survey error, we need to know the true value, in addition to the observed one, to be able to quantify the measurement error component. Administrative records, split ballot experiments, repeated measurements, and parallel or alternative measures (including physical measurements) have been used to estimate measurement bias. However, in most cases, estimation of bias is practically impossible. Thus, within one survey administration, we resort to proxy indicators for measurement error bias, such as item missingness, inconsistency of responses, context effects (including primacy and recency), mode differences, time on task, acquiescence,[2] and straightlining.[3]

Psychometricians use concepts such as validity and reliability to gauge the quality of their measures. In surveys, validity refers to the extent to which a survey question accurately measures the construct of interest, while reliability refers to variability of responses over repetitions. Chapter 13 describes how reliability and validity can be assessed through simple statistics (such as correlations and kappas) and complex modeling techniques (such as Multitrait-Multimethod Modeling and Item Response Theory).

Chapters 11 and 12 provide approaches commonly used by survey methodologists and question writers to evaluate and test survey questions. Chapter 14 discusses usability testing of survey instruments. These approaches are useful tools to reduce measurement error arising from questions and modes of data collection.

**About This Book**

This book is intended to be an introductory and practical textbook on questionnaire design. Our first objective is to present a broad overview of the existing literature, drawing on both theoretical and empirical research. Our second objective is to present practical principles, guidelines, and best practices for developing and testing survey questions.

This book consists of three themes. The first is the survey response process model (Schwartz et al., 1996; Tourangeau, 1984; Tourangeau et al., 2000), which will serve as the theoretical framework to establish the basic principles of writing different types of survey questions. These principles and best practices are supported by both keystone theoretical and experimental studies and the latest research. We present the cognitive processes related to answering survey questions (Chapter 2), followed by detailed discussion on how to write different types of survey questions (Chapters 3-5), knowing the theoretical framework of the survey response model.

The second part of this book focuses on special topics such as asking sensitive questions (Chapter 6), developing questionnaires for older people and children (Chapter 6), designing paper surveys (Chapter 7), designing web surveys and optimizing the questionnaire for mobile devices (Chapter 8), developing questionnaires for a multimode survey (Chapter 9), and conducting surveys in multiple languages and cultures (Chapter 10).

The third theme of this book focuses on methods for testing and evaluating survey questions (Chapters 11–13). Topics include, but are not limited to, focus groups, cognitive interviewing, expert review, Questionnaire Appraisal System, behavior coding, respondent and interviewer debriefing, experimental pretest, and pilot studies. Given extensive web survey coverage, we also discuss usability testing for self-administered surveys (Chapter 14). The last chapter (Chapter 15) provides a brief overview of the use of artificial intelligence and machine learning for questionnaire development and evaluation.

Even though this book is about writing survey questions, invaluable sources are available that can be used to find questions that match one's research objective and can be used as is or adapted for one's own purposes. Below are some of the question banks that we recommend:

- https://wwwn.cdc.gov/qbank/
- https://www.pewresearch.org/politics/question-search/
- www.icpsr.umich.edu

## Notes

1 A sampling frame is the listing of all units in the target population.
2 The tendency of respondents to agree with the question statement, regardless of how they actually feel.
3 The tendency of respondents to select the same response option for questions that use the same scale, especially when presented in a grid.

# 2 Survey Response Model

**Introduction**

According to the most influential conceptual framework of the survey response process (Sudman et al., 1996; Tourangeau, 1984; Tourangeau et al., 2000), respondents undergo four cognitive stages when answering a survey question (Figure 2.1). We will use a question from the Consumer Expenditure Surveys (CE) as an example to illustrate the four stages of the survey response process:

> In the last 12 months, how much did (you/your household) spend on your last purchase of living room, family, or recreation room furniture?

The first stage is **comprehension**. Respondents must understand the meaning of the survey question as intended by the question writer to provide a meaningful answer. For instance, they have to figure out what counts as "living room, family, or recreation room furniture" and what the reference period (the last 12 months) covers. They also must understand the intent of the survey question. In this instance, the question writer wants to know the expenditure of the respondent's *last* purchase of living room, family, or recreation room furniture in the last 12 months.

The second stage is **retrieval** of information. Respondents search for relevant information (say, all purchases of living room, family, or recreation room furniture that occurred in the last 12 months) in their long-term memory and move the retrieved information to their working memory. This stage follows the determination that the survey question asks about expenses of their very last purchase in the last 12 months.

The third stage is **judgment and estimation**. That is, respondents integrate the relevant retrieved information to form an attitude or provide an estimate related to a behavior when the retrieved information cannot be directly used as an answer. In our example, after respondents retrieve all episodes of living room, family, or recreation room furniture that occurred in the last 12 months, they will need to decide which episode represents the last purchase that occurred in the last 12 months and then retrieve the expenditure for that purchase. If the respondents happen to have a receipt of that last purchase and are motivated to do so, they could pull out the amount directly. If they do not have a receipt, they would need to come up with an estimate based on some strategy (e.g., the TV cannot cost more than $500). As we can see from the amount of work required at the retrieval and judgment and estimation stages of the survey response model, this question incurs rather burdensome cognitive tasks that respondents have to engage in to provide an answer.

DOI: 10.4324/9781003367826-3

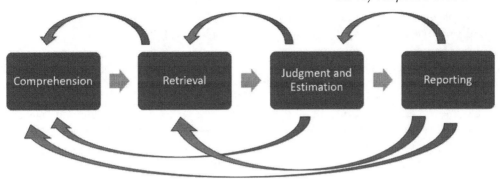

*Figure 2.1* Survey Response Model.

At the fourth stage – **reporting** – respondents edit or map the resultant judgment or estimate to one of the provided response options. Our example question asks respondents to provide a dollar amount. The respondent could report the dollar amount retrieved from the receipt, their memory, their best guess, or an estimate based on some strategy they use. Sometimes, respondents are provided a list of response options and they have to map their estimate into one of the options. At this stage, survey respondents may choose to edit what they retrieved before reporting it, for different reasons. For instance, the respondent may not feel comfortable reporting that their TV costs more than $1,000 and may decide to report that they spent $500 on the TV instead.

Next, we discuss each stage in detail. It is important to note that survey respondents do not necessarily follow the four stages sequentially and conscientiously. It is common that respondents engage in satisficing behaviors by skipping a stage completely or taking a cognitive shortcut at a particular stage (e.g., Krosnick, 1991, 1999). Sometimes respondents may jump ahead (e.g., they start the retrieval stage before the interviewer finishes reading the question) or backtrack (e.g., as respondents are retrieving information, they may go back to the comprehension stage to adjust their understanding of the survey question).

**Comprehension**

Comprehension of a survey question occurs at three levels: syntactical, semantic, and pragmatic (Tourangeau & Bradburn, 2010; Tourangeau et al., 2000). The **syntactical** process involves grammatical analysis of the question to identify its presupposition (What assumption does the question make?) and focus (What information is requested of respondents?). Survey questions with a complex syntactical structure are difficult for respondents to process and answer. Studies using eye-tracking and response times data have demonstrated that longer questions, questions with multiple clauses, negatively phrased questions, and syntactically ambiguous questions are more burdensome and take longer for respondents to understand and answer (Just & Carpenter, 1993; Kamoen et al., 2017; Lenzer et al., 2011; Yan, 2023; Yan & Tourangeau, 2008). As a result, question writers should avoid double-negative questions and double-barreled questions because of their overly complicated syntactical structure. Double-negative questions are questions with more than one negative word in the question stem and response options. An example double-negative question is shown below with the negative words bolded:

> All in all, do you favor or **oppose** Congress passing a law **not** allowing any employer to force an employee to retire at any age? FAVOR, OPPOSE.

Double-negative questions also present an analytic problem when the negative end of a scale is endorsed because it is unclear what the respondent's position truly is. In our example, when a respondent selects "oppose," it is not clear whether opposing a law not allowing any employer to force an employee to retire is the same as favoring a law allowing employers to force employees to retire at any age.

Double-barreled questions are questions asking about more than one topic. An example double-barreled question is shown below with the double topics bolded. The analytical challenge with double-barreled questions is that, when a respondent answers "yes" to this question, it is not clear which of the two things (dealing effectively with AIDS or dealing with sexually transmitted disease) they believe in.

> Do you believe that the U.S. health care system is dealing effectively **with AIDS and with sexually transmitted diseases**?

Another syntactical problem to be avoided is faulty or inappropriate presupposition carried by a survey item. For instance, a survey question asking about the number of hours respondents worked outside in their garden presupposes that respondents have a garden, which is unlikely to be correct for everyone.

**Semantic** comprehension of a survey question is understanding the meaning of each word in the question. There are several hurdles to semantic comprehension. First, technical terms (e.g., myocardial infarction) and idioms (e.g., to build a nest egg) are less likely to be understood uniformly by the general population and thus should be avoided. Second, some words have multiple meanings; for instance, the word "table" can refer to a coffee table or an Excel table. It can also be a verb as in "to table a conversation." Third, vague concepts (e.g., children, ill effects) and vague quantifiers (e.g., very often) mean different things to different people. For example, in a classic study, Belson (1981) showed that some of his respondents took the word "children" to mean young people in general regardless of relationship to themselves whereas others took the word to mean their offspring regardless of age. Schaeffer (1991) demonstrated that white respondents who reported experiencing an emotion "pretty often" actually experienced that emotion about the same number of times per month as black respondents who reported "very often." Fourth, even words commonly used in daily life

> Suessbrick et al. (2000) asked respondents about their understanding of one question used in the Current Population Survey ("Have you smoked at least 100 cigarettes in your entire life?"). About half of their respondents (54%) understood the word "smoking" as including any puffs whether inhaled or not, which is the intended meaning of the question. However, the other half (46%) thought that smoking in this question referred only to puffs that one inhaled and provided an answer based on that misunderstanding.

could be understood in a different way from the one intended by the question writer (see text box example). Fifth, sometimes question concepts do not have a straightforward mapping to a respondent's life circumstances. For instance, the CE question about expenditure of the last purchase of living room, family, or recreation room furniture in the last 12 months applies to the purchase of an end table. However, it is not clear to people whether it also applies to the purchase of a floor lamp (Schober & Conrad, 1997; Schober et al., 2004).

Respondents also need to understand the intent of survey questions, which involves the determination of implicatures or the **pragmatic** meaning of the questions. To infer the pragmatic meaning, respondents resort to principles they engage in everyday conversations, treating a survey as conversational interaction (Conrad et al., 2014; Tourangeau et al., 2000). The philosopher H. Paul Grice introduced the Cooperative Principle as the basis of human interactions (Grice, 1975). The principle assumes that participants in a conversation cooperate with each other, providing information that is relevant (Maxim of Relation), truthful (Maxim of Quality), sufficient but not redundant (Maxim of Quantity), and clear (Maxim of Manner). We assume that survey respondents apply these maxims to make inferences about the intent behind survey questions, drawing on contextual cues and generating answers based on the inferred intent. For instance, respondents are found routinely using contextual cues (such as the survey name, sponsor, prior questions, or response options) to help make sense of survey questions because the context is relevant to the goal of question-answering based on the Maxim of Relation. For example, Galesic and Tourangeau (2007) demonstrated that respondents perceived the same behaviors as more likely to represent sexual harassment when the survey was presented as "Sexual Harassment Survey" than when the survey was called "Work Atmosphere Survey." Similarly, Strack et al. (1991) showed that students made sense of a fictitious law ("educational contribution") based on prior survey items. A random half of students were asked about US tuition whereas the other half were asked about Swedish financial support. Those who were first asked about US tuition inferred that the educational contribution law was about students paying money, whereas those who got the Swedish financial support question took the law to be about students receiving money. In this case, the interpretation is not intended by the question writer.

## Retrieval

Retrieval involves searching for relevant information in long-term memory and moving the retrieved information to short-term or working memory. It is particularly relevant to answering behavioral questions, as shown in Chapter 3.

> Characteristics of events affecting retrieval: time of occurrence, proximity to temporal boundaries, distinctiveness, and importance or emotional impact.

The quality and ease of the retrieval process are affected by characteristics of information being retrieved. First, the older the information, the harder it is to retrieve and the less detailed the retrieved information is (Jobe et al., 1993). Forgetting is a major cause of respondents' underreporting requested information. Second, mundane and frequent events are harder to recall than distinctive and salient events because of blending of memories and changes of memories over time. For instance, people remember better and remember more details about the purchase of a house than a trip to a grocery store. Third, people tend to misdate when an event or behavior occurred, leading them to report an event or experience that occurred outside the reference period, a phenomenon known as telescoping (Neter & Waksberg, 1964). All these factors are relevant to setting the appropriate length of a reference period for questions asking about behaviors.

The example question from CE on expenditure of last purchase of living room, family, and recreation room furniture in the last 12 months is seemingly a cognitively difficult question because it asks people to recall a purchase that occurred during the last 12 months. However, furniture purchase is not a mundane event and is likely memorable. Still, respondents may misdate a purchase or retrieve expenditure for the wrong purchase.

Furthermore, people do not take in everything that happens in their lives. Some information is never noticed and never stored in long-term memory, and, consequently, cannot be recalled, regardless of how we ask about it. For example, Lee et al. (1999) showed empirically that parents did not encode the exact immunizations their children received and thus could not recall what immunizations their children received, regardless of whether they were asked immediately or 2 weeks after the visit and regardless of what recall cues were presented to them. Another encoding problem affecting retrieval is that information might be encoded into a different category or with a different label than what is asked in the survey question. For example, respondents may remember vacuuming three times a week, but they may not encode that piece of information as a "moderate-intensity leisure-time physical activity." As a result, they would not necessarily recall that piece of information when answering the 2022 National Health Interview Survey that asks them how often they do "moderate-intensity leisure-time physical activities." Question writers should be aware of both encoding issues when developing survey questions.

The context in which the survey questions are answered affects this stage. By context, we mean a variety of factors ranging from interview setting and interviewer characteristics to question order, visual layout of response scales, and so on. Chapters 3 and 4 have detailed discussions on the impact of context on survey answers, which are also called context effects. Chapters 7 and 8 also talk about how to guard against context effects in paper and web surveys. At this stage, context affects retrieval by serving as a retrieval cue or by priming certain information for more accessible retrieval. For instance, researchers have found that the correlation of self-reported measures of a specific domain (say, marriage satisfaction) and a general domain (life satisfaction) is higher when the specific question is asked before the general question than when the general question precedes the specific question (Schwarz et al., 1991b; Strack et al., 1988; Tourangeau et al., 1991a, 1991b; also see Mason et al., 1994). This is because answering the specific question on marriage satisfaction has made information about marriage highly accessible in working memory. Because marriage is an important part of life, highly accessible information about marriage is also used to form a judgment about life satisfaction, yielding a high correlation between the two self-reported measures.

In general, providing respondents retrieval cues has been found to improve recall. A retrieval cue is a prompt to memory and provides clues that help with search of long-term memory. Chapter 3 discusses strategies to improve recall, including providing retrieval cues and using landmark events to set a reference period.

## Judgment and Estimation

Sometimes the retrieved information can be directly used as an answer to a survey question. This happens when respondents have an existing attitude or a running tally of events. For instance, people

> Strategies survey respondents adopt to derive an estimate or a judgment: bottom-up, top-down, and impression-based.

typically can retrieve their answers directly from their memory when asked how many houses they have purchased or how they feel about broccoli. However, in the absence of an existing attitude or an estimate, respondents will have to form a judgment or derive an estimate on the spot by applying one of the following estimation strategies to integrate the retrieved information: bottom-up, top-down, or impression-based (Tourangeau, 2018; Tourangeau & Bradburn, 2010; Tourangeau et al., 2000).

With the bottom-up strategy, respondents use specific retrieved information to add up to an estimate or to derive a judgment. To answer a survey question on the number of dental visits in the last 12 months, for instance, respondents add up specific episodes of dental visits recalled (e.g., "I had dental cleaning in February, and I also had two cavities filled in August.") to yield an estimate ("2"). Similarly, when using the bottom-up strategy to generate answers to attitudinal questions, respondents combine specific beliefs or feelings retrieved about a political candidate (e.g., "This candidate supported abortion.") to derive an overall attitude about the candidate ("This candidate must be very liberal"). Also see Tourangeau (2021) for a discussion of the belief-sampling model of forming an attitude on the fly and Chapter 4 on attitudinal questions.

By contrast, with the top-down strategy, respondents project general information (e.g., a rate or a general value) to the specific situation requested by the survey question. For instance, when answering the same question on the number of dental visits in the last 12 months, respondents may apply a retrieved rate (e.g., "twice a year") to the last 12 months to derive an answer ("2") regardless of what actually happened during that period of time. In the same way, respondents may use a retrieved general value (e.g., "Democrat politicians are liberal") to derive their answer to the question about a particular Democrat candidate.

The top-down strategy could be used as an impression-based method, which is often used when all respondents could retrieve is some sort of impression or stereotype. For instance, respondents apply an impression ("I never have dental problems") to yield an answer of zero to the question about dental visits in the last 12 months, and a stereotype ("All politicians are corrupt") to give a negative rating to a particular political candidate.

For questions about behavioral frequency, the survey literature shows that the accuracy of self-reported behavioral frequencies is best when respondents can directly retrieve an answer from their long-term memory and worst when respondents adopt an impression-based strategy (Burton & Blair, 1991). Characteristics of the behavior, such as saliency or importance, frequency, and regularity of the behavior, play a role in respondents' choice of the bottom-up or top-down strategy (Brown, 2002; Sudman et al., 1996). The bottom-up strategy tends to underestimate self-reported behavioral frequency measures because retrieval of specific episodes is likely to be incomplete (Burton & Blair, 1991). The top-up strategy is more likely to overestimate self-reported behaviors because of exceptions to the rate and rate misestimation (Burton & Blair, 1991).

Furthermore, context affects judgment and estimation by suggesting a norm or a standard of comparison to be used as the basis for forming a judgment. For instance, Couper and colleagues (2007) asked web respondents to rate their health. Some of respondents were shown a picture of a healthy woman jogging, while others were presented with an image of a sick woman lying in a hospital bed. Respondents were found to rate themselves healthier when presented with the picture of the sick woman than the healthy woman. This is because respondents used the picture as a basis for comparison, leading to a contrast effect.

**Reporting**

The fourth step is reporting the judgment or estimate derived at the end of the judgment and estimation stage. Closed questions offer respondents a list of response categories. Ideally, respondents can map the recalled or derived judgment or estimate to one of the response options provided to them. Exact match of this type is desired to ensure validity and reliability of self-report measures. However, mapping is not always an easy or straightforward process.

First, respondents sometimes deliberately do *not* choose the response option that best matches their answer. This happens with two types of survey items. When asked a sensitive question invoking social desirability concerns, respondents edit their answer before reporting it to avoid embarrassment or disclosure of behaviors or attitudes that do not conform to societal norms (Tourangeau & Yan, 2007; Yan, 2021; Yan & Cantor, 2019). Chapter 6 discusses strategies for asking sensitive questions.

Sometimes surveys use gate questions to determine whether follow-up questions are applicable to respondents. Respondents are found to deliberately choose a response option that will disqualify them or their household from being eligible and, thus, avoid additional follow-up questions, regardless of whether that selected response option reflects their true opinion or situation. This is called motivated misreporting. To reduce motivated misreporting to gate items, question writers should employ a grouped question format (that is, asking all gate questions together first before asking follow-up questions) instead of the interleafed format (asking the first gate question, followed by follow-up questions, and then the subsequent gate questions, followed by follow-up questions) (e.g., Daikeler et al., 2022; Eckman et al., 2014).

Second, formal features of response options affect respondents' choice of a response. We discuss five formal features below as an example and caution that question writers should pay extreme attention to such features when designing a response scale. Response order effects refer to the effect of the order in which response options are presented on resultant answers. When a list of unordered options is presented in a self-administered survey, options displayed at the beginning of the list are more likely to be selected, resulting in primacy effects (Galesic et al., 2008; Krosnick & Alwin, 1987). However, when the same list is read to respondents in interviewer-administered surveys, options toward the end of the list are more likely to be selected because they are heard last, leading to recency effects (Holbrook et al., 2007). For response scales comprising a list of ordered options (e.g., a Likert scale running from Strongly Agree to Strongly Disagree), scale points closer to the start of a

> Formal features of response options affecting answers include order of response options, range of response options, numeric labels, colors and shade, and visual layout.

scale are more likely to be selected, regardless of the mode of data collection, producing scale direction effects (Keusch & Yan, 2018, 2019; Yan & Keusch, 2015), especially for longer scales and complex survey questions (Yan et al., 2018).

Another formal feature of response options – the range of response options – is sometimes used as a frame of reference by respondents to estimate their own or other people's behavioral frequencies. Respondents assume that the middle category of a frequency scale reflects "typical" or "average" behavior frequencies, whereas the ends of the scale reflect the extremes of the distribution. Respondents then use this information to estimate how much they themselves engage in a behavior in comparison to the "average" frequency. For example, Tourangeau and Smith (1996) showed that respondents reported having more sexual partners when they were given a high-frequency scale than when they were given a low-frequency scale. See Chapter 3 for more discussion.

In addition, the numeric labels attached to scale points are found to affect respondents' interpretation of the scale, and subsequently, the selection of a scale point. For instance, for a scale with the same number of points and the same verbal labels, respondents are less likely to choose scale points when a negative number is attached to them than when a positive number is used (Schwarz et al., 1991a; Yan, 2006; more discussion in Chapter 4). In a similar fashion, the color and shade of response options on a screen (Tourangeau et al., 2007) and the graphical layout of the response options (Lenzner & Höhne, 2021; Schwarz et al., 1998; Smith, 1993) also affect respondents' understanding and use of the scale. Respondents tend to see response options with similar color or shade as conceptually closer than when the same response options have different colors or shades (Tourangeau et al., 2007). Furthermore, respondents take the pyramid shape of a response scale to suggest that more people should be represented at the bottom of the scale than at the top of the scale (Lenzner & Höhne, 2021; Schwarz et al., 1998; Smith, 1993). Subsequent chapters on designing paper surveys (Chapter 7) and web surveys (Chapter 8) discuss the importance of visual characteristics of survey questions.

A third problem that could potentially occur at the reporting stage is a tendency to select an answer in ways independent of question content and the judgment or estimate derived at the end of the judgment and estimation step. In practice, this means that no matter what the question is asking, respondents will always select a particular answer category of a scale. This is known as response style (Van Vaerenbergh & Thomas, 2013). Well-known examples of response styles include straightlining (the tendency to select the same response option to a battery of items using the same set of response categories), acquiescence (the tendency to agree regardless of what the question is about), extreme response style (the tendency to select the end points of a response scale), and midpoint response style (the tendency to select the middle option of a response scale).

**Summary**

The survey literature has offered many general guidelines for writing good questions. We conclude this chapter with advice offered by Krosnick and Presser (2010). Similar conventional wisdom can also be found in Converse and Presser (1986), Schaeffer and Presser (2003), and Bradburn et al. (2004).

Advice on writing good questions:

1  Use simple, familiar words (avoid technical terms, jargon, and slang)
2  Use simple syntax

3 Avoid words with ambiguous meanings (i.e., aim for wording that all respondents will interpret in the same way)
4 Strive for wording that is specific and concrete (as opposed to general and abstract)
5 Make response options exhaustive and mutually exclusive
6 Avoid leading or loaded questions that push respondents toward an answer
7 Ask about one thing at a time (avoid double-barreled questions)
8 Avoid questions with single or double negations

Advice on grouping questions into a questionnaire:

1 Early questions should be easy and pleasant to answer and should build rapport between the respondent and the interviewer, if administered in a telephone or face-to-face mode.
2 Questions at the beginning of a questionnaire should be engaging and explicitly address the topic of the survey, as it was described to the respondent prior to the interview.
3 Questions on the same topic should be grouped together.
4 Questions on the same topic should proceed from general to specific.
5 Questions on sensitive topics that might make respondents uncomfortable should be placed toward the end of the questionnaire.
6 Filter questions should be included to avoid asking respondents questions that do not apply to them.

**Exercises**

1 Describe the survey response model.
2 For each stage of the survey response model, describe at least two problems respondents may have. Also, which problems have you run into before?
3 This chapter includes various best practices and guidelines for writing good questions. Which guidelines/best practices you have heard before and which ones are new to you?

# 3  Writing Behavioral Questions

## Introduction

Behavioral questions collect information on experiences and events that occurred in respondents' life. Such questions typically ask about what happened, when, where, how often, how long, how many times, or how much. In contrast to attitudinal questions (to be discussed in Chapter 4), behavioral questions are linked to an objective truth, at least in theory. However, the objective truth is often not known or may not be accessible to researchers. For instance, number of doctor visits can be verified through respondents' medical records; however, the records may have their own errors or not be available to researchers. Our discussion of developing behavioral questions will focus on the retrieval stage of the survey response model (see Chapter 2 for a description of the survey response model). Because retrieval is the recall of information from long-term memory, we begin this chapter with a brief discussion on human memory and organization of autobiographical events (events that happened in a respondent's life) followed by a discussion of factors that might affect recall and practical advice on how to improve it.

## Autobiographical Events and Human Memory

Knowledge of events may exist at different levels – it can be rather abstract for basic-level, daily events, such as eating breakfast (Rosch, 1978); generic, for repeated events that follow a particular script (e.g., doctor visits generally include talking to a receptionist, seeing a nurse, and then seeing a doctor); or very specific, for personal events that are of particular importance to respondents (e.g., high school graduation party). Thus, autobiographical memory consists of events of different levels of specificity that are likely to be recalled with different levels of accuracy. Several theoretical models describe the structure and links across autobiographical events (e.g., Conway, 1996; Kolodner, 1985; Tulving, 1983). What they all have in common is that they place autobiographical events in episodic memory, which along with semantic memory (knowledge about general events) and procedural memory (knowledge about how to do things) are systems in humans' long-term memory. The models differ in how they envision the retrieval process itself – from general to more specific memories (top down); sequential, allowing for chronological sequencing within a theme; parallel, based on relationships among events or specific episodes across themes, or a combination of all.

How autobiographical events are organized in human memory is relevant to how we structure survey questions and how we present retrieval cues to respondents. For example, experimental research has shown that for specific events, questions that ask about

DOI: 10.4324/9781003367826-4

what happened yield more accurate reports than questions about where the event took place or date of the event (Brewer, 1988; Wagenaar, 1986). We do expect that the ability to recall details and the accuracy of recall will vary by event type, as will other factors likely to affect recall and strategies to improve it.

## Event Characteristics Affecting Recall and Strategies for Improving Recall

### Event Characteristics Affecting Recall

As mentioned in Chapter 2, multiple factors affect a respondent's ability to retrieve events directly and influence the extent to which inferences are reported rather than the events themselves. Events that are important to respondents, particularly unique events or those that are emotional at the time of occurrence, are remembered more accurately than mundane events, regardless of the elapsed time (e.g., Linton, 1982; Mathiowetz & Duncan, 1988). In a self-study of memory, Wagenaar (1986) reported that the pleasantness of an event (as recorded in a diary over a 6-year period) was linked to the ability to recall the event a few years later. Similarly, Thompson et al. (1996) reported that events associated with strong emotions (both pleasant and unpleasant) were remembered better than neutral events.

In contrast, similar events require the spread of memory activation across multiple pathways (e.g., from general themes to more specific subthemes and isolated episodes); thus, little activation reaches each specific experience, and multiple events of the same type are easy to recall relative to unique events. Indeed, several early studies examining survey recall report that important and memorable events are reported better in surveys – for example, major purchases are reported more accurately than smaller ones (Sudman & Bradburn, 1973), and longer hospital stays are reported more accurately than shorter ones (Cannell & Fowler, 1965; Cannell et al., 1981).

### Strategies for Improving Recall

**Landmark Events and Other Retrieval Cues**. Studies have demonstrated that even though respondents may not know the dates of events they are asked to report, they can report accurately dates for important events (landmark events, which are usually time-tagged) and can use them to put dates around less important events. Landmark events can be personal (such as college graduation, giving birth), or public (e.g., Thanksgiving, Christmas). Studies have demonstrated that highly salient landmark events yield better estimates of an event's date than other recall strategies (e.g., Burt, 1992; Thompson et al., 1996).

> The Neighborhood History Calendar, a method designed to collect event histories of community changes over time, contained memorable public events at different levels to help respondents with their recall task. Landmark events included national (e.g., the deposition of the king), regional (e.g., natural disaster), and local events (e.g., household electrification) (Axinn et al. 1997).

**Decomposition**. Asking multiple questions and breaking the recall task into smaller subtasks improves the probability of more accurate recall (Means et al., 1989). Question decomposition helps disentangle generic memories into specific events by asking

**41a. SQATTACKHOW**

(Other than any incidents already mentioned,) has anyone attacked or threatened you in any of these ways -

(Exclude telephone threats) -

Read each category.

(a) With any weapon, for instance, a gun or knife -

(b) With anything like a baseball bat, frying pan, scissors, or stick -

(c) By something thrown, such as a rock or bottle -

(d) Include any grabbing, punching, or choking,

(e) Any rape, attempted rape or other type of sexual attack -

(f) Any face to face threats -

OR

(g) Any attack or threat or use of force by anyone at all? Please mention it even if you are not certain it was a crime.

Ask only if necessary

Did any incidents of this type happen to you?

541    1 ☐ Yes - ASK 41b
       2 ☐ No - SKIP to 42a

*Figure 3.1* Decomposition Example from the 2023 National Crime Victimization Survey Screener Questionnaire.

multiple questions rather than a single one. Figure 3.1 provides an example from the National Crime Victimization Survey (NCVS); instead of asking about assaults that respondents might have experienced in the past 6 months, the survey asks if someone has attacked or threatened the respondent by grabbing, punching, or choking them; using any weapon; or sexually attacking them. Such a strategy is used to avoid premature termination of memory search when respondents may feel they have nothing to report.

Asking multiple questions related to the event of interest also improves the probability an event will be recalled and will stimulate associations across questions. For example, instead of just asking about seatbelt wearing during the respondent's most recent car ride, multiple questions related to when was the last time the respondent drove or rode in a motor vehicle, where the trip began and ended, how long was the trip, whether the respondent was the driver or a rider and if so, where they sat in the vehicle can be asked to improve recall to the seatbelt question (Dillman, 2000).

**Event History Calendars**. Event history calendars (EHCs) have been used to improve recall in surveys for events that occurred in previous years or respondent's lifetime (e.g., Belli et al., 2001; Freedman et al., 1988). EHCs aid respondent recall through processes that capitalize on the sequential and hierarchical storage of memories, and their link to personal landmark events serves as an inherent cue. Historically, EHCs have been used in interviewer-administered surveys, but with the widespread use of web surveys, they are becoming integrated into self-administered surveys as well (e.g., National Survey of Family Growth; NSFG). Figure 3.2 presents an example from the paper EHC for NSFG 2017–2019. To facilitate monthly recall of sexual activity and the use of contraceptive methods

**National Survey of Family Growth: Life History Calendar**

| | | 2014 | | | | | | | | | | | | 2015 | | | | | | | | | | | | 2016 | | | | | | | | | | | | 2017 | | | | | | | | | | | |
|---|---|---|---|---|---|---|---|---|---|---|---|---|---|---|---|---|---|---|---|---|---|---|---|---|---|---|---|---|---|---|---|---|---|---|---|---|---|---|---|---|---|---|---|---|---|---|---|---|---|
| Before 2014 | | Ja | Fe | Ma | Ap | My | Jn | Jl | Au | Sp | Oc | Nv | Dc | Ja | Fe | Ma | Ap | My | Jn | Jl | Au | Sp | Oc | Nv | Dc | Ja | Fe | Ma | Ap | My | Jn | Jl | Au | Sp | Oc | Nv | Dc | Ja | Fe | Ma | Ap | My | Jn | Jl | Au | Sp | Oc | Nv | Dc |
| | Your Age | | | | | | | | | | | | | | | | | | | | | | | | | | | | | | | | | | | | | | | | | | | | | | | | |
| | Education | | | | | | | | | | | | | | | | | | | | | | | | | | | | | | | | | | | | | | | | | | | | | | | | |
| | Births & Other Pregnancies | | | | | | | | | | | | | | | | | | | | | | | | | | | | | | | | | | | | | | | | | | | | | | | | |
| | Marriages, Cohabs, Partners | | | | | | | | | | | | | | | | | | | | | | | | | | | | | | | | | | | | | | | | | | | | | | | | |
| | Intercourse | | | | | | | | | | | | | | | | | | | | | | | | | | | | | | | | | | | | | | | | | | | | | | | | |
| | Birth Control Methods | | | | | | | | | | | | | | | | | | | | | | | | | | | | | | | | | | | | | | | | | | | | | | | | |
| | | Ja | Fe | Ma | Ap | My | Jn | Jl | Au | Sp | Oc | Nv | Dc | Ja | Fe | Ma | Ap | My | Jn | Jl | Au | Sp | Oc | Nv | Dc | Ja | Fe | Ma | Ap | My | Jn | Jl | Au | Sp | Oc | Nv | Dc | Ja | Fe | Ma | Ap | My | Jn | Jl | Au | Sp | Oc | Nv | Dc |

**Your Date of Birth:** __________ **Date of First Intercourse:** __________

**Birth or Pregnancy Ending Dates:**

**1st:** __________ **2nd:** __________ **3rd:** __________ **4th:** __________ **5th:** __________

*Figure 3.2* National Survey of Family Growth Paper Life History Calendar, NSFG 2017–2019.

over the past 4 years, respondents are asked to record events of personal importance (e.g., marriages, pregnancies, and births) that would facilitate recall of those monthly events and guide the judgment of whether they occurred within the time frame of interest.

**Use of Diaries.** Asking respondents to keep a diary for a short period of time and record specific events is a well-known practice for frequent, nonsalient events. This approach minimizes the reliance on recall because respondents are asked to record the event of interest immediately after its occurrence (e.g., daily food purchases). Despite their promise, diaries do not always provide a good solution – one of the main concerns is that keeping a diary may unexpectedly change the behavior under study; other concerns are related to timely completion and keeping respondents motivated to complete the diary over time.

## Impact of Time Since Event on Recall and Strategies for Improving Recall

### *Impact of Time Since Event on Recall*

Respondents are often asked to report on behaviors or events that were experienced in the past rather than at the time of the interview and typically, a time frame (reference period) is provided within the question:

*Did you see a pediatrician **within the last 6 months**, that is since January 25, 2024?*

The accuracy of such responses often depends on the time lapse since the event – the longer the time lapse between the event of interest and the survey interview time, the less likely respondents are to remember it accurately, if at all (see discussion in Chapter 2). Some of the theories on forgetting suggest that this is the result of respondents experiencing similar events in between and those additional experiences interfering with the memory for the original event (Gillund & Shiffrin, 1984; Johnson, 1983). Indeed, validation studies demonstrate decrease in recall accuracy with increase of time since the event (e.g., Cannell et al., 1981; Loftus et al., 1992; Smith & Jobe, 1994).

Proximity to the reference period boundaries is another factor that interacts with length of the reference period and can contribute to a respondent's uncertainty about whether an event took place within those boundaries. Respondents can mistakenly report events that happened before the reference period or omit events as if they happened outside of the reference period. The first error is called forward telescoping (events are wrongfully telescoped within the reference period), while the second is called backward telescoping (events from inside the reference period are mistakenly taken out and not reported). Backward telescoping is less of an issue because respondents generally have less uncertainty about more recent events. Telescoping errors were first reported by Neter and Waksberg (1964) in a longitudinal study of expenditure, home repairs, and alterations. The study noted forward temporal displacement of both expenditure amounts and number of jobs and that was particularly true for larger expenditures and jobs (e.g., buying a sofa vs. paint for lawn furniture).

### Strategies for Improving Recall

**Short Reference Period**. In addition to the use of landmark events and EHCs to help facilitate recall and reduce telescoping, shortening the reference period as much as possible given the behavioral frequency of an event might be a simple solution. For example, one of NCVS's objective is to produce annual estimates of crime victimizations. However, respondents are asked to recall and report crimes they might have experienced in the past 6 months instead of in the past 12 months. NCVS then uses the survey response data to extrapolate and produce annual estimates. Many studies manipulating the length of the reference period report a decrease in the number of events per unit time with length increase (e.g., meta-analysis by Sudman & Bradburn, 1973). This is likely the result not only of forgetting but also the increase in the total number of events that need to be recalled (Neter & Waksberg, 1964).

**Bounded Recall**. Bounded interviewing (providing a list of previously reported behaviors at the next wave of data collection) is a strategy commonly used in longitudinal surveys to reduce telescoping and improve recall. Neter and Waksberg (1964) compared the bounded interviewing approach to unbounded (simply asking respondents to report on jobs and expenditures within the reference period) and found that bounded recall significantly reduced telescoping by discouraging respondents to consider previously reported events. Cross-sectional studies have also demonstrated the utility of bounded recall in reduction of telescoping. Sudman et al. (1984) first asked respondents about events in the preceding month, then about events in the current month (which was of interest) and found that fewer events were reported in the current month when the interview was bounded; Loftus and Marburger (1983) used a landmark event (the eruption of Mt. St. Helens for respondents in Washington state) as a boundary of the reference frame to reduce telescoping.

**Time on Task**. Early investigations on strategies to improve recall have demonstrated that providing respondents more time to recall events improves response accuracy (e.g., Wagenaar, 1986; Williams & Hollan, 1981). Reiser et al. (1985) showed that it took several seconds to recall a specific event in response to a request, and the more difficult the retrieval task the longer it took. Allowing respondents more time to answer survey questions increases the accuracy of responses and at the question level, this strategy translates into asking longer questions. For example, asking questions with redundant wording, thus providing respondents with more time to recall (Cannell et al., 1977; Cannell et al., 1981), or giving respondents longer deadlines to report back (Burton & Blair, 1991) have both yielded more accurate responses. Burton and Blair (1991) manipulated response time by providing respondents with the following instructions:

> *The next question is very important. After I finish reading the question, I would like you to spend at least fifteen seconds thinking about it. I will let you know when the fifteen seconds are up. If you wish to take more time, just let me know. Okay?*

**Overall Survey Length**. Several studies have demonstrated that as surveys become longer, respondents' motivation deteriorates and willingness to work on retrieval decreases over time (e.g., Galesic & Bosnjak, 2009; Peytchev, 2007). Such findings suggest that the most important behavioral questions should be placed earlier in the questionnaire, and likely that behavioral questions should precede attitudinal ones when logically possible.

**Estimation Strategies for Answering Behavioral Frequency Questions**

Besides recall, the use of an estimation strategy to answer questions about frequency of a certain behavior affects the reported answers. Chapter 2 describes three estimation strategies respondents employ to come up with the number of times events happened in the past. With the bottom-up strategy, respondent enumerate every single instance of the event of interest and add them up to yield an estimate. The top-down strategy employs a rate-based estimation, when respondents apply a rule to come up with a response that is not an exact count of events, typically used when information about a "usual" or very frequent behavior is asked or when the reference period is so large that it does not allow for individual events to be recalled. An extreme form of the rate-based estimation is the impression-based method, where respondents retrieve an impression (e.g., I always wear my seat belt) and use it to form an answer (number of times the seat belt is worn). As discussed in Chapter 2, the bottom-up strategy typically leads to underreporting because of errors of omission. However, the top-down strategy usually leads to overreporting because of the presence of stability bias (Burton & Blair, 1991; Menon, 1994), even though respondents can occasionally engage in an "anchor and adjust" strategy when they use their present status as a benchmark against which they adjust past events based on their perception of stability or change (Ross, 1989).

Respondents sometimes rely primarily on the response categories to formulate an answer. When respondents are presented with a frequency scale to report on a past behavior, they use the scale as an additional source of information, assuming that the range of the scale reflects the population distribution of the behavior of interest and the middle point of the scale represents the average for the population. This strategy results in higher frequency estimates when a high-frequency scale is presented, and lower estimates when a low-frequency scale is presented. For example, in a study by Schwarz et al. (1985), participants were asked about their daily hours of TV watching and presented either with a low frequency (Up to 0.5 hours, 0.5–1 hours, 1–1.5 hours, 1.5–2 hours, 2–2.5 hours, and more than 2.5 hours) or high frequency (Up to 2.5 hours, 2.5–3 hours, 3–3.5 hours, 3.5–4 hours, 4–4.5 hours, more than 4.5 hours) alternatives. Responses were recoded to reflect estimates of 2.5 hours or more than 2.5 hours. As expected, the scale range had a significant effect on reporting – only 16.2% of the low-frequency condition respondents reported more than 2.5 hours of TV watching, while that percentage more than doubled (37.5%) for the high-frequency condition. Interestingly however, in a follow-up study, Chassein et al. (1987) observed that the scale effect disappeared when respondents were given a chance to cue their memories by browsing through the previous week's TV program. Nonetheless, multiple studies have demonstrated that scale effects are robust and replicate over multiple domains (e.g., Billet & Waterplas, 1988; Schwarz, 1990; Schwarz & Bienias, 1990). Furthermore, proxy reports (reports about others' behaviors) are more affected by scale frequency than self-reports because people generally have better knowledge of their own behaviors than those of others (Schwarz & Bienias, 1990).

The choice of estimation strategy respondents would employ depends on multiple factors, such as number of events to be reported, similarity and regularity of events, length of the recall period, and time to answer. Any of the recall improvement strategies discussed in the previous section would help facilitate recall, regardless of the recall strategy.

**Summary**

In this chapter, we discuss reasons for recall error and strategies to improve retrieval and estimation strategies respondents engage in when answering behavioral questions. We alert the reader to the fact that response alternatives may add unintended information to the response processes and that open-ended questions might be preferable for behavioral reports where respondents are expected to provide numeric answers (thus, no extra coding is needed). Instead, some researchers may want to resort to using vague quantifiers, such as "often," "sometimes," and "most of the time"; however, vague quantifies are not recommended for behavioral questions because they do not carry a unified meaning across respondents and often represent different frequencies in different contexts – for example, "frequently" is less frequent for rare events, such as a volcanic eruption, than frequent ones, such as thunderstorms.

As discussed, both the bottom-up and the top-down estimation strategies are imperfect and lead to different types of error, but the methods for improving recall often help with data accuracy. One variable under researchers' control is the length of the reference period; manipulating it based on what strategy respondents are more likely to engage in (enumeration for infrequent events and estimation for frequent ones) may improve recall quality by offering shorter reference periods for events likely to be estimated and longer for events likely to be counted (to avoid telescoping). Another variable under researchers' control is the amount of time given to respondents to answer a question in interviewer-administered surveys – results from multiple studies suggest that respondents who try to recall specific events retrieve more information when given more time. However, this strategy is unlikely to be very successful for respondents who engage in estimation rather than enumeration.

**Exercises**

1 Discuss event characteristics that can affect recall. Compare and contrast two strategies for improving recall in the context of event characteristics and describe in what situations you would prefer one over the other.
2 What are the main strategies respondents employ when answering behavioral frequency questions? When are they more likely to engage in one over the other?
3 What are the dangers of using behavior frequency scales?

# 4 Writing Attitudinal Questions

## Introduction

### What Is an Attitude?

In addition to facts and behaviors, survey researchers are also interested in measuring opinions and attitudes. Opinions and attitudes are likely based on facts, but facts are not directly referred to in attitudinal questions and likely are not consciously sought by respondents. Attitudes are defined as "an enduring positive or negative feeling about some person, object or issue" (Petty & Cacioppo, 1981, p. 7). Attitudes have direction and intensity and consist of three components – cognitive, affective, and action (an example is shown in the text box). The cognitive component refers to what the respondent knows about the attitude object. That knowledge may not be comprehensive, or even correct, and is limited to what the respondent has accessible in memory. Somewhat related to the cognitive component is the affective component – it is the primary dimension measured in surveys and reflects how respondents feel toward the attitude object. Finally, the action component reflects the respondent's willingness or likelihood to behave in a way related to the attitude object. Unlike factual and behavioral questions discussed in Chapter 3, attitudinal questions invoke subjective responses, so whether respondents provide a truthful response cannot be measured objectively.

> **Example: Attitudes toward abortion**
>
> **Cognitive component:** 10,000 abortions occur each year in the United States.
> **Affective component:** Every woman should be able to get an abortion.
> **Action component:** Intention/likelihood of getting an abortion.

### Theories on Attitude Formation and Retrieval

How attitudes are reported by respondents has interested psychologists for a long time. Various theories are proposed to explain how people form and retrieve attitudes. Here we discuss two theories that are most relevant to the process of respondents answering attitudinal questions.

DOI: 10.4324/9781003367826-5

*The File Drawer Model*

One of the early theories on responses to attitude questions was the file drawer model (Wilson & Hodges, 1992). According to the model, evaluations and opinions on various topics are stored in the respondent's memory, and when needed, are looked up and retrieved, similar to extracting a file from a file drawer cabinet. When existing evaluations are not found in the file drawers, respondents rely on relevant information from the file drawers to form new judgments. The assumption this model makes is that most attitudes are preexisting and stable over time. However, these assumptions fail because findings from multiple surveys and experiments have demonstrated that attitudes change over time (e.g., Converse, 1964, 1970; Zaller, 1992), attitudes are extremely susceptible to context and question order effects (e.g., Sudman et al., 1996), and respondents express opinions about fictitious issues (Bishop et al., 1986; Schuman & Presser, 1981). Even though some respondents (particularly those with strong attitudes) answer attitudinal questions by retrieving an existing evaluation (as if from a file drawer), others generate their responses through some other process that does not involve recall of an existing judgment.

*The Belief Sampling Model*

Proposed by Tourangeau et al. (2000) and further elaborated in Tourangeau (2021), the model suggests that attitudes are a "haphazard assortment" (Tourangeau et al., 2000, p. 179) of existing evaluations, vague impressions, general values, and relevant feelings toward an attitude object. Thus, attitudes may be created through different paths, frequently dependent on the accessibility of information cued by preceding questions or chronically available, time respondents have on task, and respondents' motivation. As such, attitudes are inherently unstable and unreliable, as they tend to "overrepresent whatever considerations happen to be accessible when the question is asked" (Tourangeau et al., 2000, p. 181). Respondents with one-sided views on an issue are likely to produce more consistent attitudes because they will likely draw on the same considerations every time they are asked about their views. The attitudes of respondents with mixed underlying views, however, will be greatly impacted to the extent to which different considerations are brought to attention when asked about their views.

**Strategies of Answering Attitudinal Questions**

When respondents do not have an existing judgment to report, they might resort to other strategies for answering attitudinal questions as briefly described in Chapter 2: (1) general impressions/stereotypes or impression-based strategy (Sanbonmatsu & Fazio, 1990); (2) general values or top-down strategy (Zaller, 1992); or (3) specific beliefs and feelings that can be extrapolated to the attitude target or bottom-up strategy (Tourangeau & Rasinski, 1988).

Impression-based responses may occur when respondents do not have enough information or interest to form or retrieve an existing evaluation of the attitudinal target. In a study by Sanbonmatsu and Fazio (1990), respondents were presented with information about two department stores – one was described in a very favorable light, while the other was described in a very negative light – with the exception of their camera departments, which were described in the opposite light from the overall store: the terrible store had an excellent camera department and vice versa. Respondents were asked to report from which store they would choose to buy a new camera. When they had to respond under pressure, most study participants selected the wonderful store with the subpar camera department; however, when given time to think and not rely on their general impressions, participants made choices consistent with what they knew about each camera department.

Based on the top-down retrieval strategy, general values come to play when respondents do not have a preexisting opinion toward a narrow attitude target but can express an opinion that reflects their general values and ideological norms. Examples of such attitudes include opinions on various political issues, which are highly susceptible to question wording – for example, in a famous experiment by Rugg (1941) replicated over time, respondents were randomly assigned to one of the following versions of the same question:

*Do you think the United States should allow public speeches against democracy?*

*Do you think the United States should forbid public speeches against democracy?*

Interestingly, 75% of respondents answered "no" to the first question, indicating that the United States should *not allow* speeches against democracy. By contrast, only 45% of respondents answered "yes" to the second question indicating that the United States should *forbid* speeches against democracy. Such seemingly small wording changes can alter how respondents apply their general values and norms on a narrow topic for which they might not have a preexisting opinion. In this particular instance, "forbid" is such a strong word that seems to contradict the principles of "democracy." Respondents, not paying much attention to the specific attitude object, were influenced by this controversy to say no to the second question.

Similarly, respondents may construct an opinion based on an inference from a specific belief or beliefs they hold. Studies that explore this mechanism have looked at responses provided to open-ended questions and found that, for example, views on the local economy contained specific considerations of the local unemployment rate and job growth (Mason et al., 1994). Studies also examine reaction time (how long it took respondents to provide an answer) when respondents are primed with a related issue, an unrelated issue, different aspects of the same issue, or the same aspect of an issue. In a study by Tourangeau et al. (1991b) participants were asked to agree or disagree with two statements and recorded how long it took to provide a response to the second item. The study found increased response speed when the prime and target questions were very closely related, such as when representing the same aspect of an issue (e.g., abortion is murder and life begins at conception). The authors argue that speed of response would not have decreased if responses to both questions stem from a general evaluation rather than a specific belief and that respondents likely retrieve specific considerations for the speed of response to be affected by how related the two questions are.

### *Impact of Context on Answering Attitudinal Questions*

Based on the belief sampling model, attitudes are unstable and dependent on information available in working memory. Context (in particular, question order) plays an important role at each stage of the survey response model. Context effects become an issue at the comprehension stage when the question is about an ambiguous or unfamiliar attitude target (e.g., the study by Strack, Schwarz, & Wänke, 1991, described in Chapter 2). As working memory degrades with age, context effects are less pronounced in older respondents than in young ones (Knauper, 1998). On the flip side, chronically accessible information, such as previously formed judgments, will be less affected by the context.

At the retrieval stage, the information to form an attitude must be available in working memory triggered by current or prior questions. Because prior questions on related topics affect what is considered for subsequent questions, their impact is demonstrated by studies that focus on response time – answering a target question on a topic similar to the preceding questions makes respondents answer more quickly (e.g., Bassili & Fletcher, 1991; Judd et al., 1991; Tourangeau et al., 1989a,1989b). Because quick response times are associated with decreased respondent burden, a best practice in questionnaire design is to group questions on a similar topic (thus, questions that use the same attitude object together).

Context effects in forming attitudes are likely the most pronounced at the judgment stage, when respondents need to make an evaluation relative to something else. The direction of the context effect on a response to a subsequent question may vary – we distinguish between **assimilation** and **contrast** effects. Assimilation effects occur when responses to the target question are in the same direction as responses to preceding (context) questions; conversely, contrast effects (including subtraction-based contrast effects as noted in Tourangeau et al. (1991a)) occur when responses to the target question move away from responses to the preceding questions.

An interesting example of how question order affects the norm invoked in making a judgment is a study originally published by Hyman and Sheatsley in 1950 and replicated by many over the years (e.g., Schuman & Ludwig, 1983; Schuman & Presser, 1981). Respondents were asked two questions, with varied order:

*Do you think the United States should let communist reporters from other countries come in here and send back to their papers the news as they see it?*

Followed, or proceeded by:

*Do you think a communist country like Russia should let American newspaper reporters come in and send back to their papers the news as they see it?*

Figure 4.1 presents the percentage of respondents who answered "yes" to the communist reporters' question by question order. The results show a dramatic shift in responses of 37% in the original study, depending on whether the communist reporters' question is asked first or second. When the communist question is asked first, it evokes beliefs and attitudes at the time toward Russia and communism in general. However, when the same question follows the American reporters question, the norm of reciprocity is invoked, requiring the same treatment for communist reporters. This is an example of a *comparison-based assimilation effect*.

A study by Schwarz et al. (1990) is another example of context effects at the judgment stage. Study participants were asked to rate on a scale from 1 to 9 the typicality of wine, milk, and coffee as German beverages. These target questions were preceded by a context question asking typicality of beer or vodka, frequency of beer or vodka drinking in Germany, or caloric content of beer or vodka in a 2 (beer vs. vodka) × 3 (typicality rating, consumption frequency, caloric content) factorial design, where participants were randomly assigned

30   A Practical Guide to Survey Questionnaire Design and Evaluation

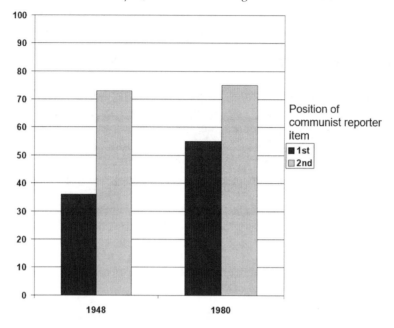

*Figure 4.1* Percent Respondents Agreeing that Communist Reporters Should be Given Access, by Question Order and Study Year.

to a condition. Table 4.1 presents the results of the averaged typicality score for wine, milk, and coffee across conditions. The study demonstrates that respondents' ratings of typicality of wine, milk, and coffee were influenced by the extreme anchors (vodka or beer) used in the preceding context question especially when the context and target questions tapped into the same underlying dimension (typicality). Compared to vodka, which is not a typical German drink, wine, milk, and coffee were rated higher on the typicality dimension than when compared to beer, which is a very typical German drink. However, there was no contrast effect when the preceding context question asked about a different evaluative dimension (i.e., caloric content).

At the response mapping stage, context affects how respondents map their attitude on the provided response scale and whether they change their true answers beforehand. An example of how contextual information influences responses at the response

*Table 4.1* Mean Typicality Rating Averaged Over Wine, Milk, and Coffee by Experimental Condition

| Preceding questions | Context stimulus | |
|---|---|---|
| | Vodka | Beer |
| Typicality Rating | 5.4 | 4.4 |
| Consumption frequency | 5.3 | 4.9 |
| Caloric content | 4.3 | 4.5 |

*Note*: Measured on a scale from 1 to 9, where 1 is not at all typical and 9 is very typical.

mapping stage is respondents' reluctancy to provide negative evaluations, resulting in overuse of the positive end of a scale (positivity bias). A study by Schwarz et al. (1991a) presented respondents with two sets of rating scale, with different numeric end points – one set had values from −5 to +5, while the other ranged from 0 to 10. Despite having the same verbal endpoints on both scales (not at all successful and extremely successful), respondents largely utilized the positive end of the scale. When the negative numeric label was used for the "not at all successful" verbal label, it likely implied presence of failure rather than lack of success. Furthermore, when the numeric labels (e.g., ±5) suggested a bipolar scale, while the verbal labels suggested a unipolar scale (e.g., not at all successful to extremely successful), respondents used only part of the scale, as supported by follow-up studies (e.g., Mazaheri & Theuns, 2009; O'Muircheartaigh et al., 1995).

### Considerations for Developing Attitudinal Questions

Issues with attitudinal questions mostly occur at the judgment stage of the survey response process described in Chapter 2; however, questionnaire designers should watch out for problems that could occur at each of the four stages.

At the comprehension stage, attitude object **ambiguity** could be a major issue. In a study by Belson (1981) asking respondents to express an opinion on whether "children suffer any ill effects from watching programs with violence in them," participants demonstrated very different interpretation of the terms "children," "ill effects," and "violence." To avoid such inconsistencies across respondents, a best practice is to define the attitude target and then follow up with a question about respondents' opinions. A possible fix to the earlier example could be:

*Do you think children under 14 are affected by watching videos or movies of people inflicting or sustaining physical injuries, using abusive behaviors or language, or damaging property?*

However, question writers need to evaluate the tradeoffs between clarity and complexity and should strive for clearly specified concepts using simple language without making the question too long or too syntactically complicated.

As illustrated in the earlier section, the report of attitudes is very sensitive to context – if most attitudes are formed on the spot (in accordance with the belief sampling model), preceding questions will determine what information is currently active in the respondent's mind and what remains temporarily available in working memory.

To avoid unexpected context effects, we recommend writing simple questions, with a clear attitude target. Grouping questions by topic also helps control context effects in most modes. When there are concerns that the question order may influence the intended interpretation of the questions, a best practice is to randomize the order to estimate the effect.

A few other considerations, independent of the survey response process, should be taken into account when developing questions to measure attitudes and opinions.

**Question balancing** provides an opportunity for respondents to consider a counter-argument. In its simplest form, a balanced question contains the positive and negative responses (argument and counter-argument):

*Do you feel a woman should be allowed to have an abortion in the early months of pregnancy if she wants one, or <u>do you feel this should not be allowed</u>?*

Alternatively, the question may present a substantive counter-argument, such as or *do you feel this should depend on the reason for abortion?* One concern with substantive counter-arguments is that it is nearly impossible to perfectly balance the question and it may not even represent the respondent's position on the issue. Because the argument introduces information that otherwise may not have been available, it is included in the respondent's evaluation of the attitude object, so what alternative is chosen among sets of counter-arguments really matters. For example, in experiments by Schuman and Presser (1981), respondents were randomly assigned to one of the following questions:

*If there is a serious fuel shortage this winter, do you think there should be a law requiring people to lower the heat in their homes, or do you think this should be left to individual families to decide?*

*If there is a serious fuel shortage this winter, do you think there should be a law requiring people to lower the heat in their homes, or do you oppose such a law because it would be too difficult to enforce?*

The level of support for that law differed significantly between the two conditions – 35% of those who received the first version of the question favored the law, while only 25% of those who received the second version of the question endorsed it. Generally, question balancing is considered a best practice and is especially useful to minimize response acquiescence[1] – instead of presenting respondents with a single statement with which they need to agree or disagree, question balancing presents a forced choice. Furthermore, many studies have demonstrated a shift toward the counter-argument, when one is presented; for example, in the series of experiments noted earlier, Schuman and Presser (1981) randomly assigned respondents to unbalanced versus balanced questions and reported significant changes in endorsement rates toward the counter-argument, when it was offered.

Attitudinal questions often use response scales as response options. Response scales consist of a series of numeric or verbal values conveying an order. An important characteristic of scales as used in social sciences is **scale polarity** – the main distinction being between *bipolar and unipolar scales*.

Bipolar scales reflect two opposing alternatives and present a clear conceptual midpoint, collecting information on both the positive and negative endpoints. The intention is to measure the direction (side of the scale) and intensity (distance from the midpoint) of respondent's opinion on an issue. An example of a bipolar scale is shown below:

*Very Positive ↔ Positive ↔ Mixed ↔ Negative ↔ Very Negative*

In contrast, unipolar scales reflect gradation on the same dimension and do not present a clear conceptual midpoint. As a result, such scales often seem unbalanced:

*Very Positive ↔ Positive ↔ Somewhat Positive ↔ Not at all Positive*

Unipolar scales are easier to construct, but do not provide an idea to which of the two opposing ends the respondent belongs. Thus, two separate questions for the positive and negative directions need to be asked.

Yet another approach for asking questions utilizing a bipolar scale is **branching** (or **scale unfolding**) where instead of presenting the full scale from the beginning, respondents are first asked about direction to determine whether they agree or disagree with a statement, and then about intensity of their agreement or disagreement (e.g., completely, generally agree, or disagree). Research on the effects of branching over data quality is mixed – some present evidence that branching is beneficial (e.g., Krosnick & Berent, 1993), while others show no effect or negative impact on validity (Gilbert, 2015; Wang & Krosnick, 2019). Some authors recommend that when branching is used, the middle category should also be presented (Malhotra et al., 2009). We recommend careful consideration when to use bipolar instead of unipolar scales, alerting the reader that branching would also increase the number of items (similar to asking two unipolar questions) and may have an impact on overall cost (Gilbert, 2015).

The decision on what kind of scale to use is often practical and dependent on the attitude object that is measured. In surveys, the traditional belief is that using two unipolar scales to measure the positive and negative directions is better than one bipolar scale (Alwin et al., 2018; Cacioppo et al., 1997; Gannon & Ostrom, 1996; Mazeheri & Theuns, 2009; Schaeffer & Thompson, 1992; Solomon, 1978). From a practical perspective, clear antonyms that are used in bipolar scales do not often exist, and the use of negative adjectives (e.g., exceptional-unexceptional) is not equivalent to an antonym comparison (e.g., exceptional-ordinary) (Paradis et al., 2009). Thus, using unipolar scales provides more flexibility to measure the positive and negative dimensions of a phenomenon and yields more reliable results (Alwin et al., 2018).

There is significant research on the use of **verbal labels** in addition to the numeric ones of a response scale. There is general support for the finding that verbal labels increase scale reliability (e.g., Alwin, 2007; Lau, 2018; Menold et al., 2014) and validity (e.g., Lau, 2018), as they unify the meaning of the scale points across respondents. The number of scale points also dictates the extent to which verbal labels can be used for all, or only the end categories. Based on studies of response order effects and scale reliability, the recommended number of scale points for both bipolar and unipolar scales is five (e.g., Pasek & Krosnick, 2010; Revilla et al., 2014), with at least the end and middle categories verbally labeled.

The inclusion of a **middle category** in the response scale depends on the type of rating scale. As previously noted, bipolar scales have a meaningful midpoint that should be included. Labels for the middle category vary from "neutral," "neither-nor," and "middle of the road" to "both equally," but they all mark a transition from positive to negative (or vice versa). Often, the middle category is used as the equivalent of "Don't Know" or "Undecided" (e.g. Dykema et al., 2019; Sturgis et al., 2014) and similar to "Don't Know," many studies have reported endorsement of the middle category when offered (e.g., Converse & Presser, 1986; Kalton & Schuman, 1982). Schaeffer and Thomson (1992) suggest that the middle category of a bipolar scale can mean many things – from a respondent's indifference to ambivalence; however, not including a middle category does not improve data quality (Wang & Krosnick, 2019).

In series of experiments conducted at the University of Michigan, Schuman and Presser (1981) examine whether the location of the middle category (in the middle of the response scale or at the very end) has an impact on responses, whether the number of substantive response options affects the endorsement of the middle category, and whether the middle category has an effect on the rest of the response options in interviewer-administered surveys. The results suggest that the location of the middle category does

*Table 4.2* Example Full and Quasi Filters

| Full filter | Quasi filter |
| --- | --- |
| Here is a statement about another country. Not everyone has an opinion on this. If you do not have an opinion, just say so. Here is the statement: The Russian leaders are trying to get along with America. Do you have an opinion on that? | Here is a statement about another country: The Russian leaders are trying to get along with America. Do you agree, disagree or not have an opinion? |

make a difference – it is endorsed significantly more when presented at the end of the question, likely because of recency effects. Furthermore, the authors report that the more points there are on a scale, the less likely the middle category is to be selected (based on significant differences in the endorsement of the middle category in a 3-point vs. 5-point scale), and that the middle category gets selected when offered, but its presence does not seem to have an effect on the substantive responses.

One way to avoid over-endorsement of the middle category is to include knowledge questions that can filter out respondents who do not have an opinion on the issue. We distinguish between **full filters and quasi filters**. Full filters typically present a statement to the respondent and ask whether they have an opinion on that. Only those who have an opinion proceed to the question that measures that opinion. Table 4.2 presents examples of full and quasi filters from the Schuman and Presser (1981) experiments. Quasi filters present the "no opinion" option within the question stem, along with the opinion options. Experiments on using full versus quasi filters demonstrate that full filters tend to filter out significantly more respondents (e.g., Schuman & Presser, 1981). Hippler and Schwarz (1989) report that strongly worded filters, such as "Have you already heard or read enough about it to have an opinion?" might suggest to respondents that a great deal of knowledge is needed to answer the follow-up attitudinal questions in comparison to a simple filter such as "Do you have an opinion on this or not?" and thus screen out more respondents.

**Acquiescence**, or agreeing response bias, is a respondent's tendency to agree or answer affirmatively regardless of the presented attitudinal statements. Acquiescence occurs regardless of mode of data collection (e.g., Liu & Keusch, 2017), or number of response categories (e.g., Schuman & Presser, 1981), and is mostly associated with Likert-type of scales (e.g., strongly agree-strongly disagree). Acquiescence may be dependent on the order of the response options; for example, Liu and Keusch (2017) report that acquiescence is more prevalent in web mode than face-to-face mode when the "agree" end of the scale is presented first. However, there are several ways to detect and minimize acquiescence. One is to use **reverse coding** – for example, respondents may be asked to agree or disagree with two contradictory statements:

Teenagers should be allowed to stay out at night as long as they want to.

Several questions later, respondents may be presented with the exact opposite statement:

Teenagers should have curfew.

Those acquiescing will agree with both contradictory statements and their responses may be flagged to later decide whether to exclude from analyses or correct for measurement error.

Another approach to avoid acquiescence is to move away from Likert scales and use **construct-specific** questions rather than agree-disagree statements:

Would you say that most men are better suited emotionally for politics than are most women, that men and women are equally suited, or that women are better suited than men in this area?

Rather than:

Tell me if you agree or disagree with this statement: Most men are better suited emotionally for politics than are most women.
(General Social Survey, 2002)

Overall, recent research consistently recommends the use of construct-specific questions because of their higher reliability and validity in comparison to agree-disagree statements (e.g., Revilla & Ochoa, 2015; Saris et al., 2010). Even though there are several studies that fail to show differences in reliability or validity (e.g., Lelkes & Weiss, 2015), we still recommend construct-specific questions for attitudes.

## Summary

Writing attitudinal questions presents multiple challenges, because attitudes are often created on the spot and the attitude target is vague, making responses highly dependent on context and what is activated in a respondent's working memory. To avoid unwanted context effects and other issues such as acquiescence, we recommend specifying the attitude target as clearly as possible and asking item-specific questions rather than agree-disagree questions. Furthermore, if there are concerns about question groupings within a content topic, we recommend randomizing the order where an impact is expected. Finally, using verbal labels in response scales tends to increase data quality and consistency across modes and we recommend it whenever possible.

## Exercises

1. What are the advantage of the belief sampling model over the file drawer model?
2. Discuss comparison-based contrast effects and assimilation effects, providing examples from your daily life.
3. Balance the following question, then create two counter-arguments:

   Do you think it is the responsibility of the federal government to make sure all Americans have health care coverage?
   (Pew Research Center, https://www.pewresearch.org/2024/06/24/americans-views-of-governments-role-persistent-divisions-and-areas-of-agreement/)

## Note

1. Respondent's tendency to say "yes" or "agree" to attitudinal questions.

# 5 Writing Demographic and Knowledge Questions

## Introduction

Questions that measure demographic characteristics are often considered quasi-factual questions, because they vary in terms of objective and subjective elements. Examples of characteristics that have objective elements are age, sex at birth, income, and education status; examples of characteristics that contain subjective elements include identification of one's race and ethnicity and gender identity. Demographic questions in surveys are collected for three main purposes: (1) to screen out respondents who do not belong to the target population (e.g., the National Survey of Family Growth seeks 15–45-year-old respondents), (2) to make weighting adjustments to known population totals, and (3) to compare subgroups on survey substantive outcomes. Those goals, along with mode of data collection, drive the placement of demographic questions. Typically, demographic questions are presented at the very end, because they are not very engaging and some are perceived as sensitive or intrusive. However, such questions can be placed at the beginning of a survey when needed to determine respondent eligibility, selection of respondents, and the questionnaire path a respondent should take (e.g., whether respondents are administered a male- or female-specific questionnaire in the National Survey of Family Growth is determined by their response to the sex at birth screener question).

Knowledge questions are factual in nature, because they contain an objective truth that is known to the researcher. Uses of knowledge questions in surveys include screening out respondents who may not be knowledgeable enough on a topic to have an opinion, measuring political knowledge (e.g., the American National Election Study: https://electionstudies.org/), scientific knowledge (e.g., the General Social Survey: https://www.norc.org/research/projects/gss.html) literacy, or education level (e.g., the National Assessment of Education Progress: https://nces.ed.gov/nationsreportcard), or obtaining information in the qualitative stage of survey development. This chapter introduces best practices for measuring selected demographic questions (race and ethnicity, gender identity, and income) and presents a discussion on uses and considerations for knowledge questions.

## Demographic Questions

A movement to standardize demographic questions across US surveys has been attempted since 1975 based on the Social Science Research Council recommendation (Social Science Research Council, 1975). Using the same demographic questions across surveys not only allows for comparability but also enables survey practitioners to use data from federal surveys, such as the American Community Survey, in their weighting adjustments. Our discussion draws heavily from US Decennial Censuses and Office of Management and Budget (OMB) guidelines for certain demographic questions and may not have direct relevance for surveys outside of the United States.

DOI: 10.4324/9781003367826-6

## Measuring Race and Ethnicity

The meaning of race varies across countries. In the United States, race has been defined biologically, anthropologically, genetically, and, lately, socially. The US Census first introduced a race question in the 1790 Census, where it collected race data in three categories: free white people, all other free persons (including free Black and a subset of Native Americans under US jurisdiction), and slaves. The free people categories in the 1850 census included white, black, or mulatto and introduced a separate form for enslaved people, who were counted under their owners. The first post-Civil War census, the 1870 census, for the first time did not count slaves and introduced "Chinese" to count people of Asian identity. In fact, each decennial census has presented a slightly different way of collecting race and ethnicity, reflecting societal changes. The 1997 OMB standards on race and ethnicity signaled a paradigm shift to self-identification, employing the social definition of race/ethnic belonging and allowing respondents to select more than one racial category. Ethnicity is

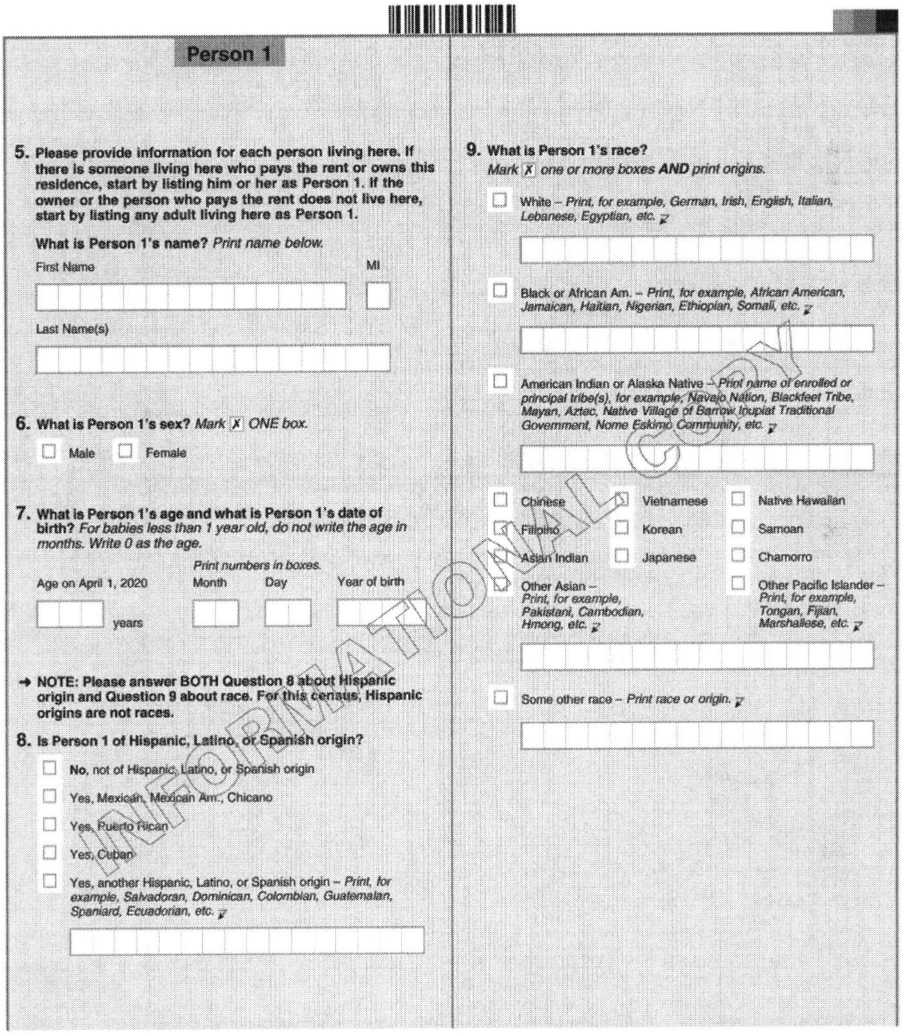

*Figure 5.1* Example Race and Ethnicity Questions from the United States 2020 Census.

defined by OMB as either "Hispanic or Latino" or "Not Hispanic or Latino." Hispanic or Latino is defined as Cuban, Mexican, Puerto Rican, South or Central American, or other Spanish culture or origin, regardless of race.

The 2020 Census race and ethnicity questions and categories are presented in questions 8 and 9 in Figure 5.1.

The 2024 revised OMB guidelines (spd15revision.gov) recommend one combined question for race and ethnicity, allowing respondents to select as many response categories as they want. The question can be presented in three formats, as shown in Figure 5.2.

**1. Minimum Categories, Multiple Detailed Checkboxes and Write-In Response Areas with Example Groups**

---

**What is your race and/or ethnicity?**
*Select all that apply* and enter additional details in the spaces below.

☐ **American Indian or Alaska Native** — *Enter, for example, Navajo Nation, Blackfeet Tribe of the Blackfeet Indian Reservation of Montana, Native Village of Barrow Inupiat Traditional Government, Nome Eskimo Community, Aztec, Maya, etc.*

☐ **Asian** — *Provide details below.*
  ☐ Chinese     ☐ Asian Indian    ☐ Filipino
  ☐ Vietnamese  ☐ Korean          ☐ Japanese
  *Enter, for example, Pakistani, Hmong, Afghan, etc.*

☐ **Black or African American** — *Provide details below.*
  ☐ African American  ☐ Jamaican   ☐ Haitian
  ☐ Nigerian          ☐ Ethiopian  ☐ Somali
  *Enter, for example, Trinidadian and Tobagonian, Ghanaian, Congolese, etc.*

☐ **Hispanic or Latino** — *Provide details below.*
  ☐ Mexican  ☐ Puerto Rican  ☐ Salvadoran
  ☐ Cuban    ☐ Dominican     ☐ Guatemalan
  *Enter, for example, Colombian, Honduran, Spaniard, etc.*

☐ **Middle Eastern or North African** — *Provide details below.*
  ☐ Lebanese  ☐ Iranian  ☐ Egyptian
  ☐ Syrian    ☐ Iraqi    ☐ Israeli
  *Enter, for example, Moroccan, Yemeni, Kurdish, etc.*

☐ **Native Hawaiian or Pacific Islander** — *Provide details below.*
  ☐ Native Hawaiian  ☐ Samoan  ☐ Chamorro
  ☐ Tongan           ☐ Fijian  ☐ Marshallese
  *Enter, for example, Chuukese, Palauan, Tahitian, etc.*

☐ **White** — *Provide details below.*
  ☐ English  ☐ German  ☐ Irish
  ☐ Italian  ☐ Polish  ☐ Scottish
  *Enter, for example, French, Swedish, Norwegian, etc.*

---

*Figure 5.2* Race/Ethnicity Question Stipulated in the 2024 OMB Guideline. *(Continued)*

## 2. Minimum Categories Only and Examples

**What is your race and/or ethnicity?**
*Select all that apply.*

☐ **American Indian or Alaska Native**
   *For example, Navajo Nation, Blackfeet Tribe of the Blackfeet Indian Reservation of Montana, Native Village of Barrow Inupiat Traditional Government, Nome Eskimo Community, Aztec, Maya, etc.*

☐ **Asian**
   *For example, Chinese, Asian Indian, Filipino, Vietnamese, Korean, Japanese, etc.*

☐ **Black or African American**
   *For example, African American, Jamaican, Haitian, Nigerian, Ethiopian, Somali, etc.*

☐ **Hispanic or Latino**
   *For example, Mexican, Puerto Rican, Salvadoran, Cuban, Dominican, Guatemalan, etc.*

☐ **Middle Eastern or North African**
   *For example, Lebanese, Iranian, Egyptian, Syrian, Iraqi, Israeli, etc.*

☐ **Native Hawaiian or Pacific Islander**
   *For example, Native Hawaiian, Samoan, Chamorro, Tongan, Fijian, Marshallese, etc.*

☐ **White**
   *For example, English, German, Irish, Italian, Polish, Scottish, etc.*

## 3. Minimum Categories Only

**What is your race and/or ethnicity?**
*Select all that apply.*

☐ American Indian or Alaska Native

☐ Asian

☐ Black or African American

☐ Hispanic or Latino

☐ Middle Eastern or North African

☐ Native Hawaiian or Pacific Islander

☐ White

*Figure 5.2 (Continued)*

### Measuring Sex and Gender Identity

Similar to race, how we collect data on a respondent's sex and gender has evolved over time, from a simple binary category (male-female) question, based on the assumptions that sex and gender do not differ from one another and sex/gender is objective in nature and does not change over time, to series of questions measuring sex assigned at birth, gender identity, and sexual orientation, based on the latest research that defines sex as a biological trait and gender as social and behavioral characteristics (e.g., Hall et al., 2021; Schudson et al., 2019).

Sexual orientation is related to both sex and gender because it is determined based on relationship of one's sex or gender and that of their partner. The National Academies of Science recommends the following measures (https://nap.nationalacademies.org/catalog/26424/measuring-sex-gender-identity-and-sexual-orientation):

*Sex at Birth and Gender Identity*

Q1: What sex were you assigned at birth, on your original birth certificate?

- Female
- Male

(Don't know)
(Prefer not to answer)

Q2: What is your current gender? [Mark only one]

- Female
- Male
- Transgender
- [If respondent is AIAN:] Two-Spirit
- I use a different term: [free text]

(Don't know)
(Prefer not to answer)

*Sexual Orientation*

Which of the following best represents how you think of yourself? [Select ONE]:

- Lesbian or gay
- Straight, that is, not gay or lesbian
- Bisexual
- [If respondent is AIAN:] Two-Spirit
- I use a different term [free-text]

(Don't know)
(Prefer not to answer)

## Measuring Income

Household income is an important concept that is highly correlated with a variety of economic, sociological, and health outcomes. However, it presents two major challenges – there are many potential sources of income, and respondents do not like to disclose how much money they have. As a result, questions measuring income are associated with high levels of missing data. In an attempt to combat these challenges and minimize measurement error, some federal surveys employ the unfolding brackets approach to collect income data. In this approach, if the respondent does not answer the initial income question, a follow-up question presenting a rounded figure is asked and respondents have to indicate if their household income is above or below that number. Similar questions could follow until a closer range for the household income can be determined. This method has been found effective in reducing nonresponse and uncertainty around income measures in many surveys (e.g., Juster & Smith, 1997; Pleis et al., 2006; Wang, 2010). Figure 5.3 presents an example from the Health and Retirement Survey.

An alternative approach many surveys employ is to provide income ranges as response options from the very beginning, instead of asking an open-ended question. For example, Figure 5.4 presents the household income question from the National Crime Victimization Survey.

---

Q015 What was your income from self-employment, before taxes and other deductions, in LAST CALENDAR YEAR?

Please include income you actually received from the business and any profits that may have been left in the business.

[INSTR: DO NOT PROBE DK/RF.]

$_____.00 .............. GO TO Q019

DK

RF

---

Q016-Q018 Question text: (Thinking about your self-employment income in [LAST CALENDAR YEAR]):

Did it amount to less than $____, more than $____, or what?

PROCEDURES: 3Up, 2Up1Down, 1Up2Down

BREAKPOINTS: $5,000, $10,000, $25,000, $100,000

RANDOM ENTRY POINT ASSIGNMENT [1 ($5,000)] or [2 ($10,000)] or [{NOT 1 and NOT 2} ($25,000)] AT X041

---

*Figure 5.3* Unfolding Brackets Example from the 2022 Health and Retirement Survey.

**90. HOUSEHOLDINCOME** (Asked of Household Respondent Only)

(Asked of household respondent.
Asked at 1st, 3rd, 5th, and 7th interview, or if never asked before. Asked at subsequent interviews if no or Don't Know/Refused at prior interview.)

Which category represents the TOTAL combined income of all members of this HOUSEHOLD during the past 12 months? This includes money from jobs, net income from business, farm or rent, pensions, dividends, interest, Social Security payments, and any other money income received by members of this HOUSEHOLD who are 14 years of age or older.

[214]

1. ☐ Less than $5,000
2. ☐ $5,000 to $7,499
3. ☐ $7,500 to $9,999
4. ☐ $10,000 to $12,499
5. ☐ $12,500 to $14,999
6. ☐ $15,000 to $17,499
7. ☐ $17,500 to $19,999
8. ☐ $20,000 to $24,999
9. ☐ $25,000 to $29,999
10. ☐ $30,000 to $34,999
11. ☐ $35,000 to $39,999
12. ☐ $40,000 to $49,999
13. ☐ $50,000 to $74,999
14. ☐ $75,000 to $99,999
15. ☐ $100,000 to $149,999
16. ☐ $150,000 to $199,999
17. ☐ $200,000 or more

*Figure 5.4* Household Income Question from the 2022 National Crime Victimization Survey.

**Knowledge Questions**

Using knowledge questions to screen out respondents who may not be knowledgeable enough to express an opinion on a topic is common in surveys. As such, knowledge screening questions can be placed anywhere in the questionnaire, or at the beginning of a series of attitudinal questions. The nature of such "no opinion" filters to a large extent determines how many respondents will get screened out. Chapter 4 distinguishes between full filters and quasi-filters with examples of each presented in Table 4.2.

When the intent is to measure political knowledge, the mode of data collection becomes an issue; in self-administered surveys, respondents can look up the correct answer or consult with others. Many studies have examined ways to prevent respondents from searching for the correct answer by specifically instructing them not to look up answers (e.g., Motta et al., 2017; Smith et al., 2020), asking for explicit commitment not to look up responses (e.g., Gummer et al., 2023b), or using pictures of politicians, instead of names (e.g., Munzert & Selb, 2017). Although some studies evaluate the efficacy of the intervention based on self-reports, many are using paradata to detect new browser widows and tab switching (e.g., Gummer & Kunz, 2022; also see Chapter 7 for a discussion), but are of course unable to detect searches on another device. The current recommendation for minimizing answer look-up is using commitment statements such as:

> It is important to us that you do not use any additional aids, such as the internet, to answer these questions. Do you agree to answer the next questions without additional aid?
> (modified from Gummer et al., 2023b)

Knowledge questions may be perceived as threatening by respondents because responses may present them in a negative light. To reduce this perceived threat, knowledge questions often begin with "Do you happen to know," "As far as you know," or "Can you recall, offhand" phrases. Such questions inherently suggest that not knowing the answer is acceptable and explicit Don't Know responses are often included as response options to reduce the possibility of guessing in closed questions.

Questions that collect numeric information are best presented as open-ended questions to avoid the risk of respondents guessing correctly somewhere in the middle of the numeric scale. In the rare occasion where Yes/No questions are appropriate, we recommend asking several questions on the same topic to reduce the likelihood of successful guessing (Sudman & Bradburn, 1982).

## Summary

Demographic questions vary in the extent to which subjective or objective elements are present, and this evolves over time, driven by societal changes. OMB has guidance on measuring important demographic characteristics, and it is a good practice to follow those recommendations, especially if federal survey data are used for weighting adjustments or comparisons. Knowledge questions have useful applications in surveys – screening out respondents, measuring knowledge of a particular field (e.g., political knowledge), and informing a qualitative portion of the questionnaire design process. However, the nature and wording of knowledge questions determine how many respondents will get screened out and should be considered carefully.

## Exercises

1 Practice bracket unfolding by developing a question asking respondents how old they were when they first had sex.
2 Discuss possible uses of knowledge questions in surveys and considerations related to placement and mode of data collection.

# Part II
# Specific Considerations

# 6 Writing Sensitive Questions and Questions for Sensitive Populations

**Introduction**

It is common for general population surveys to include sensitive questions. For instance, the National Survey on Drug Use and Health (NSDUH) includes questions on health, drug use, and criminal justice involvement. The National Survey of Family Growth (NSFG) asks detailed questions on sexual behaviors, drug use, and abortion.

Tourangeau et al. (2000) define three types of sensitive questions. The first type concerns the intrusiveness of the content of the question. A survey item is intrusive when it invades a respondent's privacy and is considered inappropriate for normal conversations (see also Tourangeau & Yan, 2007; Yan, 2021). For example, survey items about income, religion, and number of sexual partners may fall into this category. This type of sensitive question risks offending all respondents, regardless of their true status or their answers. The second type of sensitive question is related to the extent that disclosing the answer to a third party will put the person at risk of harm (Tourangeau & Yan, 2007; Tourangeau et al., 2000; Yan, 2021). For instance, people in the United States may not be comfortable providing their Social Security number because of potential stolen identity threats from disclosing that piece of information. Other disclosure risk-related examples include legal concerns about disclosing illegal drug use or citizenship status. The third type of sensitive question involves the concept of social desirability (Tourangeau & Yan, 2007; Tourangeau et al., 2000; Yan, 2021). Social desirability is the extent to which survey questions cover topics conforming to accepted social norms (DeMaio 1984; Holtgraves, 2004). Answers conforming to norms are considered socially desirable, whereas answers deviating from norms are socially undesirable. For example, society norms prescribe that good citizens are expected to vote and to *not* drink and drive. As a result, both questions on voter turnout and on driving under the influence of alcohol invoke social desirability concerns. Respondents are found to overreport socially desirable attitudes or behaviors (e.g., voting, church attendance, seat belt use, owning a library card, volunteering, and donating) and underreport socially undesirable attitudes or behaviors (e.g., drunk driving, abortion, and discrimination).

> Sometimes questions are sensitive for more than one reason. For instance, questions about criminal justice involvement are sensitive because of the intrusiveness of the topic, negative consequences of disclosure, and social stigma associated with the topic (Yan & Cantor, 2019).

DOI: 10.4324/9781003367826-8

Question sensitivity is not a stable characteristic of survey questions (Yan, 2021). The same survey questions may be perceived as more or less sensitive by people from different countries and cultures (Andreenkova & Javeline, 2019; Johnson & van de Vijver, 2002; Triandis et al., 1965), by how they are asked (Kreuter et al., 2008a), and by who answers them (e.g., Kreuter et al., 2008a). In many cases, the perceived sensitivity of a survey item depends on whether the respondent has experienced the undesirable behavior of interest. Furthermore, some questions become more sensitive over time. For instance, questions on citizenship were included in the decennial Census form from 1890 to 2000, but it became such a sensitive issue that the US Supreme Court blocked the 2020 Census from asking it (Yan, 2021).

Several ways exist to measure sensitivity of a survey question. When data are available from other surveys asking about the same concept or from previous rounds of data collection, item nonresponse rates can be used to assess question sensitivity. This is because sensitive questions such as those about income (Yan et al., 2010), citizenship (Brown et al., 2019), voting intentions (Krumpal, 2013), and number of sexual partners (Tourangeau & Yan, 2007) are shown to produce a higher level of missing data than nonsensitive questions such as those about age and education (Brown et al., 2019; Krumpal, 2013; Tourangeau & Yan, 2007). Furthermore, results from validation studies comparing survey reports to external data are also used as evidence of the presence (or absence) of question sensitivity. For instance, validation studies found that survey respondents underreported abortions (e.g., Jones & Kost, 2007) and overreported voter registration and voting turnout (e.g., McDonald et al., 2017), confirming that questions on abortion and voter turnout are sensitive. Question writers also measure question sensitivity by asking coders or judges to determine how sensitive a question concept is (Tourangeau et al., 2000). People in the target population are sometimes asked directly how sensitive a survey question is. One way to accomplish this is to probe on perceived sensitivity of target survey questions during cognitive interviews (see Willis, 2005). Alternatively, debriefing questions asking actual respondents about their perception of the sensitivity of survey questions can be included at the end of the survey (e.g., Kreuter et al., 2008a).

> Question sensitivity differs by culture, region, and country, and over time. Question sensitivity can be assessed through item nonresponse rates, validation studies, and reported perception of sensitivity.

## Strategies for Asking Sensitive Questions

Yan (2021) described the impact of asking sensitive questions from the Total Survey Error perspective. Of particular importance to questionnaire design are the established empirical findings that people tend to *not* answer some sensitive questions such as those about income (Yan et al., 2010) and misreport their answers to other sensitive questions (Bradburn et al., 2004; Tourangeau & Yan, 2007; Tourangeau et al., 2000). As a result, when writing sensitive questions, the goals are to alleviate item nonresponse and to reduce socially desirable responding. Survey researchers have been developing methods and strategies to achieve these dual goals by changing either the environment in which sensitive questions are asked or the way sensitive questions are phrased. We group the strategies and techniques into three categories: (1) strategies related to survey design protocol, (2) strategies on preparing respondents for the task, and (3) strategies on writing sensitive questions.

The first two categories aim to change the environment in which respondents are asked sensitive questions, whereas the third category focuses on how to ask sensitive questions.

**Strategies Related to Survey Design Protocol**

This section discusses specific survey design features that can be used to change the environment in which sensitive questions are asked to reduce social desirability concerns and improve perceived privacy.

> Survey design features shown to improve answers to sensitive questions include using self-administration, using a diary, and enhancing privacy and ensuring anonymity.

*Using a Self-administered Mode*

The survey literature has shown consistently that using a self-administered survey mode (e.g., web) increases disclosure of sensitive information and reduces socially desirable responding when compared to an interviewer-administered mode of data collection such as face-to-face interviewing (Bradburn et al., 2004; Tourangeau & Yan, 2007; Yan, 2021; Yan & Cantor, 2019). Self-administration removes interviewers from the survey-answering process, which eliminates respondents' need to look good in front of the interviewer and their concerns about privacy, and, thus, reduces social desirability bias in the resultant answers. For instance, data using NSFG have shown that women reported more abortions and miscarriages during the audio computer-assisted self-interviewing (ACASI) portion of the interview than when interviewed by an interviewer during computer-assisted personal interviewing (e.g., Yan & Tourangeau, 2022). Many large-scale surveys such as NSFG, NSDUH, and the Population Assessment of Tobacco and Health (PATH) include ACASI as part of the survey design for sensitive questions. One word of caution, however. Studies have shown that interviewers still affect answers to ACASI questionnaire even though interviewers only stay around and do not directly administer the ACASI questionnaire (e.g., West & Peytcheva, 2014).

In terms of different forms of self-administration, Tourangeau and Yan (2007) found no difference between computerized self-administration (e.g., web) and paper-and-pencil self-administration (e.g., mail surveys) in disclosure of sensitive information.

*Collecting Data in Private and Ensuring Anonymity*

The presence of other people (also called bystanders) at an interviewer-administered survey setting is found to increase misreporting to sensitive questions (e.g., Diop et al., 2015). In particular, the presence of parents during an interviewer-administered survey significantly increases social desirability bias in children's answers to sensitive questions (Tourangeau & Yan, 2007). As a result, Tourangeau and Yan (2007) recommend that survey interviews be conducted in a private setting, so that respondents are not concerned about someone else overhearing their answers to sensitive questions.

For self-administered surveys, respondents are usually encouraged to complete the self-administered survey in a private setting. Research has shown that *not* asking respondents to provide their full names (Ong & Weiss, 2000) or *not* showing any identifying information (Yang & Yu, 2011) increases socially undesirable answers. We recommend taking additional steps to ensure anonymity for self-administered surveys.

*Using a Diary*

Bradburn et al. (2004) suggest using the diary approach to collect sensitive information because it does not invoke the same level of social desirability concerns as survey questions directly asking about sensitive topics. For instance, asking respondents to keep a diary on their time use yields more accurate information on their church attendance than a direct question asking them to self-report church attendance. Similarly, asking respondents to keep a diary on expenditures produces more accurate information on alcohol expenditure and drinking than direct survey questions. However, the major limitation with using this approach to reduce social desirability bias is that not all sensitive behaviors can be easily measured with such an approach. Besides, the diary approach has other undesirable measurement properties (see Yan & Machado, 2023, for a review of different types of diaries). For instance, diaries are not filled out every day as expected and desired by survey researchers, and the process of filling out a diary could create demand characteristic by changing the behavior of interest.

**Strategies on Preparing Respondents for the Task**

*Commitment, Instructions, and Honesty Pledge*

Commitment and instructions are two techniques proposed in the 1980s to improve respondents' question-answering performance in interviewer-administered surveys (Cannell et al., 1981). The idea behind instructions is to let respondents know what is expected from them and how they achieve those expectations. With commitment, respondents are asked to formally commit to be diligent in doing what is expected from them. The two complement each other. Cannell et al. (1981) showed that combining commitment and instructions increased disclosure of embarrassing information for respondents regardless of their education status.

> Cannell et al. (1981) used instructions for two questions:
>
> - *Let me just mention that, to be most accurate, you may need to take your time to think carefully before you answer.*
> - *On this next question, we'd like to get numbers as exact as possible.*

Two studies investigated the use of commitment and instructions on web surveys. Clifford and Jerit (2015) presented web respondents with a question:

> "It is important to us that participants in our survey pay close attention to the materials. Are you willing to carefully read the materials and answer all of the questions to the best of your ability?"

and respondents could select Yes or No. They found that asking for commitment reduced the number of socially desirable responses only for respondents with low education.

Cibelli (2017) did not find an effect of commitment on improving disclosure of sensitive information in her web studies. It is important to note that these studies vary in how instructions were conveyed and how commitment was sought.

McDonald et al. (2017) tested a slightly different type of commitment – they asked a random half of their web respondents during a pre-election survey to take an honesty pledge ("Are you willing to keep track of whether you voted in the upcoming November election and to be honest when you report this?"). In the subsequent post-election survey, respondents were asked whether they voted in the November election. Comparing self-reports of voter turnout to records shows that the honesty pledge reduced the overreport of voter turnout by 5.3 percentage points for the full sample and 10.9 percentage points for nonvoters.

These studies demonstrate the potential of using commitment, instruction, and honesty pledges to reduce socially desirable responding. However, it is critical to test the instructions and procedures of obtaining commitment and pledge before they are fielded.

> Cannell et al. (1981) described one commitment procedure used in a face-to-face survey:
>
> That's the last of this set of questions. The rest of the questions are on how media like newspapers, TV, and radio fit into your daily life. We are asking people we interview to give us extra cooperation and that they try hard to answer accurately so we can get complete and accurate information about this topic. You are one of the people we hope is willing to make the extra effort. Here is an agreement that explains what we are asking you to do. (HAND AGREEMENT) As you can see, it says, "I understand that the information from this interview must be very accurate in order to be useful. This means that I must do my best to give accurate and complete answers. I agree to do this." We are asking people to sign an agreement and keep it for themselves so that we can be sure they understand what we are asking them to do. It is up to you to decide. If you are willing to agree to do this, we'd like you to sign your name here. (POINT OUT LINE) Down below there is a statement about confidentiality, and I will sign my name there. (POINT OUT LINE) (IF R HAS NOT ALREADY SIGNED) Are you willing to make the extra effort to continue the interview?

*Priming*

Priming is a concept in psychology to describe an automatic and unconscious process of exposure to one stimulus affecting responses to a later stimulus. Two studies have examined the use of a priming task to change respondents' motivation to report honestly. Rasinski et al. (2004) gave undergraduate students a vocabulary task before asking them to complete a seemingly unrelated questionnaire on alcohol consumption. A random half of the respondents received neutral words; the other half received a combination of neutral words and words related to honesty. They found that respondents primed to be honest (through the vocabulary task with words related to honesty) reported more sensitive behaviors involving excessive alcohol consumption. Acquisti et al. (2012) primed a volunteer sample of *New York Times* readers on privacy through a photo identification task. Participants were asked to identify either phishing emails or endangered fish before completing a Web survey. They found that the privacy priming through identification of phishing emails decreased respondents' propensity to admit socially undesirable behaviors (Study 2c). Question writers are encouraged to prime respondents' motivation to report truthfully.

*Bogus Pipeline*

The bogus pipeline technique aims to convince respondents that the researchers have a way of knowing if they lie. For example, Bauman and Dent (1982) warned respondents beforehand that their breath sample would be used to determine whether they had smoked before asking them about smoking. Tourangeau et al. (1997) told respondents that their inaccurate answers could be detected by a physiological recording device. Hanmer et al. (2014) told respondents through an introduction to the survey that their answers would be checked against public records kept by election officials. In all of these studies, the collection of additional information before survey administration was never used in reality to check against the truth, hence the name "bogus pipeline." All the studies reported that the technique effectively reduced social desirability bias in answers to sensitive questions.

**Strategies on Writing Sensitive Questions**

This section describes strategies on how to phrase sensitive questions, including manipulations on lead-ins or introductions, question wording, and response options.

*Desensitizing the Question*

Desensitizing a target-sensitive question by preceding it with an even more sensitive question has been found to elicit more disclosures of socially undesirable answers. For instance, Acquisti et al. (2012) empirically showed that significantly more respondents reported littering in a public space when the question was asked after sensitive questions on one's sexual life such as having an affair with a friend's spouse than when the question was preceded by less intrusive questions (e.g., failing to tip a waiter, failing to do chores). This is because a question becomes less sensitive and threatening when it is preceded by a more sensitive and threatening question. Although Bradburn et al. (2004) listed this approach as a potential strategy, they also acknowledged that this approach has limitations because it may lead to survey breakoffs. We suggest that question writers consider this approach with caution.

*Choosing the Appropriate Time Frame*

For socially undesirable behaviors, Bradburn et al. (2004) suggest starting with a question asking about "ever" before asking about "current" status. This is because questions about events that happened in the past are less salient and threatening than questions about current behaviors. The PATH Study adopts this approach by first asking if one ever smoked a cigarette, and for those answering yes, whether they now smoke every day, some days, or not at all (https://www.icpsr.umich.edu/files/NAHDAP/pathstudy/36231-1001-Questionnaire-English.pdf). In contrast, for socially desirable behaviors, Bradburn et al. (2004) suggest first asking about "current" behavior before asking about "ever."

## Using Forgiving Introduction

Forgiving introductions, also called "face-saving," or "permissive" introductions, are recommended when asking sensitive questions (Bradburn et al., 2004; Tourangeau & Yan, 2007). They are intended to reduce perceived sensitivity of the questions by normalizing or justifying the undesirable behavior or attitude and to eliminate any concerns about negative consequences of giving a truthful answer.

> Question writers can utilize question order, time frame, forgiving introduction, question wording, response options, and indirect methods to encourage truthful response and to reduce misreporting to sensitive questions.

Forgiving introductions take several forms and can be summarized into four main groups. The first is the "everyone does it" approach. A humorous exemplification of this approach is shown by Barton (1958) ("As you know, many people have been killing their wives these days. Do you happen to have killed yours?"). Holtgraves et al. (1997) presented a survey question on vandalism with this type of forgiving introduction: "Almost everyone has probably committed vandalism at one time or another." The second form of forgiving introduction uses an authority to justify the behavior: "Many doctors now believe that moderate drinking of liquor helps to reduce the likelihood of heart attacks or strokes" (Bradburn et al., 2004). The third type of forgiving introduction shows two or more sides of a story using the "some... others..." format. A typical example is provided by Peter and Valkenburg (2011): "Some people use erotic or pornographic materials often, while others do this rarely or never." The fourth type of forgiving introduction provides a face-saving excuse for not doing something socially desirable or for doing something socially undesirable. Holtgraves et al. (1997) provided an example of such a face-saving introduction to an item about global warming: "You may not have had enough time to learn about the GATT treaty because of a heavy load of school work." All these studies have found that providing forgiving instructions increases reporting of socially undesirable behaviors.

## Question Wording Strategies

Several strategies have been used to improve the wording of sensitive questions. The first strategy **assumes the socially undesirable behavior and asks about it** (Bradburn et al., 2004; Tourangeau & Yan, 2007). For instance, to measure the number of cigarettes people smoke each day, we can ask respondents directly: "How many cigarettes do you smoke each day?" The second strategy employs **face-saving question wording**. One example is provided in Holtgraves and colleagues (1997): "Have you had the opportunity to learn the details of the Clinton Health Care Plan?" The third strategy **uses long questions with words familiar** to respondents, especially when asking socially undesirable behaviors (Bradburn et al., 2004). For instance, Blair and colleagues (1997) first asked respondents to provide their own word for intoxication and then used that word in the question below on frequency of intoxication:

> *Occasionally, people drink on an empty stomach or drink a little too much and become (RESPONDENT'S WORD FOR INTOXICATION). In the past year, how often did you become (RESPONDENT'S WORD FOR INTOXICATION) while drinking any kind of alcoholic beverage?*

This question was found to outperform the standard questionnaire item ("In the past year, how often did you become intoxicated while drinking any kind of alcoholic beverage?").

*Response Option Strategies*

As discussed in the earlier chapters, respondents use response options to make inferences on the norm of the behaviors. A high-frequency scale (0, 1–4, 5–9, 10–49, 50–99, 100 or more) conveys a higher norm than a low-frequency scale (0, 1, 2, 3, 4, 5 or more). As a result, respondents were found to report more sexual partners when given the high-frequency scale than the low-frequency scale (Tourangeau & Smith, 1996). Furthermore, respondents reported more sexual partners when no response list was provided than when a low-frequency list was used (Tourangeau & Smith, 1996). Consequently, we recommend that question writers **use the open-ended question format or a high-frequency scale** when asking frequency of socially undesirable behaviors (Bradburn et al., 2004; Tourangeau & Yan, 2007; Yan, 2021; Yan & Cantor, 2019).

**Face-saving response options** are used to lower the threat of truthfully disclosing socially undesirable behaviors. Zeglovitis and Kritzinger (2014) provided two additional face-saving response options to a question asking about voter turnout besides the yes/no dichotomous response options: "I thought about voting this time but didn't" and "I usually vote but didn't this time." The addition of face-saving response options significantly increased the percentage of respondents reporting not voting in the last election.

The **unfolding brackets technique** is recommended for sensitive questions asking about income, assets, and other financial information as discussed in Chapter 5. Figure 5.2 provides a great example of this technique. Yan et al. (2010) showed empirically the positive impact of using unfolding brackets to reduce missing data to income questions.

*Using Indirect Questions*

Answers to direct questions reveal respondents' involvement in socially (un)desirable behaviors. For instance, a "Yes" answer to a survey question asking about having had an abortion in the last 5 years clearly reveals that the respondent has had an abortion. By contrast, indirect methods aim to protect the anonymity of respondents' answers by breaking the link between answers and involvement in the socially (un)desirable behaviors.

There are several types of indirect methods. The **randomized response technique (RRT),** originally proposed by Warner (1965), relies on a randomizing mechanism (e.g., asking the respondent to flip a coin or throw a die) to determine that the respondent is supposed answer the sensitive question. There are different ways to do it. Greenberg et al. (1969) described two approaches. The first approach is to ask respondents to agree or disagree with either a sensitive statement (e.g., I have had an abortion) or the complement statement (e.g., I have not had an abortion). The second approach uses an unrelated and nonsensitive statement instead of the complement statement (e.g., "I was born in North Carolina"). A third approach is to instruct the respondent to answer the sensitive question truthfully when the randomization results in a certain outcome (e.g., when the coin flip is tails), but to give a predetermined answer (such as always responding "No") otherwise (e.g., Boruch, 1971; Fox & Tracy, 1984). Holbrook and Krosnick (2010) provided an application of using RRT to measure voter turnout. The randomizing mechanism provides protection for the respondent's true status with respect to the sensitive question because there is a stochastic uncertainty as to which question was answered. A related variation – **the cross-wise model** – presents both the sensitive and the nonsensitive question to respondents and provides two response options for respondents to choose from. The two response options are "my answers are the same for both questions" and "my answers are different for both questions" (Jann et al., 2012).

The **item count technique (ICT)** is another type of indirect method in which respondents are randomly assigned to receive a long list of questions including the sensitive question of interest, or the same list without the sensitive question (Droitcour et al., 1991; Miller, 1984). Respondents are then asked to provide the number of items from the list they answered positively. A respondent's true value on the sensitive question is protected because the answer is an overall count variable of all "Yes" responses. The prevalence of the sensitive behavior is estimated by taking the difference in the counts between the two lists. Variations of this method include using two pairs of lists (e.g., Biemer & Brown, 2005) and **item sum technique** designed for continuous variables (Trappmann et al., 2014).

Two major disadvantages are common to indirect methods. First, a larger sample size is needed because of the randomization. Second, estimates at the aggregate level can be calculated, but individual responses are not known, making it impossible to analyze the data at the individual level. Methods have been developed for multivariate regression analysis of data obtained from the ICT, enabling researchers to assess how the probability of answering Yes to the sensitive question varies as a function of respondents' characteristics (Imai, 2011), but the application is not straightforward and may not be applicable to other types of indirect methods.

## Strategies for Writing Questions for Older and Younger Respondents

Older and younger people are two sensitive populations. There is a growing literature demonstrating that older and younger respondents differ in cognitive functioning and are differentially affected by questionnaire features during the survey response process (Schwarz et al., 1999). As a result, question writers should take into consideration the cognitive abilities of their target population.

### Asking Older Respondents

It is established that aging is related to a decline in basic functions, such as attention and working memory capacity (Salthouse & Babcock, 1991) and higher level functioning such as speech and language abilities, reasoning, and decision-making (Kutschar & Weichbold, 2019). The decline in cognitive functioning poses challenges at every stage of the survey response process, making it harder for older respondents to answer survey questions (see a review by Knäuper et al., 2016). For instance, older respondents are more likely to encounter comprehension issues with negatively worded items and complex content (Fox et al., 2007). Older respondents encounter greater difficulty remembering where or when they experienced an event or

> Question writers should be mindful about declining cognitive functioning among the aging population. Survey questions should be simple and short. And older adults should be given more time to answer survey questions.

learned a fact, partially because of decline in both long- and short-term memories and partially because they are likely to have more to retrieve (Craik, 1999). Older respondents have also been found to have difficulties with judgment and mapping – they are more likely to provide missing data or "Don't know" answers (e.g., Kutschar & Weichbold, 2019), imprecise answers (Andrews & Herzog, 1986), inadequate answers (Holbrook et al., 2006; Olson et al., 2018), and answers that cannot be easily coded into categories (Olson et al., 2018). Finally, older respondents are found to have difficulty using numeric response options (Fox et al., 2007) and bipolar scales (Fox et al., 2007; Krestar et al., 2012).

On the positive side, declining working memory capacity makes previously used information less accessible to older respondents. Consequently, older respondents are less likely to be affected by question order effects (Knäuper et al., 2007), as discussed in Chapter 4. However, when answering questions on less salient and less relevant topics, they are more likely to be affected by the order of response options (Knäuper, 1999) and the number and range of response options (Knäuper et al., 2004).

Given the difficulties older respondents have answering survey questions, we suggest writing simpler and shorter questions and using fewer response options. We also suggest allowing older respondents to take time to answer questions; several studies have demonstrated that older adults who take longer to answer questions provide better quality data than those who answer faster (e.g., Yan et al., 2015).

### Asking Younger Respondents

Children's cognitive development is closely related to age. Theories differ on age cutoffs when describing children's cognitive development stages. We adopt the cutoffs used by de Leeuw et al. (2004). Children under the age of 7 have not developed the cognitive functioning required to answer survey questions. As a result, we do not recommend surveying this age group directly; instead, we suggest proxy reporting by parents and guardians, combined with special data collection techniques aimed for children, such as playing assessment, drawings, story completion and puzzle tasks, and observational studies.

Children between the ages of 7 and 12 are better with logical and systematic thinking but are still growing in terms of cognitive processing and memory capacity. At that age, respondents have been shown to have difficulties with vague words (de Leeuw et al., 2004), negatively phrased questions (Borgers et al., 2000), indirect questions (Borgers et al., 2000; Scott, 1997), ambiguous questions (Borgers & Hox, 2001; Scott, 1997), and questions with more response options (Borgers & Hox, 2001). Interestingly, children with 4–6 years of education had less missing data to sensitive questions but more missing data to questions that were coded as not sensitive by researchers (Borgers & Hox, 2001). Children in this age group have a short attention span, may satisfice when they find the survey uninteresting or too long, or provide socially desirable or acquiescing answers because they can be easily influenced (Borgers et al., 2000; de Leeuw et al., 2004). They do not have difficulty navigating grid questions on the web (Maitland et al., 2016) and produce data of sufficient reliability and validity for questions using emojis to illustrate response

> Question writers should be mindful about the cognitive development of children and write questions appropriate for their age.

options (e.g., Massey, 2022). Thus, if surveying children between 7 and 12 years of age, we suggest using simple language and offering two to three response options. If response scales with more than two or three options are to be used, consider using emojis instead of verbally labeling the long response scales.

Children aged 13–17 have well-developed cognitive functioning, including formal thinking, negations, and logic, and are considered able to answer survey questions on their own (Borgers et al., 2000; de Leeuw et al., 2004). Studies show that youth of this age group provide equally reliable answers to questions about tobacco and health as adults (Tourangeau et al., 2019). In addition, they have been able to navigate web instruments and provide insights on their interactions and experiences with the web survey and adults (Yang et al., 2021). However, the setting of interviews is important for youth of this age group. Studies have found that youth reported more risk behaviors when interviewed at schools than at home (Brener et al., 2006; Fendrich & Johnson, 2001).

Youth of this age group provide more reliable answers to demographic questions, questions with yes/no response options, and questions using simple words (Tourangeau et al., 2020b). We suggest writing questions that are short, clear, and use simple words, and using shorter response options. To assist youth, we suggest providing a brief and clear introduction using child-friendly language and a bullet point list of simple instructions on what is expected from them (O'Reilly et al., 2013). We also suggest keeping data collection private if interviews are done at the home of youth.

**Summary**

Survey questions are sensitive because they are personal or intrusive, there is a disclosure risk, and they invoke a social norm. In many cases, the perceived sensitivity of a survey item depends on whether the respondent has experienced the behavior of interest. We reiterate below strategies question writers can use to alleviate item nonresponse and to reduce socially desirable responding.

Strategies pertaining to survey design protocol include the following:

1 Using a self-administered mode
2 Using a diary if appropriate
3 Collecting data in private and ensuring anonymity

Strategies on how to prepare respondents for the task of answering sensitive questions include the following:

1 Providing instructions, asking for commitment, asking for an honesty pledge
2 Priming
3 Bogus pipeline technique

Strategies on writing sensitive questions include the following:

1 Embedding the question
2 Choosing an appropriate time frame
3 Using a forgiving introduction

58  *A Practical Guide to Survey Questionnaire Design and Evaluation*

4  Implementing wording strategies such as using questions presupposing behavior, using long questions with familiar words, and using face-saving wording
5  Implementing response option strategies such as open-ended format or a high-frequency list for questions asking about frequency or numbers, using unfolding brackets for questions on income and assets, and providing face-saving options

For respondents aged 65 and above and respondents under the age of 18, we suggest using short questions and fewer response options, and allowing more time to answer.

**Exercises**

1  How does social desirability affect survey responses?
2  Describe two ways you can reduce the effects of social desirability when asking respondents about drug use.
3  How would you write survey questions asking older respondents and teenagers about their drug use?

# 7 Design of Paper Surveys

**Introduction**

Starting with this chapter, we focus on considerations for developing surveys for various modes of data collection and cultures and languages. We reiterate the importance of following best practices, guidelines, and recommendations discussed in Section 1 of this book. This section deals with mode-, culture-, and language-specific considerations. We start with designing paper surveys.

Paper surveys continue to be a popular mode of data collection, especially in recent years. They are commonly sent to sampled members by mail (and thus are also called "mail surveys") but can also be delivered to sampled members by interviewers. In this book, we use the terms *paper surveys*, *paper questionnaires*, *mail surveys*, and *mail questionnaires* interchangeably.

When mailed to sampled members, paper surveys present several significant advantages over other modes: lower cost and ability to reach a large geographical area. Most importantly, paper surveys are an effective mode for the non-internet population. However, paper surveys can also present some challenges because the burden of understanding how to accurately navigate the survey falls on the respondent, who determines the pace and order of questions, having the ability to review all items and response options at once. That loss of control over the questionnaire order can change the intended interpretation of questions (see Chapter 4 for a discussion on context effects). In addition, the lack of help by an interviewer and the need to deal with skip logic often affects respondents' motivation – not surprisingly, mail surveys exhibit more measurement error (satisficing answers, item nonresponse, primacy effects, straightlining, errors of omission and commission) than other modes of data collection (de Leeuw, 2018).

Therefore, an important task for questionnaire designers is to design paper questionnaires in a way that makes them easy to follow and understand by applying visual principles that reduce nonresponse and measurement errors. The visual presentation of information significantly impacts whether people will respond to a paper survey and their ability to comprehend the questions, retrieve information, formulate judgments, and select responses (DeMaio & Bates, 1992; Dillman et al., 1993, 2014); thus, it is important to understand the elements and principles of visual design before we discuss their application.

Self-administered questionnaire design (such as paper questionnaires and web questionnaires) includes four types of visual design elements: *words* (e.g., the question stem), *numbers* (e.g., response option scales, reference periods), *symbols* (e.g., an arrow to

DOI: 10.4324/9781003367826-9

communicate where respondents should focus next), and *graphics* (e.g., radio buttons, shaded background, text boxes). Each of these elements has *properties* that can be manipulated to attract more or less attention – these include size, font, color, contrast, location, shape, orientation, and motion. For example, **bolding** utilizes contrast and color to attract attention.

Dillman et al. (2014) identify three steps that respondents undertake to process visual elements:

- *Basic Page Layout* – Respondents do a quick scan of the page and preattentively process color, size, and other visual elements. For example, respondents notice the basic page layout, dark versus light areas on the page, and different shapes and sizes of elements. This step is associated with bottom-up processing, where only the visual elements influence how information is perceived.
- *Information Organization* – Respondents organize information by segmenting the page into regions and perceiving relationships across elements. At this step, respondents begin to distinguish header, logos, survey title, instructions, sections that group questions together, and response option boxes. This step is associated with top-down processing, where the context and respondent's cultural knowledge and expectations influence the meaning assigned to visual elements.
- *Task Completion* – Respondents' focus changes from the whole page to a smaller area for focused processing where attention is on components of each question. At this step, respondents initiate question comprehension, using all information associated with the question and assigning meaning to the visual elements. This step is also associated with top-down processing.

To design surveys that take into consideration these three processing steps and to a certain extent control a respondent's perception at each step, the Gestalt grouping principles can be applied:

- *Proximity* – Elements close to each other belong to the same group.
- *Similarity* – Objects that look similar in size, shape, color, and contrast belong to the same group.
- *Continuity* – Lines follow the smoothest path.
- *Closure* – People will perceive a whole object even when it is incomplete, filling in missing information.
- *Connectedness* – Objects connected by other objects are perceived as a group.

In the next sections, we focus on best practices related to physical format, question organization within the questionnaire, and layout, including front and back cover, taking into consideration the Gestalt grouping principles and the processing of visual elements model.

**Questionnaire Format**

A simple booklet in portrait format has been proven to work best in terms of respondents not missing pages of the questionnaire or having trouble fitting it in the mail-back envelope (Dillman et al., 1998). This is a standard reading format in most Western cultures and is processed automatically by respondents; thus, they do not have to understand how to handle the questionnaire while trying to answer survey questions. A consideration during the design of a mail questionnaire is that booklet formats require pages to be added or deleted in units of four, so paper size becomes an important factor (Dillman et al., 2014).

Furthermore, the booklet size determines whether pages should be in single- or double-column format. For booklets of size 7"×8.5" (folded legal size paper), one column is recommended; for booklets of size 8.8"×11", two-column format is recommended to allow more questions per page, especially when the questions are relatively short. For complex or longer questions, one-column format performs better, regardless of the booklet size. In addition, one-column formats are used when the goal is to match as closely as possible a scrollable web survey for mixed-mode surveys employing both modes. Figure 7.1 provides an example page of a double-column format from the 2023 National Survey of College Graduates.

**Questionnaire Layout**

One of the main goals of good visual layout is to create a common stimulus for everyone, similar to how respondents in interviewer-administered surveys are exposed to the same stimulus (Dillman, 2000). This means ensuring that people understand intended groupings across questions such as what response options belong to which question, and how to navigate through the questionnaire. Thus, completing a self-administered mail survey entails understanding the written words *and* the graphical symbols and visual cues of the questionnaire. Dillman (2000) outlines three steps for bringing these two components together:

*Step 1*: Define a desired navigation path for reading all information presented – this step involves thinking carefully about what instructions should be presented within the question itself (rather than at the beginning of the questionnaire or as separate entities) and visually and consistently presenting the response options in a way that makes clear to respondents that after reading the question they need to select from the listed categories.

*Step 2*: Create visual navigation guides that will assist respondents in adhering to the prescribed navigational path and correctly interpret the written information. This step involves several important design decisions:

- the size of elements to attract attention – for example, bolding or larger front are often used for the question stem, while response options are presented in lighter or smaller font;
- consistent use of light color and spacing to signal grouping of questions or distinguishing between questions;
- starting the survey at the upper left quadrant and placing information that is not important in the lower right quadrant;
- consecutive and simple numbering of questions from the beginning to end;
- listing answer categories vertically or horizontally in one row, avoiding double or triple banking and ensuring equal spacing between response categories;
- placing nonsubstantive response options (such as "Don't Know," "Undecided," or "No Opinion," if offered) separately from substantive response options using space or a horizontal line; and

- using different shapes for the answer categories to convey if a single (e.g., circle or radio button) or multiple responses (e.g., check boxes) are needed.

*Step 3:* Develop additional visual navigation guides when an established navigation behavior is interrupted because of skip logic and change of reference period. These guides include major visual changes such as:

- directional arrows;
- increased font size;
- repetition of the qualifying condition (e.g., "If Yes");
- indent of the follow-up question, so only questions that apply to everyone start at the left margin of the page; and
- visually emphasizing words or phrases that introduce a change in the pattern through bolding or underlining (e.g., moving to series of questions asking about "the past 2 weeks" from questions asking about "the past 12 months").

Experiments have been conducted to test how to best design skip instructions to minimize errors of omission (wrongly skipping a question) or commission (wrongfully responding to a question that should be skipped out) by respondents (Gohring & Smyth, 2013; Redline et al., 2003, 2005). The results show that including advanced warning of shift in navigation, using directional arrows and larger, bold font, and indentation minimizes total error rates.

Figure 7.1 demonstrates the application of these steps. It starts with a section title in the upper left corner, alerting respondents where to start. The question numbering helps navigate from question to question, and the bolded question stem clearly indicates when a new question is being asked. Instructions are largely included within the question stem, while answering instructions (e.g., "Mark Yes or No for each item") or examples are visually separated by using italics. The response options are left white, suggesting to respondents that action is needed on their part – either checking a box, writing a number, or providing an open-ended response. Navigation arrows are used for more complex scenarios, such as skip logic and response tables to clearly indicate how to navigate depending on a response and which box belongs to which answer category.

The creation of subgroupings through contrast and color is important. A standard practice in questionnaire design is to use darker color or bolding for the question stem and lighter color or smaller print for the response options, as demonstrated in Figure 7.1. In addition, standardized spacing between questions and within response options also helps reinforce subgrouping within questions. For open-ended questions, the response boxes should differ depending on the nature of the open-ended question – a descriptive open-ended question should present a large box, providing respondents with plenty of space to write in their response (question A6 in Figure 7.1); one that asks for a numeric response should present a smaller box, commensurate with the desired format for the answer (e.g., two fields for month and four fields for year, as in question A4, Figure 7.1). When multiple open-ended responses are required to the same question (e.g., instead of asking for the title of respondent's last job, question A5 could have asked for all job titles ever held), an effective way to convey that multiple responses are needed is to provide multiple answer boxes, instead of one large box (Dillman et al., 2014).

33213034    INFORMATION ONLY - DO NOT USE TO REPORT

## Part A – Employment Situation

**A1.** During the week of February 1, 2023, were you working for pay or profit?

*Working for pay or profit also includes being a student on paid work-study, self-employed and did not get paid that week, on vacation from work, traveling while employed, on personal leave, sick leave, or other temporary leave.*

Use an X to mark your answer.

- ₁ ☐ Yes → *Go to question A8*
- ₂ ☐ No

**A2.** *(If No)* Did you look for work during the four weeks preceding February 1, 2023 – that is, between January 4ᵗʰ and February 1ˢᵗ?

- ₁ ☐ Yes
- ₂ ☐ No

**A3.** Do any of the following reasons describe why you were not working during the week of February 1, 2023?

*Mark Yes or No for each item.*

|   | Yes | No |
|---|---|---|
| 1 Retired............................................ | ₁ ☐ | ₂ ☐ |
|     If Yes → Year retired ☐☐☐☐ |  |  |
| 2 On layoff from a job ..................... | ₁ ☐ | ₂ ☐ |
| 3 Student.......................................... | ₁ ☐ | ₂ ☐ |
| 4 Family responsibilities ................. | ₁ ☐ | ₂ ☐ |
| 5 Chronic illness or permanent disability ....................... | ₁ ☐ | ₂ ☐ |
| 6 Suitable job not available.............. | ₁ ☐ | ₂ ☐ |
| 7 Did not need or want to work ........ | ₁ ☐ | ₂ ☐ |
| 8 Other reason, *specify* ⤳ ............... | ₁ ☐ | ₂ ☐ |

**A4.** Prior to the week of February 1, 2023, when did you last work for pay or profit?

₀ ☐ ← *Mark this box if you never worked for pay or profit and then go to page 11, question D1*

Last worked — Month ☐☐  Year ☐☐☐☐

**A5.** What was the title of the last job you held prior to the week of February 1, 2023?

*Example: Financial Analyst*

**A6.** What kind of work were you doing on your last job – that is, what were your duties and responsibilities? Please be as specific as possible, including any area of specialization.

*Examples: Analyzed financial information, prepared technical reports, specialized in asset management.*

**A7.** Using the JOB CATEGORY list on pages 20-21, choose the code that **best** describes the last job you held prior to the week of February 1, 2023.

Code ☐☐☐ → *Go to page 8, question A42*

Note: Job category codes range from 010 to 500

**A8.** Although you were working during the week of February 1, had you previously retired from any position?

*Examples of retirement include voluntary retirement, early retirement, or mandatory retirement.*

- ₁ ☐ Yes → Year retired ☐☐☐☐
- ₂ ☐ No

*Figure 7.1* Example Page from the 2023 National Survey of College Graduates.

The principles of visual design can also be applied to emphasize or deemphasize certain question elements – for example, question A4 in Figure 7.1 utilizes underlining to draw respondent's attention to the word "never" and help with task comprehension.

**Question Order**

Similar to other modes, organizing questions by topic is important for minimizing respondent burden and conveying professionalism. Typically, the most salient topics are asked first to engage respondents, meet their expectations related to the introduced survey title, and keep them motivated.

One of the critical decisions related to question order is what is the first question, as it is likely to drive a respondent's decision whether to proceed with the questionnaire. The first question should apply to everyone, be easy to answer, be relevant to the survey topic, and be interesting to most respondents. Table 7.1 shows examples of acceptable and unacceptable first questions from Dillman (2000). The acceptable first questions in this example are general, likely to engage a large audience, and easy to answer. In contrast, the unacceptable first questions require tremendous cognitive burden – free recall and a ranking task that are likely to create a negative first impression.

As discussed in Chapter 5, even though demographic questions are easy to answer, they should not be asked at the beginning of a survey because their direct link to the survey topic is not obvious to respondents. Such questions are typically placed toward the end of the questionnaire on the premise that respondents who have already invested time and effort will not abandon the survey at the end. An exception could be made when there is a need to ask demographic questions first to establish eligibility before completing the survey (see Chapter 5).

In addition to grouping together questions on a similar topic, it is also helpful, within a topic, to combine questions with similar structure – for example, questions on self-rated

*Table 7.1* Examples of Acceptable and Unacceptable First Questions

| *Acceptable first questions* | *Unacceptable first questions* |
|---|---|
| Thinking about this community, how would you rate it as a place to live?<br>• Excellent<br>• Good<br>• Fair<br>• Poor | Please think about all the things that make this community a pleasant place to live. Then please write down the five most important aspects of community that make this community a pleasant place to live, and rank them from 1 (meaning most important) to 5 (the least important of the five attributes). |
| How long have you lived in this community?<br>• More than 6 months<br>• Less than 6 months | Please describe in your own words what you consider good about living in this community. |

*Source*: Dillman (2000).

health that use the same Likert scale can be grouped together, as can questions with Yes-No response options or those that otherwise use the same response categories. Often, such groupings take the form of grids, such as the one presented in Figure 7.2. To avoid respondents skipping a question in error, shading of every other line in the grid is used to create visual distinction between the questions. Grouping similarly structured questions together reduces cognitive burden by teaching respondents how to answer a particular type of question and letting them answer a series of such questions rather than changing the instructions for a different type.

However, one should also be aware of context effects (see Chapter 2), not only for questions of close proximity but also across the whole instrument, given a respondent's ability to review the questionnaire and change previous responses. A decision on what questions should be presented together on one page or two facing pages is also important for managing context effects. Separating questions on different pages creates a break in the information carryover and may be a way to avoid unwanted question order effects.

| 58. Have you ever...? | Yes | No |
|---|---|---|
| a. Had chest pain when walking uphill or upstairs that is relieved by rest | ☐ | ☐ |
| b. Had calf pain when walking uphill or upstairs that is relieved by rest | ☐ | ☐ |
| c. Had shortness of breath when walking uphill or upstairs that is relieved by rest | ☐ | ☐ |
| d. Needed to sleep on two or more pillows to help you breathe | ☐ | ☐ |
| e. Been awakened at night by trouble breathing | ☐ | ☐ |
| f. Had swelling in your feet or ankles *(If female, except during pregnancy)* | ☐ | ☐ |
| g. Felt your heart racing, fluttering, or skipping beats | ☐ | ☐ |
| h. Had five or more headaches that were at least 4 hours long; one-sided, pulsating, intense, or worsened by activity; and associated with nausea, vomiting, or sensitivity to light or sound | ☐ | ☐ |

*Figure 7.2* Example of a Question Grid Format.

## Questionnaire Front and Back Cover

The questionnaire cover is a respondent's first impression of the questionnaire and likely a major factor in the decision to complete the survey (Grembowski, 1985; Nederhof, 1988). Dillman (2000) recommends using a front cover that:

1 Is simple, yet makes the questionnaire immediately distinguishable and memorable.
2 Includes a title, by which respondents can easily identify the survey. The survey name should appeal to a large proportion of the sample members rather than simply describe the goal of the researchers – for example, the initial proposal for the American Community Survey (ACS) was "The Continuous Measurement Survey," which rightfully was not considered appealing to the general US population.
3 Includes the name and address of the survey sponsor, ensuring legitimacy and allowing respondents another option to return the questionnaire if they misplace the postage-paid mail-back envelope.

Similarly, the back cover should be simple, not competing for attention with the front cover, and should include an invitation for comments and a thank you note. It should *not* contain any final questions. Figure 7.3 presents examples of well-designed front and back covers.

When the questionnaire is very short, it may not make sense to add a cover, but rather to display the questionnaire name and logo in a header and start the survey on the first page. The same approach applies to the back cover, where the thank you note can be added after the last questions. Examples of such designs are the Decennial Census and the ACS questionnaire (Figure 7.4).

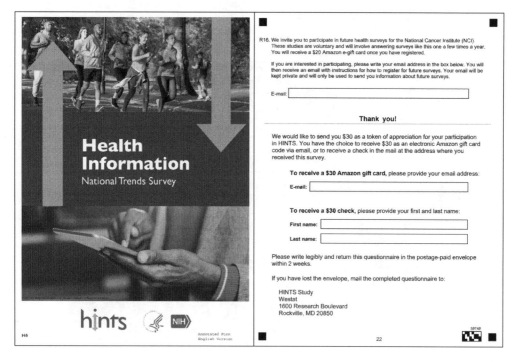

*Figure 7.3* Example from the 2022 Health Information National Trends Survey Front and Back Cover.

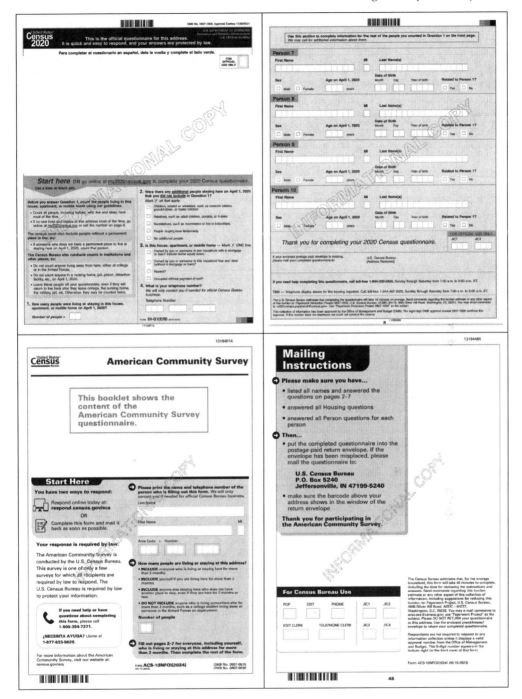

*Figure 7.4* Example Cover and Back Pages from the 2020 Census and the 2024 American Community Survey.

## Summary

Controlling a respondent's navigation through a mail questionnaire is important for minimizing measurement and nonresponse errors. This is done through a series of visual design features such as use of symbols, numbers, directional arrows, size, proximity, color, contrast, and pagination. To minimize respondent burden associated with navigation, the preferred questionnaire format is a booklet with an engaging front and back cover that appeals to most sample members. We encourage survey practitioners to adhere to these best practices to ensure high-quality data collections through paper questionnaires.

## Exercises

1. Describe the three steps in questionnaire visual processing.
2. Describe the most important elements in questionnaire layout.
3. Discuss advantages and disadvantages of single vs. double-column format and when would you prefer one over the other.

# 8 Design of Web and Mobile Web Surveys

## Introduction

Web surveys are a computerized self-administered mode of data collection. Unlike interviewer-administered data collections, web surveys do not have an interviewer reading survey questions to respondents and recording their answers. Respondents must have a device and internet access to complete a web survey. Once logged in, respondents read survey questions presented on the screen and enter their answers via the device's keyboard.

Web surveys differ from paper surveys (which are described in detail in Chapter 7) – another self-administered mode of data collection – in many important ways. First and foremost, web surveys take advantage of computerization by automating skip logic, conditional branching, and conditional or dynamic fills using previous answers or available information. Second, web surveys can easily build in randomization mechanisms to present question order and response order and implement split-ballot designs by assigning respondents to different question wording or different question formats. Third, web surveys can build in data quality checks (such as outlier detection and consistency checks) to validate and provide feedback to respondents' answers in real time (e.g., Peytchev & Crawford, 2005). Fourth, web surveys are able to embed other features such as a URL/hyperlink, a calendar, a map, or a running tally for respondents to use. For instance, respondents can click on a hyperlink to see a definition or an example. A calendar can be shown to facilitate respondents' selection of a date. A map can be used to search and select a grocery store instead of recalling the store's address. A running tally spares respondents from doing arithmetic by showing them the sum of their entries.

More importantly, web surveys can build in interactive features and interventions to prevent undesirable respondent behaviors. For instance, when respondents select the same response option to a series of survey items using the same set of response categories (also called "straightlining"), the web instrument can trigger a prompt to remind respondents that they need to carefully think about how to respond to each survey question and to offer them an opportunity to go back and change their answers. Similar prompts and interventions can be built in to prevent respondents from speeding through the web instrument or moving forward to the next question without providing an answer. Clarification (through definitions and examples) and feedback can be presented to respondents based on their response behaviors. For instance, if a respondent spends a long time on a given screen, a prompt can be triggered that provides help (e.g., a definition, or instructions on how to proceed).

DOI: 10.4324/9781003367826-10

Despite their differences from interviewer-administered surveys and paper questionnaires, web surveys should follow the same questionnaire design principles and best practices discussed in earlier chapters when it comes to writing survey questions. However, because respondents interact with web surveys without the help of interviewers, the visual design of web surveys is critical to their success. This chapter focuses on visual design of web surveys.

## Designing Web Surveys

The basic visual design principles discussed in Chapter 7 apply to the visual design of web surveys. Respondents are more likely to pay attention to elements that are more visible. Numbers, words, symbols, and graphical features such as size, color, brightness, and shape all influence how respondents interpret and answer questions in web surveys (Christian & Dillman 2004; Christian et al., 2007; Dillman & Christian 2005; Redline et al. 2003; Tourangeau et al., 2004). Tourangeau et al. (2004, 2007, 2013) describe five more heuristics respondents use to interpret visuals, to understand question format, and to answer web surveys: (1) middle means typical or central; (2) left and top means first; (3) near means related; (4) like means close; and (5) up means good. Through eye-tracking, Höhne and Yan (2020) found evidence that violation of these heuristics led to increased effort on respondents' part.

Couper (2008) emphasized that the overarching goal of visual design of web surveys is to focus respondents on the primary task of answering web questions while still making secondary tasks (navigation, help, review of progress, etc.) available if needed. Under this overarching goal, we discuss visual design decisions researchers need to make when designing a web survey to be accessed on a personal computer.

### *Page Layout*

One of the first visual design decisions web survey designers have to make is web page layout. The two basic types of page design are scrolling and paging. The **scrolling design** displays all survey questions on one web page (see Figure 8.1 for a screenshot of a survey employing the scrolling design). This design loads the web page once and requires respondents to scroll to see and to answer all questions. The **paging design** displays one question per web page or screen. As a result, it does not require scrolling, but it needs to load every web page and upload answers back to the server when respondents click or tap the Next button to move forward. A major advantage of a paging design is the ease to build in interactive features such as conditional fills and automated skips based on answers to earlier questions, prompting for missing data or out-of-range values, and so on. In general, a paging design is preferred unless the questionnaire is short and does not involve skips (Tourangeau et al., 2013). A common compromise is to display a few questions on each web page. Toepoel et al. (2009) recommend placing 4 to 10 questions on a single web page to avoid the necessity of vertical scrolling.

Below are recommendations from Tourangeau et al. (2013), Dillman et al. (2014), and Geisen and Romano Bergstrom (2017) on page layout regardless of which page design is used. Some are very similar to best practices for designing paper surveys listed in Chapter 7.

- Put the most important information on the top left section of a web page because it is the most visually prominent part of the screen.
- Headers can be used for branding or orientation purposes, or links for additional information.

- Use a white or light color background (such as light blue) and avoid background graphics.
- Use boldface, darker, or larger print for question text.
- Use regular, lighter, or smaller print for response options.
- Use the same font size, font type, and spacing for all response options.
- Use spacing to separate question text from response options.
- Use capitalization or italics for emphasis; underlining is not recommended in web surveys because it conveys the presence of a hyperlink.
- Use italics for instruction.
- Font size should be large enough to permit comfortable reading, and typeface should be readily readable.
- Left-justify the questions and number them if multiple questions are displayed on a page.
- Put the input field (e.g., a radio button, a check box) to the left of the corresponding label.
- Where possible, present all the response options in a single column or a single row.
- Include a "Next" and a "Previous" button on the bottom of each page with the "Next" button to the right and the "Previous" button on the left. If possible, make the "Previous" button somewhat less visually prominent than the "Next" button.
- Allow respondents to stop the survey on any page and finish completing it at a later time.

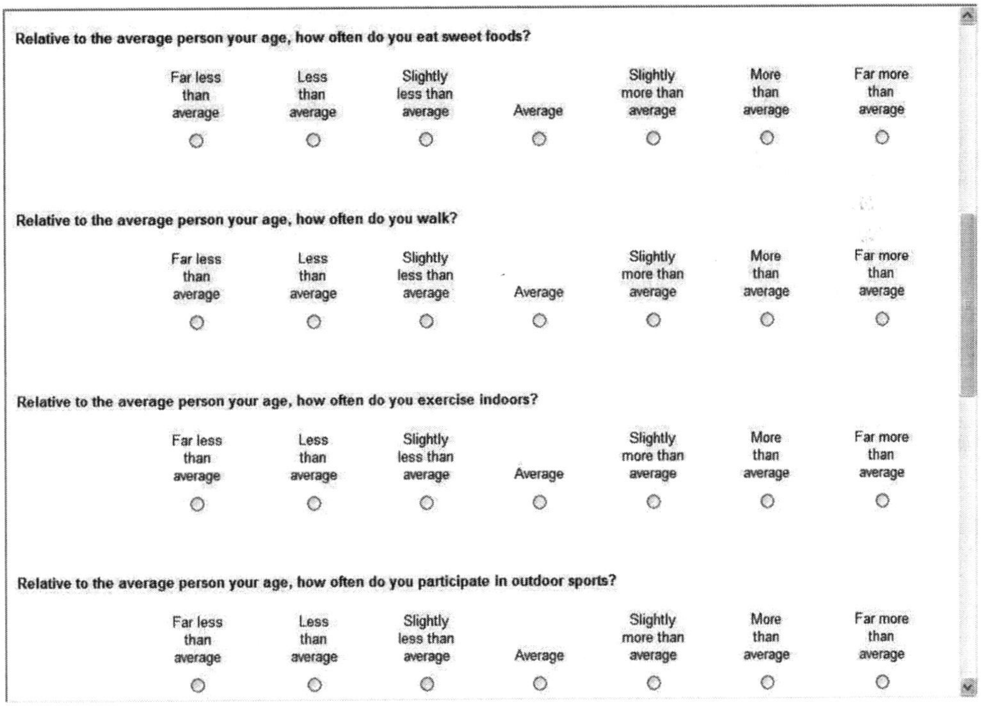

*Figure 8.1* Example of a Web Survey using a Scrolling Design.

Auto-advancing is a relatively new feature feasible for a paging design. With auto-advancing, the web survey automatically advances to the next page after respondents have answered the question on the current page. Auto-advancing only works for questions requiring a single response. Check-all-that-apply items, open-ended questions, and pages with multiple questions cannot use this feature. Literature evaluating the performance of auto-advancing does not show an advantage of this feature in terms of respondent satisfaction and data quality (Giroux et al., 2019). As a result, we do not recommend this feature.

### *Grids*

For web surveys intended to be accessed and completed on a personal computer, questions sharing the same set of response options are often shown in a grid or matrix format on a computer screen with response options as columns and question stems as rows (see Figure 8.2 for an example). Studies show that grids lead to shorter completion times and higher item-total correlations than other formats such as the one-question-per-screen format (Tourangeau et al., 2004). However, there is evidence that grids may increase item missing data (Toepoel et al., 2009) and that the high item-total correlations may reflect measurement error (Tourangeau et al., 2004).

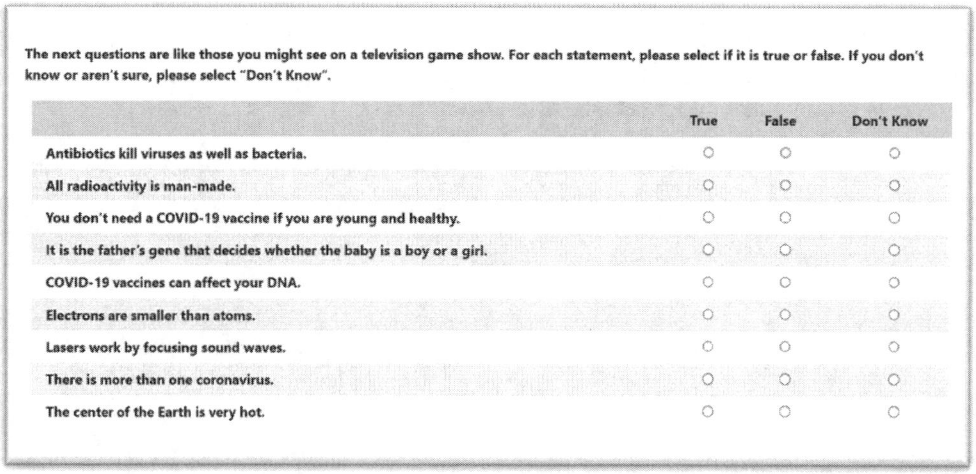

**The next questions are like those you might see on a television game show. For each statement, please select if it is true or false. If you don't know or aren't sure, please select "Don't Know".**

| | True | False | Don't Know |
|---|---|---|---|
| Antibiotics kill viruses as well as bacteria. | ○ | ○ | ○ |
| All radioactivity is man-made. | ○ | ○ | ○ |
| You don't need a COVID-19 vaccine if you are young and healthy. | ○ | ○ | ○ |
| It is the father's gene that decides whether the baby is a boy or a girl. | ○ | ○ | ○ |
| COVID-19 vaccines can affect your DNA. | ○ | ○ | ○ |
| Electrons are smaller than atoms. | ○ | ○ | ○ |
| Lasers work by focusing sound waves. | ○ | ○ | ○ |
| There is more than one coronavirus. | ○ | ○ | ○ |
| The center of the Earth is very hot. | ○ | ○ | ○ |

*Figure 8.2* Example of a Grid.

We extracted guidelines and best practices from the survey literature for designing grids and display them below:

- Grids should be used sparingly and design should be as simple as possible (Tourangeau et al., 2013).
- Shade every other row or gray out completed items (Tourangeau et al., 2013).
- Have at most five rows per page and at most five columns for response categories (Grady et al., 2019).

- Make sure that all columns (response options) are visible to avoid horizontal scrolling (Couper, 2008).
- Make sure that column headings are visible when scrolling vertically (Couper, 2008).
- Allow the table to adjust to the size of the browser (Couper, 2008).
- Ensure that columns for scalar response options are of equal width (Couper, 2008).
- Consider breaking the grid into smaller pieces if it becomes too complex (Couper, 2008).

**Definitions and Examples**

Providing definitions and examples is shown to be effective in increasing data quality to difficult survey questions and complex constructs for both interviewer-administered surveys (e.g., Schober & Conrad, 1997) and self-administered surveys (e.g., Redline, 2013). Definitions and examples can clarify misunderstanding of survey questions and improve recall by providing more retrieval cues. Definitions including atypical examples or examples of low-accessibility subcategories of events that respondents would otherwise not recall have a bigger impact on respondents' answers than definitions containing typical or high-accessible examples (Phillips, 2021; Tourangeau et al., 2014).

Schaeffer and Dykema (2020) recommend integrating definitions into the survey question and placing them before the question requesting an answer regardless of mode. However, empirical research is mixed as to the placement of definitions and examples in web surveys. Redline (2013) found evidence that definitions placed at the end of a survey item were less likely to be attended to than those placed before the survey item. But Metzler et al. (2015) showed that definitions and examples placed after the question stem were the most effective, and those placed before the question stem were the least effective in improving response quality.

Definitions and examples can be displayed on web screens to respondents in a variety of ways. They can be displayed permanently on the computer screen. Alternatively, they can be obtained by a click or tap on a hyperlink (as shown in Figure 1 of Conrad et al., 2006) or by hovering over a term (see Figure 8.3, also Figure 1 of Peytchev et al., 2010, for an example). Research shows that definitions and examples that are more visible to respondents or take less effort to access are more likely to be attended. This finding reflects the impact of visibility – people are more likely to use information that is more visible. As a result, we recommend always displaying definitions and examples on screen, if they are offered.

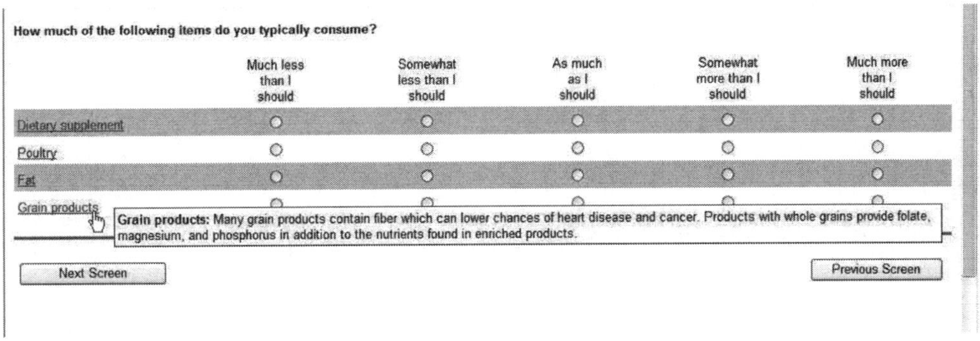

*Figure 8.3* Example of Definition Display When Respondents Hovered Over the Term.

### Images

Studies have shown that image content affects respondents' answers to survey questions in many intended and unintended ways. First, images can affect respondents' interpretation of survey questions by clarifying the meaning of a question or a key term and by making vague ideas concrete. Couper and colleagues demonstrate that respondents used images to interpret the range of objects and activities implied by the question (Couper et al., 2004a). For instance, respondents shown an image of people dining in a fine restaurant reported fewer eating-out events than those shown an image of people eating fast food in a car. Second, images introduce context effects (contrast and assimilation effects) by changing the context of the survey question. Couper et al. (2007) found that respondents who saw an image of a fit woman jogging reported poorer health than those presented with an image of a sick woman lying in the hospital bed. Lastly, images can influence respondents' moods or emotions. An image of bright sunlight elevated respondents' reported mood, whereas an image of stormy weather lowered it (Couper et al., 2003).

In addition to the content of images, the placement of images also triggers different context effects (refer to Chapters 2 and 4 for detailed discussions of context effects). Couper et al. (2007) found that the sick woman picture led to a contrast effect when it was placed next to the survey question (see Figure 1 in Supplementary Materials of Couper et al., 2007) or on a screen before the survey question. However, the same image led to an assimilation effect when it was placed in the header (see Figure 2 in Supplementary Materials of Couper et al., 2007); that is, respondents reported poorer health when the sick woman's picture was placed in the header and better health when the fit woman's picture was shown in the header. This is because people do not consciously process images placed in the header (known in the literature as "banner blindness").

Although technology makes it easy to display images on a web page, we caution question writers to be judicious in including images in a web survey (see Couper, 2008, for more examples of using images in surveys). Images should be chosen carefully or avoided (Tourangeau et al., 2013), because of their potential impact on question interpretation. With technology advances, it is now easier to embed multimedia content such as video clips. Although we are not aware of empirical literature experimenting on the content and placement of multimedia content, we believe that the same caution recommended for images applies to the inclusion of multimedia content – it should be chosen carefully or avoided.

### Response Format

*Designing Input Fields*

The design of input fields is essential for respondents to answer closed questions on the web. The basic principle for designing input fields is to match them with the intended task and to use them to serve as both visual guides to the respondent about how to answer and as devices for imposing restrictions on how answers are to be provided (Tourangeau et al., 2013). Couper (2008) described four basic input formats available in HTML forms: radio buttons (Figure 8.4), check boxes (Figure 8.4), drop boxes (Figure 8.4), and text fields and text areas (Figure 8.5).

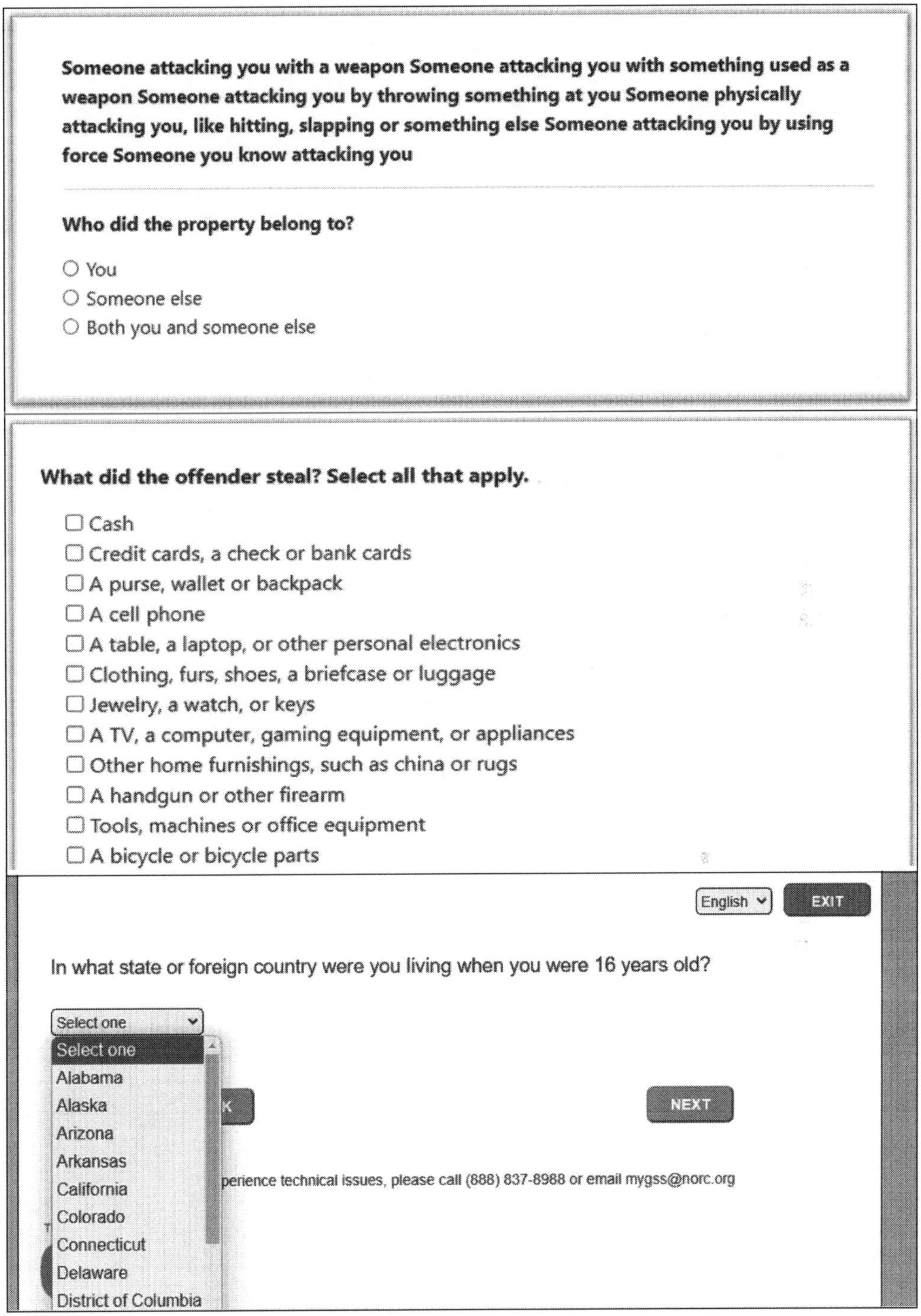

**Someone attacking you with a weapon Someone attacking you with something used as a weapon Someone attacking you by throwing something at you Someone physically attacking you, like hitting, slapping or something else Someone attacking you by using force Someone you know attacking you**

**Who did the property belong to?**

○ You
○ Someone else
○ Both you and someone else

---

**What did the offender steal? Select all that apply.**

☐ Cash
☐ Credit cards, a check or bank cards
☐ A purse, wallet or backpack
☐ A cell phone
☐ A table, a laptop, or other personal electronics
☐ Clothing, furs, shoes, a briefcase or luggage
☐ Jewelry, a watch, or keys
☐ A TV, a computer, gaming equipment, or appliances
☐ Other home furnishings, such as china or rugs
☐ A handgun or other firearm
☐ Tools, machines or office equipment
☐ A bicycle or bicycle parts

---

[English ▾]  [EXIT]

In what state or foreign country were you living when you were 16 years old?

[Select one ▾]
Select one
Alabama
Alaska
Arizona
Arkansas
California
Colorado
Connecticut
Delaware
District of Columbia

[NEXT]

perience technical issues, please call (888) 837-8988 or email mygss@norc.org

*Figure 8.4* Examples of Input Fields (Radio Buttons, Check Boxes, Drop Box). The drop box example is provided by the General Social Survey.

**Radio buttons** are appropriate for single-selection survey items with a comparatively short list of response options. Couper (2008) listed several key features of radio buttons web survey designers should be aware of. First, radio buttons come in a group or set, and selecting one button deselects any other button in the set that was previously selected. Second, once one of the buttons in the set is selected, the selection cannot be turned off and can only be transferred to another button in the set. In other words, once a respondent checked off a button in the set, they can no longer skip that question. Third, radio buttons cannot be resized.

**Check boxes** have very different features from radio buttons even though they also tend to come in a group or set. Although radio buttons operate dependently as described earlier, check boxes operate individually; each check box in the set acts as a toggle and can be turned on or off independently of what happens to the other check boxes in the set. As a result, check boxes are appropriate input fields for check-all-that-apply items. A client- or server-side script is needed if the web survey designer wants to restrict the number of boxes to be checked (e.g., select no more than four options) or wants to include mutually exclusive options in the set (e.g., having "none of the above" in the list of check boxes).

**Drop boxes** are widely used in web surveys and have various names such as select lists, combo boxes, and pulldown menus. Drop boxes are appropriate for closed survey questions with a long list of options that can be organized in a meaningful way (e.g., states; years and months). Ideally, the answer is known to the respondent, and the respondent's task is to search for it from the list. Couper (2008) lists several features that web survey designers should know how to use. First, there is more than one way to find and select items on the selection list. Second, no data are transmitted to the server unless a selection is made. Third, web survey designers can choose how many items to display initially. However, research demonstrates that initial display of options affects distribution of answers (Couper et al., 2004b). In particular, respondents are more likely to choose one of the options visible from the outset. As a result, we recommend that web survey designers do *not* make the first option visible in a drop box and do not leave the initial response blank. Instead, we recommend guiding respondents with an instruction (such as "Select one") as the first visible field. Fourth, drop boxes allow single or multiple selections from the list. However, Couper (2008) recommends avoiding the use of multiple selections in a drop box.

**Text fields** and **text areas** are appropriate for open-ended questions because they allow respondents to enter unformatted responses. Text boxes are suitable for short and constrained input; they are best for one-word answers or for entry of a few numbers. By contrast, text areas are best when respondents are expected to enter a large amount of text (see Figure 8.5 for an example). Research shows that respondents use the visible size of the text field and text area to infer what kind of information and how much is desired (e.g., Christian et al., 2007; Couper et al., 2001). As a result, a larger text field or text area should be used when web survey designers desire longer answers from respondents. In addition, we recommend using masks or instructions to guide respondents to enter the information in the desired format (e.g., Christian et al., 2007). For instance, when asking the respondent to provide a telephone number, a mask displaying "xxx-xxx-xxxx" above or below the text field will tell respondents in what format to enter the phone number. When asking about dates, a smaller text field should be used for the month and a larger one for the year. Symbolic instructions (e.g., MM, mm/dd/yyyy) should be used above, below, or inside the text field to increase the likelihood that respondents provide date information in the desired format. When possible, we recommend utilizing type-ahead to offer respondents suggestions as they type; type-ahead is found to improve the quality of information entered by respondents (Yan & Machado, 2023).

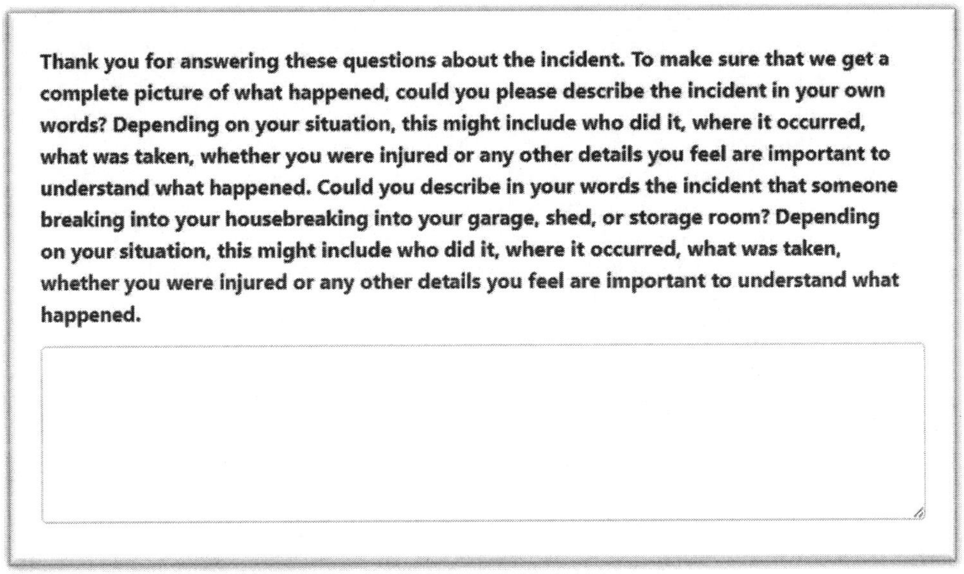

Design of Web and Mobile Web Surveys 77

> Thank you for answering these questions about the incident. To make sure that we get a complete picture of what happened, could you please describe the incident in your own words? Depending on your situation, this might include who did it, where it occurred, what was taken, whether you were injured or any other details you feel are important to understand what happened. Could you describe in your words the incident that someone breaking into your housebreaking into your garage, shed, or storage room? Depending on your situation, this might include who did it, where it occurred, what was taken, whether you were injured or any other details you feel are important to understand what happened.

*Figure 8.5* Example of a Text Area.

Using active scripting, one can implement additional input formats such as visual analog scales, drag-and-drop methods, calendar, and map-based input. **Visual analog scales or slider bars** (Figure 8.6) are scales designed as a continuum on which the respondent selects a location on an unnumbered dimension. Respondents click at the pointer and then drag it to whatever position they desire. There are two advantages of using a visual analog scale in comparison to radio buttons. First, respondents are able to express their position with more precision. Second, respondents are not prone to interpretation introduced by numerical or verbal labels. Despite these benefits, studies evaluating visual analog scales do not find measurement advantages with the visual analog scales –

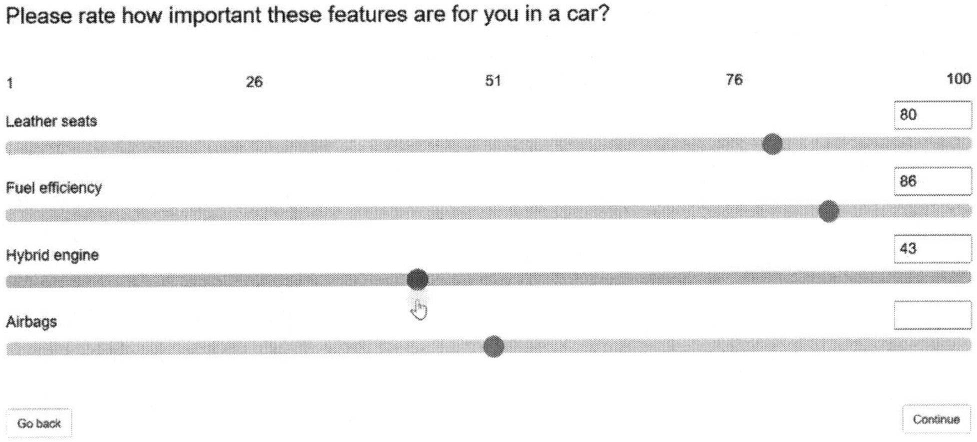

Please rate how important these features are for you in a car?

| | 1 | 26 | 51 | 76 | 100 |

Leather seats — 80
Fuel efficiency — 86
Hybrid engine — 43
Airbags —

[Go back]  [Continue]

*Figure 8.6* Example of a Slider Bar.

they produce the same distributions as radio button scales but lead to higher rates of missing data and longer completion times (Couper et al., 2006). In addition, the default position of the slider bar affects longer scales by attracting more responses to the initial values (Bosch et al., 2019a; Liu & Conrad, 2019; Maineri et al., 2021) and mobile web respondents (Maineri et al., 2021).

With **drag-and-drop methods**, a respondent drags a movable object (e.g., a picture, a card) and drops it to a desired location (Neubarth, 2010). Drag-and-drop methods can be used for ranking and rating tasks, card sorting tasks, and magnitude scaling, to name just a few. Kunz (2015) compared two implementations of the drag-and-drop approach: respondents either dragged and dropped the selected response option or dragged and dropped the question stem to the conventional grid format using radio buttons. Kunz (2015) found that both drag-and-drop implementations yielded comparable internal consistency to the grid format. In addition, the drag-item format produced more missing data, more differentiated answers, and more extreme answers than the drag-response format and the grid format. Respondents took longer when using either drag-and-drop implementation and viewed either less favorable than the grid format.

Web surveys can also use **calendars** as an input format to allow respondents to choose a specific date on the calendar instead of writing the date to a text field. When used for this purpose, the calendar should be initialized to reduce the number of clicks. For instance, initializing the calendar with the current date is not helpful for respondents who need to select a date 10 years ago. A life history calendar or **event history calendar** can also be implemented in a web survey in the same way it is used in paper surveys to facilitate respondents entering information about important life events. Chapter 3 has an example of a paper life history calendar and one can find an example for web surveys in Brüderl et al. (2016). That study shows that combining the use of an event history calendar and dependent interviewing on a web survey produces more accurate data and leads to decreased respondent burden (Brüderl et al., 2016).

Maps can also be embedded in web surveys, enabling respondents to provide precise and accurate spatial information such as home address, medical provider last visited, name and location of grocery stores or restaurants where food was obtained, and so on. Early research shows that maps can potentially be a valid and reliable tool for collecting geoinformation, but further work is needed to overcome technical difficulties and improve user experience (Bearman & Appleton, 2012; Dasgupta et al., 2014).

*Requiring Answers and Offering "Don't Know"*

Regardless of which input field is used, web survey designers must decide in advance whether respondents are required to provide an answer before moving forward to the next question. In general, allowing respondents to move forward without providing an answer runs the risk of increasing missing data to individual questions. By contrast, requiring an answer to every item before allowing respondents to move forward is found to increase breakoffs (that is, respondents quit answering the survey before completing it) and reduce the length of verbatim answers to open-ended questions (Sischka et al., 2022). Dillman et al. (2014) advise against requiring response to questions unless absolutely necessary for that survey and recommend allowing respondents to back up in the survey.

A related decision is whether and how to offer a "Don't know" response option. Allowing respondents to skip a question without answering is considered an implicit

"Don't know" response. Explicitly offering a "Don't know" option together with other substantive options increases the percentage of respondents selecting that option, and, thus, increases the overall amount of missing data (e.g., de Leeuw, 2018). If one must explicitly offer a "Don't know" option, the recommendation is to visually separate the "Don't know" option from the substantive answers either using a line (de Leeuw et al., 2016; Dillman et al., 2014; Tourangeau et al., 2004) or a special button (de Leeuw et al., 2016). A middle ground is an interactive approach tested in de Leeuw et al. (2016). The interactive approach does not explicitly offer a "Don't know" option, allows respondents to skip the question without providing an answer, and follows up with a polite probe when the question is left blank. This approach led to the lowest amount of missing information (de Leeuw et al., 2016). However, such a design does increase the survey length and could potentially increase the perception of response burden.

We encourage web survey designers to think about the tradeoffs across missing data, breakoffs, and poor data quality before deciding whether answers are required for survey items and whether a "Don't know" option should be offered explicitly. We recommend implementing the interactive approach tested by de Leeuw et al. (2016) on selected key items and allowing respondents to move forward if they do not wish to provide an answer.

*Response Option Alignment*

Response options can be displayed vertically from top to bottom – this is called vertical alignment (or vertical orientation). Response options can also be displayed horizontally from left to right, leading to horizontal alignment (or horizontal orientation). Studies comparing these two alignments did not find significant differences in answers and in data quality measured through scale reliability, straightlining, missing data, and the resultant factor structure (Hu, 2019; Mockovak, 2018; Revilla & Couper, 2018). One study found some evidence of stronger primacy effects for vertical alignment (Toepoel et al., 2009), but another study failed to find the difference (Hu, 2019). Hu (2019) also demonstrated that horizontal alignment led to longer response time than vertical alignment. Couper (2008) recommended vertical alignment of response options, indented below the question text, and with the input fields to the left of the labels. Regardless of which alignment web survey designers decide on, it should be used consistently throughout the survey (Couper, 2008).

*Visual Design of Response Scales*

When processing and using response scales, respondents attend to various types of information in a hierarchy with verbal labels taking precedence over numerical labels and numerical labels taking precedence over visual cues (Toepoel & Dillman, 2011). Visual cues, such as graphical layout of a scale (Lenzner & Höhne, 2022; Schwarz et al., 1998; Smith, 1993), color and shade of response options (Tourangeau et al., 2007), and spacing between response options (Tourangeau et al., 2004) are found to affect answers. Tourangeau et al. (2013) recommended that visual cues should be consistent with the intended use of the response scale. We recommend keeping a simple visual design of response scales and pretesting before the web survey is fielded.

## Interactive Features and Designs

Web surveys offer new opportunities to include interactive features and designs to improve respondent experience and data quality. **Progress indicators** or progress bars are one interactive feature that can be embedded in a web survey to convey respondents' progress as they complete the questionnaire (see Figure 8.7). Progress indicators can be graphic (such as a bar growing as respondents move further along the web survey) or text only (e.g., 12% completed). Research examining the effect of progress indicators consistently shows that progress indicators boost completion rates only when they provide encouraging news but depress them when conveying discouraging feedback (Villar et al., 2013; Yan et al., 2011). We do not recommend the use of progress indicators, especially in long surveys.

Sometimes respondents are asked to provide numeric answers that are expected to sum to a fixed total. For instance, respondents are asked how much time they spent on various activities yesterday and their answers are expected to sum up to 24 hours. This type of task essentially distributes a total quantity across several parts. A **running tally** can be embedded into the web survey that shows the total quantity as respondents provide numeric answers (see Figure 8.8). Research demonstrates that running tallies promote answers that add up to the requisite total, but do not necessarily improve accuracy of component quantities (Conrad et al., 2005). In addition, this format is prone to primacy effects in that respondents enter higher numbers when the text boxes are shown earlier than later on the list (Wells & DiSogra, 2011).

**Human-like interactive features** can be implemented in web surveys to improve data quality. We described earlier an interactive approach that prompts respondents who move forward without providing an answer in an attempt to **encourage substantive answers** and to reduce missing data (de Leeuw et al., 2016). Similar interactive designs can be implemented to reduce other undesirable response behaviors. Conrad et al. (2017) tested an interactive feature aiming to **reduce speeding**. Respondents who went through the web survey too quickly were shown a message asking them to give the question enough thought. This interactive feature reduced respondents' tendency to rush through later items in the questionnaire. Another human-like interactive feature is **offering help** to respondents who are not producing any input such as clicking and typing for a relatively long period of time. Offering help has been shown to increase accuracy of answers (Conrad et al., 2007). Yet another feature is **interactive probing** – respondents who were probed for additional thoughts after answering an open-ended question provided more words, more themes, and more elaboration in their verbatim answers than those who were not

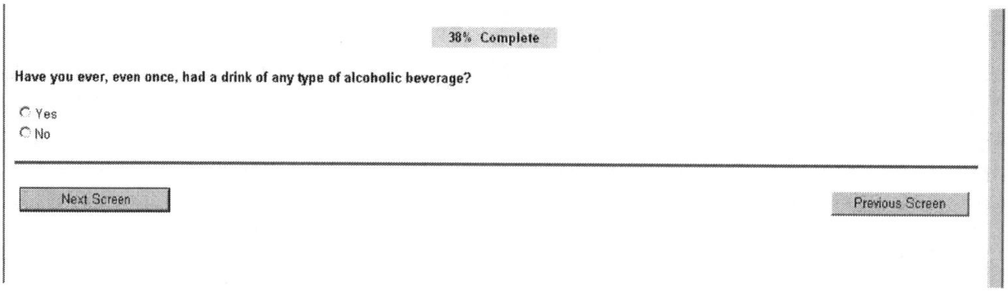

*Figure 8.7* Examples of a Progress Indicator.

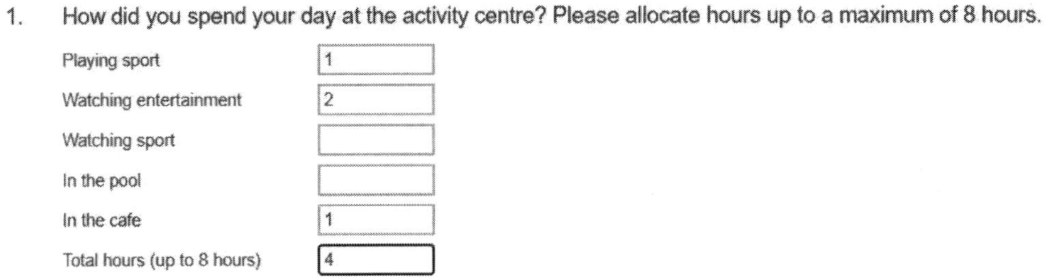
1. How did you spend your day at the activity centre? Please allocate hours up to a maximum of 8 hours.
Playing sport
1
Watching entertainment
2
Watching sport
In the pool
In the cafe
1
Total hours (up to 8 hours)
4

*Figure 8.8* Example of a Running Tally.

probed (Holland & Christian, 2009). Finally, survey- and item-specific error messages are recommended to help respondents troubleshoot any issues they may encounter while completing the survey (Dillman et al., 2014).

***Other Issues***

Because most web survey breakoffs occur on the first pages (e.g., Yan et al., 2011), welcome screens are important for engaging respondents. Welcome screens should include the title of the survey, a brief description of the survey, and instructions on how to proceed; Figure 8.9 presents an example of the welcome screen. To encourage participation, the welcome screen should be made visually appealing and have the same logo and similar visual and graphic included in the contact materials sent to respondents.

The closing screen should also be designed to be visually appealing. The messages on the closing screen should inform respondents that they have completed the survey and convey the researchers' gratitude and details on how the incentive, if offered, will be delivered.

Rich paradata – data generated as a byproduct of the data collection process – can be collected from web surveys such as device and browser respondents use to complete the web survey, time taken to answer each question (and the entire survey), sequence of

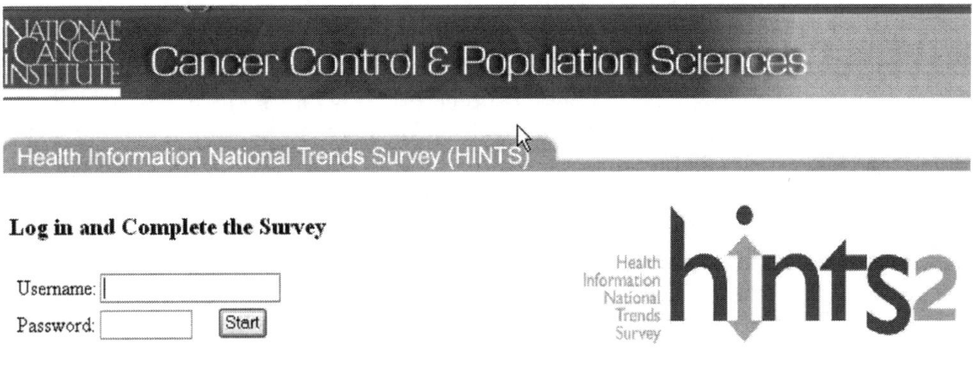
NATIONAL CANCER INSTITUTE
Cancer Control & Population Sciences
Health Information National Trends Survey (HINTS)
Log in and Complete the Survey
Username:
Password:
Start
Health Information National Trends Survey
hints2

*Figure 8.9* Example of a Welcome Screen.

clicks respondents make on each web page, and whether and how answers to each question are changed (McClain et al., 2019). We recommend collecting and using paradata to understand how respondents interact with the web survey.

**Optimizing Web Surveys for Mobile Devices**

Not everyone accesses and completes the web survey sent to them on their personal computer. The proportion of respondents completing web surveys on a mobile device (such as smartphones and tablets) is on the rise in recent years, especially when survey organizations and practitioners are increasingly taking advantage of QR codes on materials sent to respondents. QR codes make it easy to access the web survey directly from a smartphone by scanning the QR code. Gummer et al. (2023a) estimated that the share of respondents answering web surveys on a mobile device increased by 0.3 percentage points each month and around 24 percentage points between 2012 and 2020. Furthermore, they did not find any evidence suggesting that this increasing trend would slow down any time soon and recommended optimizing web surveys for smaller devices (Gummer et al., 2023a). Given this trend, survey researchers have been conducting empirical research examining the impact of using a smaller device on survey answers. At the same time, survey researchers are also working on guidelines for optimizing web surveys for mobile devices.

Empirical research comparing web surveys completed on personal computer to those on mobile devices found that mobile web respondents took longer to complete web surveys than those using personal computers (Antoun & Cernat, 2020; Keusch & Yan, 2017), especially when a page has more than one survey item or required data entry (Toninelli & Revilla, 2020). Furthermore, mobile web respondents tended to have higher unit nonresponse, higher breakoffs, and higher item nonresponse than respondents using their personal computer (Tourangeau et al., 2017, 2018). But there were few differences in substantive answers (Toepoel & Lugtig, 2014) and satisficing behaviors such as straightlining, acquiescence, and response order effects (Clement et al., 2020; Keusch & Yan, 2017; Tourangeau et al., 2017, 2018). A systematic review provides evidence for improved respondent satisfaction for optimized surveys (Antoun et al. 2018). Optimized designs reduced the time taken to complete web surveys (Toninelli & Revilla, 2020) and led to high-quality data (Andreadis, 2015).

Antoun et al. (2018) proposed five design heuristics for optimizing mobile web surveys. The first has to do with readability, which recommends that all text should be large enough to promote easy reading. According to the second heuristic (ease of selection) touch targets should be large enough to tap accurately. The third heuristic on visibility across the page stipulates that all content should fit the width of the screen so that it is visible without horizontal scrolling. The heuristic of simplicity of design features states that design features should be simple for researchers to deploy and for respondents to use. The fifth heuristic speaks to predictability across devices, which requires questionnaires to function in a predictable way across devices.

We extracted practical guidelines from research on optimizing web surveys:

- Use a scrolling design with eight to nine questions per page (Mavletova & Couper, 2014).
- Use larger controls, larger controls enclosed in wide buttons, or wide buttons without any control to improve respondents' tapping accuracy (Antoun et al., 2020).
- Avoid grids and use item-by-item format (Dale & Walsoe, 2020; Vehovar et al., 2022).

- Avoid horizontal alignment of response options (Dillman et al., 2014).
- Avoid features such as visual analog scales and date-picker wheels (Antoun et al. 2017).
- Use a modular design to break a long survey into a series of shorter surveys (Toepoel & Lugtig, 2022).

**Innovations to Web and Mobile Web Surveys**

The advancement of technology, coupled with an increasing use of mobile devices to complete web surveys, opens up the possibility of new input methods and the collection of additional information. A few studies examined the feasibility of allowing respondents to provide oral answers through **voice input**. Oral answers can be obtained via the voice recording feature of Android smartphones and the dictation feature of iPhones (Revilla et al., 2020), or an open-source tool "SurveyVoice" (Gavras et al., 2022). Relative to text input through the smartphone keypad, voice input led to higher nonresponse but reduced completion time (Revilla et al., 2020). Furthermore, oral answers differ substantially from written answers in terms of length, structure, sentiment, and topic (Gavras et al., 2022). Clearly, despite its potential, more research is needed to understand the quality of oral data obtained via voice input and at this stage, we do not recommend voice input.

Smartphone cameras can be used to take pictures of surroundings (Bosch et al., 2019b, 2022), food consumed (Yan et al., 2024), and receipts (Jäckle et al., 2019; Yan & Machado, 2023). Pictures provide richer and more detailed information. However, compliance is not high (Bosch et al., 2022; Jäckle et al., 2019; Yan et al., 2024) and taking and uploading pictures increased completion time (Bosch et al., 2022). Again, more research is needed to improve respondents' experience and increase compliance. Smartphone cameras were also used as a barcode scanner to scan barcodes on food items in a food study (Yan et al., 2017). Close to half of the food items acquired were entered into the web diary survey by using the smartphone camera to scan barcodes. Food item description obtained through barcode scanning was complete and did not need additional data cleaning and processing.

When respondents use their smartphones to complete a web survey, additional information can be collected through smartphone sensors such as GPS location data (Yan & Machado, 2023) and acceleration data. Acceleration data are used to detect motion (Höhne & Schlosser, 2019; Höhne et al., 2020a; Kern et al., 2021) and to validate the compliance with and performance on fitness tasks (Elevelt et al., 2021). In addition, open-source tools can be used to collect more information on respondent behaviors while completing the web survey such as whether respondents left the web survey to look up answers and whether respondents switched between different tabs (Höhne et al., 2020b, 2020c). The additional information on respondent behaviors sheds light on how respondents go about completing a web survey and can potentially be used in measurement error adjustments.

**Summary**

Web surveys are a computerized self-administered mode of data collection. Because interviewers are not present to guide respondents through the web instrument, visual designs are critical to the success of web surveys. Visual elements such as numbers, words, symbols, and graphical features (e.g., size, color, brightness, and shape) all influence how respondents interpret and answer questions in web surveys. Couper's (2008) recommendation to use visual designs to focus respondents on the primary task of answering survey questions while making secondary tasks available if needed should guide visual design decisions.

We recommend that web and mobile web survey designers use the principles, guidelines, and recommendations discussed in this chapter to make informed decisions that are appropriate and beneficial to their particular survey requirements. Furthermore, it is essential that web and mobile web surveys are tested on a variety of devices, platforms, browsers, connection speeds, and user-controlled settings. It is particularly important to evaluate carefully any interactive feature and audiovisual capabilities implemented in web surveys to ensure that they function as expected.

**Exercises**

1 Propose three ways of collecting information on data of birth in a web survey and discuss the pros and cons of each method.

   a Which one(s) will you use for a web survey optimized for mobile devices? Why?

# 9 Designing Multimode Surveys

## Introduction

Multimode or mixed-mode surveys are gaining popularity in today's environment of declining response rates and increasing cost of data collection (Tourangeau, 2017; Williams & Brick, 2018). As noted by de Leeuw and Berzelak (2016), the single-mode paradigm no longer applies in the 21st century. Utilizing more than one mode of data collection provides researchers the opportunity to combine the strengths of different modes. Properly designed and implemented, multimode surveys have the benefits of reducing coverage error, improving response rate and reducing nonresponse error, improving measurement, lowering cost, and improving timelines (de Leeuw, 2018; Dillman et al., 2014; Tourangeau, 2017).

To be consistent with the literature (de Leeuw & Berzelak, 2016; Dillman et al., 2014; Tourangeau, 2017), we differentiate contact modes (i.e., modes used to make contact with sampled members) from response modes (modes used to obtain information from sampled members). There are three possible ways to mix contact and response modes. First, researchers use multiple contact modes to invite sampled members to complete the survey via one single response mode. For instance, sampled members are sent an email inviting them to participate in a web survey, followed by postcard and telephone reminders. Sometimes, advance letters are mailed to sampled members announcing the survey and then interviewers make phone calls asking for their cooperation to complete the survey over the phone. Second, one single contact mode is used to make contact with sample members, who have the freedom to respond via more than one response mode. For instance, sampled members are sent a series of postal mailings that ask them to complete a survey online or over the phone. Third, researchers use multiple contact modes to reach sample members and offer them multiple response modes to complete the survey. For instance, sample members are invited through letters to complete a survey on the web. Nonrespondents to the web survey request are followed up by interviewers, who visit their houses and administer the survey in person through computer-assisted personal interviewing.

This chapter focuses on the use of multiple response modes for a survey because it poses a challenge for questionnaire design. When multiple response modes are offered, they can be offered at the same time (as in concurrent or choice designs) or in sequence (as in sequential designs). With sequential mixed-mode designs, respondents are offered one mode first – typically the least expensive mode such as web – and then a different but more expensive mode later. A good example is the American Community Survey, which starts with mail and web, followed by telephone and face-to-face interviews as nonresponse follow-ups.

DOI: 10.4324/9781003367826-11

With concurrent or choice designs, sample members are typically offered two or more response modes at the same time and are given a choice to decide how they want to respond. Sometimes, respondents are encouraged to use one of the response modes offered, known as a "choice+" design. Round 6 of the Health Information National Trends Survey (HINTS) tested the use of such a choice + design (HINTS, 2023). Respondents were provided two response modes and could choose to either complete the survey online or return the enclosed paper questionnaire. However, respondents were offered a bonus incentive of $10 if they chose to use the web mode.

A special case of concurrent or choice designs is the use of different response modes for different parts of the questionnaire, where all respondents get the same mix of modes. This is a common strategy for surveys including both sensitive and nonsensitive questions. For example, the 2002–2019 National Survey of Family Growth (NSFG) has had interviewers administer nonsensitive questions and switch to (audio) computer-assisted self-interviewing for sensitive questions (CDC, 2020).

Cross-national surveys are likely to employ a multimode design offering multiple response modes. Because countries have different infrastructures, technology penetration and use, and traditions in data collection and fieldwork requirements, it is unlikely they can use the same response mode. For instance, the International Social Survey Programme allows a self-administered survey and in-person interviews across participating countries.

## Design Approaches for Multimode Surveys

Using multiple response modes may have the advantage of improved measurement when all sampled members use one response mode to answer nonsensitive questions and another mode to answer sensitive questions, as in the example of 2002–2019 NSFG. However, when people use different response modes to answer the same questions, survey researchers are concerned about mode effects arising from two sources (de Leeuw, 2018; Hox et al., 2017; Tourangeau, 2017). Mode effects can be induced by differential selection; that is, respondents to one mode are different from those responding in another mode in characteristics related to the variables of interest. Mode effects can also occur because of differential measurement; that is, people giving different answers to the same questions in different modes, especially when the modes differ from each other in important dimensions such as channel of communication and presence of interviewers. The survey literature reports the largest mode differences between interviewer-administered modes (e.g., face-to-face and telephone) and self-administered modes (e.g. web and mail) (de Leeuw, 2018). Compared to an interviewer-administration, self-administered modes reduce social desirability bias in the subsequent answers (Tourangeau & Yan, 2007), minimize acquiescence responding (Cernat et al., 2016), and increase correct answers to knowledge questions (Fricker et al., 2005; Liu & Wang, 2014). In addition, data from self-administered surveys are not subject to the biasing impact of interviewer characteristics such as interviewer gender (Davis et al., 2010; Tourangeau et al., 2003; West & Blom, 2017), race (Davis et al., 2010; West & Blom 2017), vocal characteristics, and paralinguistic cues (Charoenruk & Olson, 2018). There is some evidence of less random measurement error for attitudinal items in self-administered than in interviewer-administered surveys (Klausch et al., 2013).

An important goal, and also the biggest challenge, of designing questionnaires for multimode surveys is to reduce mode effects resulting from differential measurement.

Question writers can take two design approaches to achieve that goal (Couper, 2008; de Leeuw, 2018; Tourangeau, 2017; Tourangeau et al., 2013). The unified mode (unimode) approach attempts to minimize differences in questionnaire design and implementation across modes, even if it means that researchers cannot take full advantage of a particular mode (Dillman et al., 2014). Under this paradigm, equivalent question structure, question wording, response options, instructions, and presentation of questions are used to develop unified stimulus in all modes to all respondents (Dillman & Edwards, 2016). The objective of this approach is to maintain measurement equivalence across modes (Hox et al., 2017). The best practices approach, by contrast, aims to minimize the error within each response mode separately by using each response mode to its full potential, even if it means that different questions are used across modes. The objective of the best practices approach is to minimize the overall systematic measurement error (Hox et al., 2017).

Researchers have different views and preferences when it comes to which design approach to take. Couper (2008) advocated for the best practices approach over the unimode approach because the latter runs the risk of question writers designing down to the lowest common denominator to achieve equivalence. Tourangeau et al. recommended the unimode design when the analytic goal is to make comparisons or when questions are subjective in nature (Tourangeau, 2017; Tourangeau et al., 2013). The best practices approach is recommended when the analytic goal is to make overall estimates or when questions are factual in nature (Tourangeau, 2017; Tourangeau et al., 2013). De Leeuw et al. (2018) noted that the unimode approach is now the current best practice in multimode survey design.

## Challenges in Multimode Surveys

The unimode design gets around mode-specific question structure and question format and aims to use same question format and wording across modes. However, it is easier to achieve unified stimulus across modes when the modes are similar to each other (e.g., web and mail) than when they are different (e.g., mail and telephone). We identify design features that are likely to contribute to differences across modes, and, thus, warrant attention from designers of multimode surveys.

### *Don't Know and Refused Options*

One challenge facing question writers designing multimode surveys is to determine whether and how to offer nonsubstantive options such as "Don't Know" and "Refused," especially when interviewer- and self-administered modes are both employed in a multimode design. Typically, in interviewer-administered surveys, "Don't Know" and "Refused" options are not explicitly offered to respondents. Interviewers are often trained to probe respondents when they first volunteer a "Don't Know" answer but to accept it when respondents cannot come up with another answer. Likewise, if a respondent prefers not to answer a question, the interviewer may have special instructions to repeat the question prior to accepting the nonresponse. However, for a mail survey, survey designers have to choose between explicitly offering "Don't Know" and "Refused" options (with the consequence of producing higher rates of item nonresponse in the resultant data) or not offering them at all (which artificially reduces the prevalence of nonsubstantive responses to almost zero). As described in Chapter 8, for a web survey, designers can (1) explicitly display the options, (2) not offer them and require respondents to provide an answer before moving to the next question, (3) not offer them but allow respondents to move forward without answering, and (4) not offer them but present respondents with a friendly probe after a question is left unanswered. The first option leads to increased endorsement of "Don't Know" and "Refused" answers, whereas the second option runs the risk of increasing breakoffs. In addition, the second option is problematic for surveys that tell respondents they can skip any item they want as part of the informed consent procedure. Option 3 does not provide any information about the reason for the item nonresponse, but is the least burdensome for respondents. Finally, option 4 takes advantage of the computer technology, is most comparable to the setup in interviewer-administered surveys, and is shown to decrease missing data without negative impact on respondents' satisfaction with the survey (de Leeuw et al., 2016). However, option 4 can also lead to respondent fatigue and breakoffs.

Martin et al. (2007) advocate using identical response categories across all modes and suggest offering nonsubstantive options in all modes if they are explicitly offered in one mode. Similarly, Dillman and Edwards (2016) suggest presenting nonsubstantive categories in all modes. In contrast, de Leeuw et al. (2015, 2016, 2018) recommend not offering nonsubstantive options for all modes and utilizing the potential of computerization of web surveys to program in a polite probe if the web mode is part of the response mode mix. For multimode surveys mixing interviewer-administered modes with web, we support the recommendation of de Leeuw et al. For multimode surveys including a mail survey, we recommend not displaying nonsubstantive options for all modes involved.

*Grids*

Matrix or grid questions take up less space in paper questionnaires and are an efficient visual format on a computer screen. With grid questions, respondents are able to see all items in the grid and perceive them to be closely related using the "near means close" heuristic (Tourangeau et al., 2004). However, such visual grouping of items in a matrix or grid provides a different context to respondents in self-administered modes relative to interviewer-administered questionnaires, which have interviewers read questions to respondents one at a time, obscuring the "grouping." Furthermore, grids on a computer screen or on paper are more prone to straightlining – that is, the tendency for respondents to select the same answer to all items included in the grid.

Grids can be used in multimode designs utilizing only paper and web surveys but we recommend that they be simplified by reducing the number of items (that is, the rows) in the grid and that they be formatted in the same way. For multimode designs involving both web and interviewer-administered modes, the auto-advance feature can be used on the web to make the grid questions comparable to interviewer-administered surveys (Berzelak, 2014; de Leeuw, 2018; de Leeuw & Berzelak, 2016; Giroux et al., 2019). However, as mentioned in Chapter 8, empirical research on auto-advance or horizontal scrolling matrix is inconclusive in terms of its impact on completion time and item nonresponse rates (Giroux et al., 2019). More research is needed to understand the circumstances under which auto-advance techniques are beneficial. Finally, for multimode designs employing paper and interviewer-administered surveys, we recommend limiting the use of grids on paper, if possible.

*Check-all-that-apply Questions*

Self-administered questionnaires, such as mail and web surveys, commonly use check-all formats for questions when asking respondents to mark all answers that apply. In contrast, telephone and face-to-face interviews typically ask respondents to answer yes/no for each individual item; this is called a forced-choice format. Experimental research has shown that check-all-that-apply formats in both mail and web surveys decrease the number of answers provided compared to forced-choice formats (Dillman & Christian, 2005; Smyth et al., 2006). There is some evidence that similar answers can be obtained between web and telephone surveys when a forced-choice format is used (Smyth et al., 2008). Thus, we recommend that researchers use a forced-choice format for check-all-that-apply questions across all modes of data collection.

*Open-ended Numeric Questions*

Open-ended numeric questions, also called discrete value questions (Schaeffer & Dykema, 2020), request numeric answers from respondents such as numbers, dates, measurements (e.g., height or weight), amounts, or expenditures. In interviewer-administered surveys, respondents are not required to provide the requested information in a specific format. Instead, interviewers enter information in the right format based on verbal interactions with respondents. However, in self-administered surveys, respondents need to enter the number using the correct format and may also need to select a unit (e.g., inches or centimeters). As a result, questions requesting numeric answers pose additional challenges in self-administered surveys, especially paper questionnaires. Respondents are found to write illegibly, outside of the answer box, or in the wrong box. They may also enter decimal points, ranges, or qualifying words when only a single whole number is requested. Therefore, for multimode surveys, careful thoughts are needed to develop well-designed answer boxes and good textual instructions for self-administration. Additional tools are available and recommended in a web-based survey to check if answers are provided in the required format such as dropdown boxes, placeholder examples within the answer box, edit checks, and error prompt messages. For multimode surveys, we recommend simplifying the request, considering limiting the use of such types of questions, and taking advantages of masks (see Chapter 8) and verbal instructions for self-administered modes.

*Open-ended Verbatim and Field-coded Questions*

In interviewer-administered surveys, interviewers may ask an open-ended verbatim question (e.g., "What do you think are the most important problems facing this country?"), and respondents are expected to provide a narrative answer. Interviewers further probe respondents, if necessary. Interviewers then either record respondents' answer verbatim or code respondents' answers to one of the existing response options, called field coding. For self-administered surveys, respondents are shown the same open-ended question and provided a text box to write their verbatim answers. Studies show that respondents tend to write shorter answers in self-administered surveys (McGonagle et al., 2017) or skip the open-ended question altogether, compared to interviewer-administered modes. Furthermore, as mentioned in Chapter 8, respondents use the size of the text box as a cue to determine how much they are expected to write (Couper et al., 2001; Smyth et al., 2009). For multimode surveys involving self- and interviewer-administered modes, visual design and motivational instructions are needed for the self-administered modes to encourage respondents and to improve reports (Dillman et al. 2014; Smyth et al., 2009).

Because field coding pertains only to interviewer-administered modes, researchers designing a multimode survey employing both interviewer- and self-administered modes have two options regarding field-coded questions. One is to leave the field-coded question open-ended for all modes involved. This option requires additional post-survey processing costs. The second option is to convert the field-coded question into a closed question using the code frame as response options. The limitation of this approach is that the distribution of answers would be affected by the code frame (Schuman & Presser, 1981). We recommend that researchers adopt one option and use it consistently across all response modes.

### *Closed Questions*

For closed questions, we recommend using identical response categories, in the same order, across all modes (Dillman & Edwards, 2016; Martin et al., 2007). Some questions include response options in the question stem when administered by interviewers. For instance, the self-reported health question will be asked by an interviewer as written below:

> Would you say that in general your health is excellent, very good, good, fair, or poor?

When this question is presented in a self-administered mode, researchers have to decide whether to include the response options in the question stem to match the interviewer-administered modes. Martin et al. (2007) recommend presenting response categories with the question, whereas Dillman and Edwards (2016) recommend making reasonable accommodations to deal with different memory capabilities and avoid redundancy. We recommend including response options for interviewer-administered modes and excluding them for self-administered modes. In other words, the same question will be shown on paper or computer screen as:

> Would you say that in general your health is…?
>
> - *Excellent*
> - *Very good*
> - *Good*
> - *Fair*
> - *Poor*

### *Introductions, Preambles, and Transition Statements*

Interviewer-administered surveys tend to include conversational inserts and statements before starting a new question topic. They are termed introductions, preambles, or transition statements. Below are two examples from American National Election Studies:

> Now I'd like to ask you about the good and bad points of the major candidates for President.

Next, I am going to read you a list of federal programs. For each one, I would like you to tell me whether you would like to see spending increased, decreased, or kept the same. The first program is: Social Security.

When mixing self- and interviewer-administered modes, we recommend building in introductions, preambles, and transition statements to unify the design across modes and wording them appropriately for each individual mode (Dillman et al., 2014; Martin et al., 2007). The two example transition statements can be reworded for self-administration as follows. Please note that, for the second example, the actual questions are presented as a grid on paper or web:

The following questions ask you about the good and bad points of the major candidates for President.

For each of the federal programs listed below, please indicate whether you would like to see spending increased, decreased, or kept the same:

|  | Increased | Decreased | Kept the same |
|---|---|---|---|
| Social Security |  |  |  |
| ... |  |  |  |

### *"If Needed" Information, Definitions, Instructions, and Examples*

Interviewer-administered questionnaires often include "if needed" information that is provided only to those for whom it applies. Examples of such information include repeat of question stems, definitions, examples, clarifications, and instructions. Often survey designers leave it to the interviewers to decide when to offer such information. For self-administered surveys, especially paper questionnaires, survey designers need to make a priori decision whether to display the "if needed" information constantly or at a prespecified interval (e.g., every two questions). As discussed in Chapter 8, definitions and examples can be displayed continuously on every screen, accessed through a clickable reference, or as a rollover feature (that is, respondents roll over a term to view the definition).

Martin et al. (2007) recommend that substantive instructions and explanations be kept consistent across modes. The same examples, in the same order, should be presented in a question in all modes, unless evidence exists that adding or deleting examples and definitions does not bias response distributions. They also recommend that the use of selective emphasis is consistent across modes even though the convention used to communicate it (e.g., boldface, underlining, capitalization, italics) may vary across modes.

### **Evaluation and Testing of Multimode Surveys**

Similar to single-mode surveys, questionnaires for multimode surveys need to be evaluated and tested before being fielded. Methods and strategies available to test single-mode questionnaires are discussed in Chapters 11–13 and apply to multimode questionnaires. Unlike single-mode surveys, question evaluation and testing for multimode surveys needs to ensure that questions perform as expected not only within a single mode but also across all modes. Therefore, we recommend that questionnaires be tested in each mode for comprehension, recall, judgment, and mapping as a way to understand within- and across-mode issues. Furthermore, for multimode surveys, question equivalence across modes is important. As a result, question testing and evaluation efforts should focus on areas where the instruments are substantially different across modes with the goal of identifying refinements that diminish those differences and increase equivalence or comparability across modes. We also recommend using quantitative evaluation methods described in Chapter 13 to assess question equivalence across modes. When a multimode survey includes a self-administered mode, other important features of the questionnaire such as visual design and navigation issues should be tested via usability testing (see Chapter 14). Before fielding a multimode survey, additional testing is needed to evaluate the specifications and data capture and to ensure the smooth and correct integration and coordination across systems.

## Summary

The biggest challenge of designing questionnaires to be used in multiple response modes is to reduce mode effects. Below we list guidelines by Dillman et al. (2014) on integration of unified mode construction into the development of mixed-mode surveys:

1. Avoid mode-specific question structures when possible and use the same question format and wording across modes.
2. Use similar visual format across modes.
3. Use similar wording and visual formats across web and telephone surveys.
4. When mixing web and mail, leverage web technologies when they will help respondents navigate the questionnaire or reduce errors, but not when they will likely result in measurement differences.
5. When mixing web or mail with telephone, build in conversational cues and transition statements to unify the design across modes.
6. When mixing web or paper with telephone, give priority in both modes to the short and simple stimuli needed for telephone.
7. If there is even a small chance of mixing modes, design the questionnaire for the possibility of mixed-mode data collection.
8. Recognize that even with unified mode design, some measurement differences may still occur across modes.

We recommend that researchers follow these best practices and guidelines provided in the earlier sections when designing questionnaires for multimode surveys. In addition, we recommend that researchers collect or use auxiliary information (e.g., paradata) that can be used to estimate mode differences and to possibly adjust for them (de Leeuw, 2005,, 2018; Hox et al., 2017).

## Exercises

1. Develop question(s) to measure household income during the past 12 months that are to be fielded with multimode design offering both web and face-to-face interviews.
2. A feeling thermometer is a 101-point scale that allows people to indicate their feelings about a person or a group. It has been used regularly in American National Election Studies.

Below is an introduction provided to respondents by interviewers in a face-to-face interview. How would you adapt it for a multimode design that offers both web and face-to-face interviews?

I'd like to get your feelings toward some of our political leaders and other people who are in the news these days. I'll read the name of a person and I'd like you to rate that person using something we call the feeling thermometer. Ratings between 50 degrees and 100 degrees mean that you feel favorable and warm toward the person. Ratings between 0 degrees and 50 degrees mean that you don't feel favorable toward the person and that you don't care too much for that person. You would rate the person at the 50 degree mark if you don't feel particularly warm or cold toward the person. If we come to a person whose name you don't recognize, you don't need to rate that person. Just tell me and we'll move on to the next one.

# 10 Design of Multiregion, Multiculture, and Multilanguage Surveys

## Introduction

With globalization trends over the past 40 years, multiregion, multiculture, and multilanguage (3MC) surveys have been gaining popularity. Not surprisingly, such surveys present challenges when it comes to estimating comparisons because it is often impossible to disentangle differences that are the result of cultural factors, measurement (as a result of using a different language), or both. In this chapter, we explore language and cultural differences using the survey response model described in Chapter 2, discuss different approaches to survey translation, and explore how bilingualism may affect survey responding.

We start this chapter with the introduction of some new terminology. Culture plays an essential role in comparative research – we employ Hofstede's definition of culture as "the collective programming of the mind which distinguishes members of one group from another" (Hofstede, 1980). Cross-cultural psychology distinguishes between collectivist and individualist cultures. A large body of research juxtaposes collectivist cultures of East Asia to individualist cultures of Western Europe and North America (e.g., Fiske et al., 1998; Kitayma & Cohen, 2007; Nisbett, 2003 for reviews). A collectivist culture conceptualizes the self as interdependent in a group and defines it based on relationships with others (e.g., Markus & Kitayama, 1991). In contrast, Western cultures conceptualize the self as independent, with unique attributes. These differential perceptions of the self are facilitated by the language structure (e.g., deemphasis of individual actors in Asian languages) and are reflected in basic psychological and cognitive processes, such as causal attribution, impression formation, and prediction (Nisbett, 2003; Oyserman et al., 2002, for reviews); organization of autobiographical memory (e.g., Han et al., 1998) and monitoring of self versus others (e.g., Ji et al., 2000). Next, we discuss some relevant differences in basic cognitive processes, followed by implications for the survey response process model.

## Cultural Differences in Cognitive Processes

### Social Orientation

Collectivists and individualists have different world views – Westerners possess an analytic view, focused on objects and their attributes, whereas East Asians have a holistic view, focused on continuities and relationships (Nisbett, 2003). These views are reflected in simple observation, recall, and recognition tasks, providing further evidence of differences in cognitive processes. In a study by Masuda and Nisbett (2001), Japanese and

DOI: 10.4324/9781003367826-12

American students were presented with eight color-animated underwater vignettes. In each, there was at least one "focal" fish that was larger, faster, and brighter. The scenes were about 20 seconds long and were shown twice, after which participants in the study were asked what they saw. Japanese participants started by describing the surroundings, while American participants first described the focal fish. Even though both groups made the same number of references to the focal fish and movement, Japanese participants made 60% more references to the background elements and 200% as many references to relationships involving inert background objects. An interesting finding was uncovered with a recognition task given to participants at a later point – Japanese participants took more time in recognizing the focal fish when the background elements changed, while it made no difference for American participants whether the environment in which they saw the focal object was the original or new one. Similar results were observed in follow-up studies by the authors, demonstrating that East Asians pay more attention to the background than Westerners, which is reflected in differential perceptions of relationships among events, that in surveys translate into differential context effects, as demonstrated later in this chapter.

*Categories vs. Relationships*

Psychological research has demonstrated additional differences in how Westerners and East Asians organize the world – Westerners show preference for grouping objects based on taxonomy or common category membership, while East Asians prefer groupings based on relationships (Chiu, 1972; Ji et al., 2002). For example, when presented with sets of three words, such as panda-monkey-banana, and asked to identify the two most closely related, US students used taxonomy (animal kingdom) to group panda and monkey together, while Chinese students used thematic relationship (monkeys eat bananas) to group monkey and banana together (Ji et al., 2002). Furthermore, such grouping preferences can be manipulated by the language used in administration of the cognitive task – Ji et al. (2004) found that relationship-based grouping shifted to categorical when Mainland and Taiwan Chinese participants were asked to perform the task in English. Such findings are likely to have implications for the organization of autobiographical memory and thus how bilingual survey respondents recall events and make judgments.

*Language and Cognition*

The link between language and cognition has long fascinated scientists. Aristotle's view on language as a tool to communicate thoughts evolved to theories suggesting that thinking is silent, subvocal speech (Watson, 1925), and later on, to theories stating that language determines the way we think (Allport, 1954; Einstein, 1954; Whorf, 1956). In the 1950s, the idea that we can think only in terms of concepts that are represented in our language received most attention. Its best-known proponent, Benjamin Whorf, made popular the principles of linguistic determinism and linguistic relativity, which constitute what is known as the Sapir-Whorf hypothesis (Whorf, 1956). The principle of linguistic relativity states that cultural differences in cognition are correlated with differences in languages across cultures; the principle of linguistic determinism states that people think differently *because* of differences in their languages. Most of the evidence for this hypothesis was based on cross-cultural comparisons; however, the analyses of language samples were not always methodologically objective (see Longacre, 1956). Today, there is a revived interest in a much weaker version of linguistic determinism – that language and thought are interdependent, but their relationship is not yet fully understood.

Large national surveys are often administered in more than one language (e.g., the National Survey of Family Growth, the National Survey of Drug Use and Health). To the extent to which language influences thought processes, responses provided by bilingual respondents would depend on the language of survey administration. To study such language influences, we need to assume that the different language versions are free of translational problems and convey the same concepts and ideas. Thus, any observed differences between responses provided by the same respondent in different languages can be attributed to language priming a particular mind frame and influencing the cognitive processes.

## Cultural Differences in Survey Response Process

We next examine evidence of language and cultural differences at each stage of the survey response process model.

### *Comprehension*

As described in Chapter 2, question comprehension requires processing the syntactic structure of a question and making sense of the semantic (literal) and pragmatic (intended) meaning. The latter (pragmatic meaning) involves general knowledge about the world and reflects the meaning system of a culture. The use of contextual information differs across cultures – for example, East Asians have been found to be more sensitive to the conversational context than Westerners (for a review, see Schwarz, 2003), and this has been found to have consequences for question comprehension when partially redundant information is presented. For example, in a study focused on responses to general and specific questions, Haberstroh et al. (2002) asked Chinese and German students to report their academic and general life satisfaction using the academic-life or life-academic question order. In contrast to German students who used information brought to mind by the academic satisfaction question to answer the general life satisfaction question, Chinese students, being more sensitive to the conversational context and detecting the potentially redundant questions, disregarded the information they already provided about their academic life when reporting general life satisfaction.

In a follow-up study, students in Heidelberg, Germany, were presented only with the redundant question order (satisfaction with academic life, followed by satisfaction with life). Beforehand, a random half of the study participants received an independent prime (reading a paragraph and circling all first person singular pronouns: "I go to the city…"), while the other half received an interdependent prime (reading the same paragraph, where first person singular pronouns were replaced by first-person plural pronouns, and circling those pronouns: "We go to the city…"). The pattern of priming effects paralleled the country comparisons from the previous study – when primed with interdependent pronouns, German students responded like Chinese students, disregarding the information already provided about their academic life when reporting on their general life satisfaction. Such pragmatic differences between cultures can not be captured by translation (and back translation) and thus should be examined with cognitive pretests.

For bilingual respondents, language can serve as a situational cue for the cultural system associated with it and drive question interpretation based on the cultural frame induced by it. For example, Ross et al. (2002) used language to shift the interpretive frame in Chinese students in Canada by manipulating the language of the interview – those interviewed in Cantonese or Mandarin provided more collectivist statements and higher endorsement of Chinese values than those interviewed in English. This phenomenon is known as **cultural frame switching** and can affect question comprehension among bilingual respondents. Survey researchers should be aware of the potential impact of cultural frame switching and provide definitions in their survey questions to standardize the understanding of key terms, or when needed, control the language of the interview.

In a theoretical model about the effect of language at each stage of the survey response process model, Peytcheva (2020) notes that **codability** (the ease with which a concept is expressed in a language) may also affect comprehension through how the question target is interpreted based on whether a concrete word for it exists. For example, Asian languages have separate terms for family members that have only one English equivalent and are able to distinguish if an uncle is the mother's brother or the father's brother, and if younger or older. Thus, Chinese respondents may think of such relatives differently from American respondents who use the same label. This may lead to inclusion errors in a household roster construction because of failure to draw a lexical distinction across referents in English.

*Retrieval and Judgment*

Differences between East Asians and Westerners in how they perceive the world are also reflected in the retrieval and judgment stages. Culture influences what we attend to (e.g., background elements vs. focal fish in the example above), how we encode the information and organize it in memory, and what retrieval cues are effective. Furthermore, studies have demonstrated that culture influences the response formation strategy – if we should estimate or enumerate, and which cues to use in memory reconstruction. In a study on encoding and estimation across cultures (Ji et al., 2000), Chinese and American students were asked to report on the frequency of various observable (public) and unobservable (private) behaviors. Behaviors in both categories were selected to be of equal frequency in both countries.[1] Participants were presented with either a high (fewer than 10 times to 18 times or more) or low-frequency scale (0–1 times to 10 times or more). Figure 10.1 presents the percent above the comparison point (10 times or more), averaged across the three observable and unobservable behaviors. It clearly shows that when there is a need to estimate, both Chinese and American respondents rely on the frequency scale; however, Chinese respondents only need to estimate when the behavior is private and unobservable. Because East Asians place value on fitting within a group and monitoring the fit, Chinese participants are presumed to be well aware of their public behaviors.

Furthermore, studies examining language and memory demonstrate that for bilingual respondents, recall is better when the language of interview matches the language spoken during the relevant life event. This phenomenon, called **language-dependent recall**, was first reported by Bugelski (1977). When Spanish-English bilingual immigrants were cued with Spanish words, 43% of their thoughts were related to post-immigration events; when cued with English words, 70% of their thoughts were related to the post-immigration period. Similar findings were later reported by other studies (e.g., Marian & Nesser, 2000; Schrauf & Rubin, 1998, 2000). Related, a study by Ross et al. (2002) reported more culture-consistent memories when the interview was in the language associated with that culture – the study observed more collectivist memories for Chinese students in Canada when they were interviewed in Mandarin and more individualist memories when they were interviewed in English.

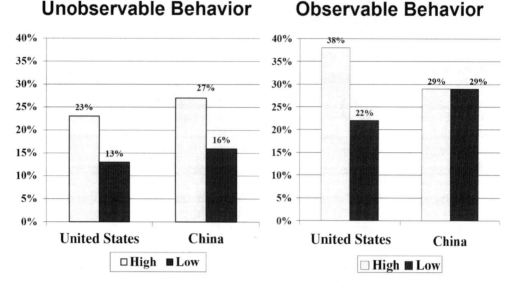

*Figure 10.1* Percent above Scale Comparison Point of Observable and Unobservable Behaviors.

Studies also show that the **spatial frames of reference** used in a language to describe object positions and relations influence nonlinguistic coding (e.g., Levinson, 2003). For example, speakers of languages with different dominant frames of reference perform memory and spatial reasoning tasks differently, utilizing the language frame of reference (e.g., Levinson, 2003; Pederson et al., 1998; Wassmann & Dasen, 1998). For example, speakers of languages that use absolute frames of reference (e.g., North, South, East, West) preserve the absolute coordinates of objects when performing memory tasks related to the position or motion of objects. For survey practitioners, this means that language, through its inherent frame of reference, is likely to influence memory and recall through differential perceptual tuning. Studies have shown that language can affect perception such that individuals become more or less attuned to certain features of the environment (Goldstone, 1998; Sloutsky, 2003). This may mean that what information is accessible during the recall and judgment tasks may be dependent on what language was used during initial information encoding and later, during the survey interview.

*Reporting*

The chronic availability of information is culture-specific. Not only do what respondents pay attention to (e.g., background vs. focal actors) and how information is encoded (e.g., categories vs. relationships) play a role but what cultural values and norms are salient and accessible at the time of the survey can also influence responses. Cross-cultural psychology studies reveal that Asians are less likely to use the extreme values on a rating scale (Chun et al., 1974; Hayashi, 1992; Stening & Everett, 1984; Zax & Takahashi, 1967). A plausible explanation for this phenomenon is that the need to maintain harmony encourages moderate responses; an alternative explanation might be related to differential scale anchoring – if Asians are considering the broader context, they would be more likely to stay in the middle of the response scale. Interestingly, within-US comparisons across ethnic and racial groups demonstrate that Hispanics and African Americans display stronger extreme responding tendencies than their White counterparts (e.g., Marin et al., 1992).

In addition to extreme responding, acquiescence has been found to be stronger for Hispanics (Marin & Marin, 1991; Marin et al., 1992) and African Americans (e.g., Bachman & O'Malley, 1984) than Whites.

Socially desirable responding is also driven by culture. Limited editing of the truth is acceptable in some collectivist cultures and is related to the value of maintaining harmony and saving face. In fact, the Marlowe-Crowne social desirability scale has been reported to be positively correlated with the collectivist orientation scale and negatively correlated with individualism measures (Johnson, 1998). Not surprisingly, East Asians receive higher scores on the Marlowe-Crowne social desirability scale than US-born respondents (Middleton & Jones, 2000).

In addition, language can play a role at the reporting stage through **codability**. For example, Kay and Kempton (1984) demonstrated that the color-naming practices in a language determine the speaker's ability to make distinctions among color chips on the blue-green color continuum. Similarly, Hoffman et al. (1986) examined to what extent the existence of a stereotype in a language influenced impressions about a person and reported that when terms were readily available in a language, participants were more likely to have stereotyped impressions and more likely to elaborate on a person's characteristics using terms consistent with the stereotype, relative to when no verbal label for a stereotype was available. For survey practitioners, this means that scales might be utilized differently by speakers of different languages as a result of different scale label codability.

In addition to the mechanisms presented at each step of the survey response model, survey practitioners should be aware of other factors such as mode effects,[2] scale length,[3] and questionnaire translation when designing surveys in 3MC contexts. We next focus our attention on creating questionnaires for 3MC surveys.

## Questionnaire Development for 3MC Surveys

When it comes to 3MC questionnaire development, practitioners are faced with three possibilities: (1) adopt an existing questionnaire; (2) adapt an existing questionnaire for comparative data collection, or (3) create a new questionnaire that would accommodate differences across regions, cultures, and languages. Next, we discuss each of these options.

### *Adopting*

Adopting refers to the direct translation of a source questionnaire to a target language without making wording or construct changes. Compared to the development of a new questionnaire in a target language, this approach is easy, inexpensive, and offers the advantage of having the questionnaire pretested at least in the source language. However, translations often do not account for cultural suitability, and monocultural questions may lead to meaningless direct translations.

Various language-specific factors may make the translation process challenging. These include:

a  Imperfect mapping – Languages do not always have word-for-word correspondence; different cognates exist across different languages (e.g., education), and country-specific terms (e.g., the food stamp program in the United States).

b  Language vagueness and ambiguity – Some languages do not offer detail to specify a concept (e.g., Kay & Kempton, 1984, showed that "moana" in Samoa means a color between blue and green, making its speakers unable to distinguish across color chips on the blue-green continuum based on color characteristics); the same word in one language can have more than one meaning (e.g., "free" may be translated as "libre" (at liberty, unrestricted) or "gratis" (without charge) in French.
c  Social context – Asian languages are highly contextual, and the same word acquires meaning based on the context (e.g., the translation of seemingly simple expressions as "please" and "thank you" in Japanese would require prior knowledge of the context within which they will be used – a child talking to their mother will use a different expression than an employee talking to their boss, or two friends talking to each other).
d  Numeracy – Different languages offer different complexities when it comes to numbers – taken to an extreme, there are languages that only have terms for one, two, and many, limiting their speakers' ability to make comparisons (Hunt & Agnoli, 1991). Furthermore, some cultures have lucky and unlucky numbers (e.g., the pronunciation of the number four in Cantonese is homophonous to the word "death"), further complicating the use of numeric scales in cross-cultural comparisons.

Several approaches can be used to translate a survey instrument from a source language into a target language:

- **On-the-fly translation** – Used when languages do not have a written component (e.g., some African languages) or an official translation of the survey is not available and bilingual interviewers try to be helpful, despite being trained to only interview in one language. This approach lacks standardization and is closed to qualitative rather than quantitative data collection.
- **Single translation** – A single translator provides a single translation. Although cost-effective, this approach does not account for personal language and cultural biases and may not be ideal for languages like Spanish that are spoken in different parts of the world and have regional and cultural variations.
- **Parallel translation** – Two or more translators work in parallel to provide independent translations of the survey instrument. This approach requires reconciliation of differences, and how this process would be conducted (i.e., who makes the final decision), should be planned in advance. Typically, the translators and at least one translation reviewer go through the whole questionnaire and agree on a final version.
- **Split translation** – Multiple translators translate different sections of the survey, often with at least one overlapping module to establish common terminology. This is a cost-effective way to minimize translator bias and save time in long survey instruments. Similar to the parallel translation, a review meeting is required to produce a final instrument.
- **Committee approach** – The committee translation approach, the most comprehensive of all, uses a team of translators, reviewers, and adjudicators with a mix of skills and substantive topic expertise to produce an optimal translation of the survey instrument. For further discussion on the advantages and practicalities of this approach, see Survey Research Center (2016).

Regardless of the undertaken translation approach, evaluation of the translation in each target language should be undertaken. Ad hoc methods include qualitative evaluations such as focus groups, cognitive interviews, behavior coding, and interviewer and respondent debriefings during a pretest (see Chapters 11 to 13 for discussion of these methods). Post hoc methods include Item Response Theory, factor analysis, and Multi-Trait-Multi-Method analyses, to name just a few.

*Adapting*

In contrast to adopting, adapting allows for deliberate changes in the source or target questionnaire to better reflect cultural nuances. Such changes could be related to modifying individual questions and their response options, or creating new questions. Similar to adopting, adapting a questionnaire is cheaper than developing a new instrument. There are several types of adaptation:

- **Terminological** – This type of adaptation is related to country-/region-specific issues (e.g., school system, sociodemographic characteristics across regions and languages).
- **Language driven** – This type of adaptation is driven by structural differences across languages (e.g., grammatical gender in languages; spoken language norms).
- **Convention driven** – This type of adaptation is related to the culture-dependent processing style (e.g., left to right vs. right to left vs. top to bottom reading style).
- **Culture driven** – Such adaptation is a result of cultural norms, sensitivities, values, and practices (e.g., the picture completion section of the Wechster Intelligence Scale for Children uses an inanimate object with a missing part in Japan, instead of a human with a missing body part, as in other countries).

*Developing a New Questionnaire*

If a questionnaire does not exist in a source language, the development of a new questionnaire provides an opportunity to tailor the questionnaire to the cross-cultural context within which it will be used. A disadvantage of developing a new questionnaire is the high cost associated with the development and testing of the new items within their respective context. Several approaches can be undertaken for new questionnaire development within the 3MC context:

- **Sequential design** – A source questionnaire is developed and pretested in one language, then adopted or adapted into other languages. Items in the source questionnaire cannot be changed, and cultural suitability is often not tested. This is the most common approach for new questionnaire design or when an existing questionnaire is exported into a cross-cultural context. The Eurobarometer is an example of a sequentially developed survey, using questions from other studies, but also new questions. Once the French and English versions are completed, the instrument is translated into other languages.
- **Parallel design** – The source questionnaire is developed by a multicultural group, using a common language. Even though the questionnaire is developed in one language, it is culturally anchored by participants of the development team, and cultural suitability is addressed at the early stages. Typically, the questionnaire undergoes an advanced translation and is pretested in different cultures/languages before it is finalized. The International Social Survey Programme and the European Quality of Life survey use a parallel approach.

- **Simultaneous design** – Questionnaire development and translation occur at the same time. Question writing begins with a common concept, and questions are developed for each language. There is a lot of back and forth among languages to minimize culture-specific elements, but sometimes this may result in misspecification of concepts. This approach is typically applied in two-culture projects because it is a laborious and expensive procedure. The World Health Organization Quality of Life Assessment instruments WHOOQOL-100 and WHOQOL-BREF are examples of simultaneous instrument development.

Which approach is undertaken depends largely on the context within which the survey will be used (national vs. cross-national) and its analytic goals (national results vs. cross-country comparisons). It is important that whatever approach is undertaken, it is followed by a pretest, and all changes implemented after the pretest should be fully documented.

## Summary

Cultures differ in cognitive processes, and these differences are often manifested when respondents from different cultures complete the same questionnaire. In addition to differential processing and memory organization styles that can affect question comprehension, retrieval, judgment, and reporting, language of the survey questionnaire impacts each step of the survey response model. Even though not a lot of empirical research exists in the survey literature, studies from cross-cultural psychology are indicative of potential issues researchers should be aware of when launching a cross-cultural survey.

Different questionnaire design models exist for exporting a survey in a cross-cultural context, each with its advantages and disadvantages (mostly related to cost and complexity). Regardless of the design model, pretesting is an important part of using surveys in a 3MC context. Careful documentation of all design decisions is also very important in comparative research.

## Exercises

1. Describe the main differences between collectivist and individualist cultures.
2. Describe two mechanisms through which language can influence the survey response model.
3. Describe the main differences between adopting and adapting a survey questionnaire. Which one is likely to yield higher-quality data and why?

## Notes

1. Examples of observable behaviors included coming late to class, going to the library, and catching a cold; examples of unobservable behaviors included having nightmares, telling a lie, and faking an agreement.
2. Socially desirable reporting and acquiescence have been reported to vary by mode of data collection—self-administered modes such as web and mail induce lower levels of social desirability and acquiescence (see Chapter 6).
3. Differences between Hispanics and non-Hispanics on the endorsement of extreme responses have been found for 5-point scales, but not for 10- or 7-point scales (Clarke, 2000; Hui & Triandis, 1989).

# Part III
# Questionnaire Evaluation and Testing

# 11 Lab-based Methods

## Introduction

The ultimate test that all survey questions must pass is reliability and validity, as discussed in Chapter 1. To ensure that survey questions measure the concepts they intend to measure and can be understood and answered by respondents, focused evaluation and testing needs to be done. A wide variety of question evaluation and testing methods are available to researchers: they differ in the amount and type of information produced, number of testing participants needed, mode and location of the test, type of personnel required, and most importantly, timeline and cost of the test (Tourangeau et al., 2020a). In addition, these methods do not always necessarily yield consistent findings about question performance (e.g., d'Ardenne & Collins, 2020; Maitland & Presser, 2016, 2020; Tourangeau et al., 2021; Yan et al., 2012a). The survey field has not yet reached a consensus on what is the best method or methods to use and in what combination and sequence. However, the best practice is to test and evaluate survey questions using at least one method, and preferably multiple methods, when possible (e.g., Tourangeau et al., 2020a; Yan et al., 2012a). We recommend the decision-tree paradigm proposed by Tourangeau et al. (2020a), which takes into consideration the pros and cons of each question and evaluation method, the nature of questions to be tested, and personnel, timeline, and budget of their survey to determine which method or methods to use. The next three chapters provide a concise description of every method that can be used by researchers to make informed decisions on how to evaluate and test their survey items.

In this chapter, we describe three lab-based evaluation methods – focus groups, cognitive interviews, and eye-tracking. They are conventionally labeled as "lab-based" methods because they used to be mostly conducted in a laboratory setting. However, virtual or remote sessions of focus groups and cognitive interviews conducted via videoconferencing software have gained popularity since the COVID-19 pandemic. We describe these advances and discuss their pros and cons as compared to the conventional lab setting.

## Focus Groups

Focus groups are discussions of small groups of about 8–10 people who share interests, characteristics, behaviors, attitudes, or circumstances required by researchers. The discussion is moderated by a trained moderator who follows a prepared guide that lists questions and issues to be discussed during the session. Focus groups are effective in uncovering what people think about a particular topic and the language and terms they use to describe and discuss the topic (Tourangeau et al., 2020a). They are typically recommended for the early stages of new content questionnaire development (d'Ardenne & Collins, 2020; Tourangeau et al., 2020a

DOI: 10.4324/9781003367826-14

Focus groups do not require a probability sample; instead, they typically recruit participants using flyers, ads, and databases maintained by facilities specialized in conducting them. When using focus groups for question development and question evaluation, it is critical to recruit participants from the survey's target population. For instance, parents of school-aged children are recruited if the target population of the intended survey is parents of school-aged children. At the same time, diversity in participant characteristics is desirable. For instance, for a focus group of parents of children aged 12–14, parents with a wide spectrum of characteristics (e.g., age, sex, education, race and ethnicity, household income, whether the parent lives in an urban area or a rural area) are recruited. Quotas are commonly used to ensure diversity. Sometimes, segmentation is important to ensure the success of focus groups. For instance, when researchers need to hear from both parents and children, parents and children are segmented so that one focus group is conducted with parents and a second one with children. Another common segmentation variable is the language spoken by testing participants – for instance, focus groups are held separately for English- and Spanish-speaking participants in each respective language. For each focus group, 10–12 participants are recruited to ensure that each group has 8–10 participants. Participants are typically offered an incentive to participate in focus groups.

> d'Ardenne and Collins (2020) conducted 12 focus groups in three locations with a total of 103 participants. Quotas were set to ensure diversity in terms of sex, age, religion, and ethnic origin. The focus groups explored participants' understanding of the term "violent extremism" and their attitudes toward extremism and tested six draft questions on the topic and participants' willingness and ability to answer.

The moderator's guide is critical to the success of focus groups. It is typically prepared ahead of time and scripts questions and issues to be discussed. When focus groups are used for question evaluation purposes, the moderator's guide typically includes survey questions to be evaluated or concepts to be measured by those survey items. In addition, the moderator's guide includes discussion questions to collect targeted information on respondents' knowledge of the topic, the language and terms respondents use to discuss the topic, and respondents' feedback on the survey questions.

A moderator leads the focus group discussion, closely following the moderator's guide. It is the moderator's job to ensure that all participants feel comfortable within the group and have the opportunity to speak, and that the discussion stays focused. A typical focus group session lasts 90 minutes. The sessions are usually recorded (either audio- or video-recorded), so they can be reviewed or transcribed for further information extraction and analysis. Organizations and researchers differ in actual practices and implementations of focus groups, but general guidelines on how to conduct focus groups are described in detail in Krueger (1994) and Krueger and Casey (2014).

Focus group information is collected via verbatim answers to discussion questions. Answers are qualitative in nature; data reduction and summary are labor intensive, time-consuming, and subjective. Qualitative analytical methods (such as content analysis and thematic analysis) can be used on text transcribed from the recordings of focus groups to generate themes and identify issues.

Although focus groups have the advantage of getting information from several people in a short period of time, one must be mindful about the possible impact of group dynamics on the type and quality of information obtained, especially when focus groups are used for question evaluation and testing. Kaplowitz et al. (2004) found that a key challenge with focus groups is digressions – people tended to share personal stories instead of focusing on the process of how they went about answering survey questions. d'Ardenne and Collins (2020) found that focus groups failed to uncover comprehension issues with target survey questions. They suspected that the group setting made it easier for individual participants to hide their comprehension issues. For instance, if some members volunteered examples of what a word meant, those with comprehension issues did not have to speak up. In addition, participants may feel embarrassed and less comfortable admitting their lack of understanding in a group setting.

**Cognitive Interviews**

Cognitive interviews evolved from the use of verbal reports as data, originally proposed by cognitive psychologists (Ericsson & Simon, 1984). Under the Cognitive Aspects of Survey Methodology movement (Jabine et al., 1984), the approach was first applied to understand autobiographical survey questions (Loftus, 1984). Heavily drawing on the four-stage survey response process model described in Chapter 2 (Tourangeau, 1984; Tourangeau et al., 2000), cognitive interviews are in-depth, semistructured administration of survey questions with the purpose of producing insights into the cognitive process of the question-answering sequences. The goal is to learn how people answer survey questions and in particular, what problems they run into at each stage of the survey response process. Cognitive interviews are appropriate for testing whether survey items are understood as intended by question writers and whether respondents are willing and able to answer them accurately. They are also appropriate for establishing why known data issues occur and exploring how these issues can be fixed.

The actual practice of conducting cognitive interviews varies by survey organization and practitioners, which sometimes leads to inconsistent conclusions with respect to survey item performance (Beatty & Willis, 2007; DeMaio & Landreth, 2004; Presser & Blair, 1994; also see Yan et al., 2012a). However, a common process involves a survey item being presented to a respondent, the respondent verbalizing the process of coming up with an answer (a technique known as "think aloud"), and the respondent being further probed on their interpretation of a certain term or the whole question, the basis of their answer, and their reaction or feedback on the survey item. This is called the concurrent approach. The other extreme is to take the retrospective approach – a questionnaire (or a block of questions) is administered without any interruptions and respondents are asked to go back to each question for think aloud and additional probing.

Regardless, researchers will need to make decisions on key elements of the process that will be appropriate for their circumstances. First, they must decide how much think-alouds (i.e., respondents verbalizing their thought process) and probing (i.e., respondents being asked follow-up questions to ensure that the same type of targeted information is obtained from everyone) should be used. Although the think aloud approach has the advantages of minimal impact on verbal reports from cognitive interviewers, minimal interviewer training requirements, and open-ended format, it does require nontrivial training of respondents because it is unnatural to everyday speech and places the main burden on them. Because cognitive interview participants differ in their ability to verbalize their thinking, it is difficult to tell in advance whether a respondent can carry out the task or to ensure that the same type of information is collected from everyone. By contrast, the probing technique maintains control of the interview and places less burden on cognitive interviewers at the risk of incurring reactivity and biasing respondents' answers.

In addition, as mentioned earlier, researchers must decide whether to use the concurrent approach (i.e., respondents are asked to think aloud and are probed right after they finish answering a survey question) or the retrospective approach (i.e., respondents think aloud and are probed after they finish answering a module or the full questionnaire). The concurrent approach is more appropriate for testing interviewer-administered questionnaires, whereas the retrospective approach evaluates self-administered questionnaires. However, both have disadvantages – the concurrent approach disrupts the natural flow of the survey-taking process and inevitably changes how respondents interact with the questionnaire, while the retrospective approach allows for time to pass, risking participants not being able to remember what they were thinking as they answered a particular question. Because of that, it is common to ask respondents to answer four or five related items together first and then probe for their thought processes for answering these items.

> **Example cognitive probes provided in Willis (2005)**
>
> *Probes for comprehension issues*
>
> 1 Can you tell me in your own words what that question was asking?
> 2 What does the word [TERM] mean to you as it is used in this question?
>
> *Probes for recall, judgment, and estimation issues*
>
> 3 How easy for difficult is it to remember [TOPIC]?
> 4 How did you come up with that answer?
>
> *Probes for reporting issues*
>
> 5 How easy or hard was it to find your answer on that list?
>
> *Probes for sensitivity of question*
>
> 6 In general, how do you feel about this question?
> 7 Is this okay to talk about in a survey or it is uncomfortable?

Probing questions are further classified by when they are written and the goals they strive to accomplish (Willis, 2005). Proactive probes are used to probe for specific information (e.g., respondents' interpretation of a particular term in the question wording). They can be drafted ahead of time (anticipated probes) or formulated during the interview (spontaneous probes). By contrast, reactive probes are based on respondent answers or behaviors that suggest a problem or an issue. They can also be scripted in advance (conditional probes) or formulated on the spot (emergent probes). Because anticipated and conditional probes are written up as part of the cognitive interview protocol, they are effective for inexperienced interviewers and for standardizing probes across respondents and interviewers. Willis (2005) is a good resource for example probes that can be used to uncover problems respondents have with the question-answering process.

Similar to focus groups, cognitive interviewing utilizes small convenience samples of participants who meet the definitions of the intended target population. Diversity in demographic characteristics is desired. When it comes to sample size, Blair and Conrad (2011) demonstrated empirically that more problems were uncovered with more participants – about a quarter of known problems were found with a sample size of 5, a third of problems were revealed with 10 participants, half of the problems with a sample size of 20, and 80% of the problems were discovered with 50 participants. However, there seems to be a diminishing return after 50 cognitive interviews. Willis (2005) recommended 8–12 interviews per round and iterative testing stopping after three rounds. According to Willis (2005), 1-hour cognitive interviews are effective to assess question performance.

Cognitive interviews are conventionally done in person. Conducting cognitive interviews over the phone is feasible, but less common. It is customary to audio or video record cognitive interviews. Occasionally, notetakers are used to observe the interviews and take notes.

Survey practitioners differ in how they analyze cognitive interviews. Some transcribe the recorded interviews and adopt a qualitative approach. Willis (2015) lists five qualitative approaches researchers can take to analyze cognitive interviews:

1 Text summary, which describes dominant themes, conclusions, and problems using raw data
2 Cognitive coding, which first codes raw data to learn the behavior of the respondent
3 Question feature coding, which also utilizes coded data and focuses on the behavior of the tested survey items
4 Theme coding, which creates labels to describe the observed phenomena
5 Pattern coding, which discovers associations in responses

By contrast, a more diagnostic approach focuses on detecting problems and identifying their nature on the spot. Yan et al. (2012a) described a diagnostic approach aimed at quickly identifying whether respondents experienced a problem answering evaluated survey questions and, if yes, what type of problems they had. According to their protocol, both the cognitive interviewer and the observer were asked to check a box indicating whether they thought the respondent had experienced a problem in answering each tested question. The interviewer and observer also indicated the nature of the problems – whether it involved difficulties with comprehension, retrieval, judgment or estimation, reporting, or some combination of these. This approach offers a quick summary of potential problems that can be further investigated using one of the qualitative approaches by Willis (2015).

Cognitive interviewing is especially effective at detecting comprehension issues. It can also suggest fixes to uncovered problems and allow researchers to test new or revised versions of previously tested questions (a process referred to as iterative testing in Esposito [2004]). However, since this method uses a small convenience sample, the results cannot be generalized to the full population, and it is not possible to quantify the extent to which a particular problem would persist in the target population. Web probing, an extension of traditional cognitive interviewing to be used on a larger population, seems to resolve this challenge. We refer interested readers to Chapter 13 for more details on web probing.

**Remote Focus Groups and Cognitive Interviews**

Both focus groups and cognitive interviews are traditionally conducted in person. Recruited participants come to a designated place (such as a focus group facility or a cognitive lab) to meet the focus group moderator or the cognitive interviewer in person. However, both are increasingly conducted virtually or remotely. Remote focus groups are mostly conducted through video-conferencing software whereas remote cognitive interviews can be conducted via video-conferencing software or by telephone.

Remote testing via video-conferencing software has advantages and disadvantages that researchers must be aware of before making the decision whether to utilize it. In terms of recruitment and coverage, remote focus groups and cognitive interviewing require participants to have Internet access, an appropriate device (equipped with a camera, a working microphone, and a speaker), and the necessary technology skills and knowledge to download and use the video-conferencing software designated by researchers. As a result, one disadvantage of remote testing is the exclusion of people without technology access and knowledge.

Remote testing allows researchers to reach a wider population and save the costs associated with travel reimbursement and snacks; thus, is easier and more cost-efficient than traditional in-person testing. However, with remote methods, researchers do not know where participants are and whether they are alone in a room or with someone else. Researchers also lose control of participants' environment and cannot control the impact of their environment on their participation and contribution to the testing.

Remote methods have the additional benefits of centralized scheduling (rather than dispersed scheduling for facilities or respondents in different locations), one training of all cognitive interviewers (instead of separate training for each geographical location), and centralized and systematic monitoring of focus groups and cognitive interviews. This centralization is very useful when tests are to be done in multiple locations or by multiple moderators and interviewers.

Participants are typically asked to turn on their cameras so that the moderators or cognitive interviewers can observe nonverbal cues. Technology makes it easy for people to share their screens, watch videos, participate in polls, and draw or comment on shared documents in addition to providing comments, feedback, and thoughts orally. However, researchers must be mindful of differential group and interview dynamics for remote methods and watch out for signs of fatigue and loss of interest in the remote session.

Another important difference between in-person and remote testing is the way consent is obtained. For in-person testing sessions, moderators or cognitive interviewers typically explain the consent form to participants in person and ask them to sign it. A number of ways exist to collect informed consent with remote methods. Consent forms can be emailed or mailed to the participant before the remote testing is scheduled to occur, and participants can be requested to reply to the email as an expression of consent or send the signed form back. Alternatively, moderators or cognitive interviewers can explain the consent form at the beginning of a remote testing session and then obtain and record oral consent from participants.

There are a few guidelines on conducting focus groups and cognitive interviews remotely (e.g., Lobe et al., 2020; Roberts et al., 2021; Shepperd et al., 2021). They all point to the importance of better internet connectivity, better video-conferencing software, and lack of audio and video problems. However, research is still needed to systematically assess the comparability of remote and in-person testing in terms of data quality, interviewer effects, and cost.

## Eye-tracking

As the name implies, eye-tracking methodology uses infrared cameras to track people's eye movements as they read and answer survey questions. These cameras record where people look, how long they look at it, and where they look next. The cameras also record the size of respondents' pupils at each gaze. As a result, eye-tracking provides a direct window into respondents' survey response process.

When used for question testing and evaluation, survey methodologists rely on fixation count (i.e., how many times people look at a targeted area), fixation duration (i.e., how long people look at it), rereads, and pupil dilation (the extent to which peoples' pupils get bigger) to identify bad questions that are difficult to understand or answer. The assumption is that questions eliciting more and longer fixations, more rereads, and larger pupil dilations perform poorly. For example, Lenzer et al. (2011) empirically demonstrated that text features that reduce readability of survey questions (such as complex syntax, ambiguous nouns) incurred longer fixation times and more fixations. Kamoen et al. (2011, 2017) showed that negative wording elicited more and longer rereads than positive wording. Yan (2023) found that negative response options (e.g., "very dissatisfied") incurred significantly larger pupil dilations in addition to receiving significantly more and longer fixations than positive response options (such as "very satisfied").

Besides identifying bad survey questions, eye-tracking can also be used to uncover usability problems with a survey instrument. For instance, eye-tracking can show whether respondents have paid any attention to a particular element of the survey instrument (e.g., the progress bar or the help button), and for how long. The results can help improve the usability of web or paper instruments.

Tourangeau et al. (2020) listed several drawbacks of the eye-tracking methodology. First, eye-tracking requires a new data collection, which will increase the cost of question evaluation and testing efforts. Second, eye-tracking requires the investment of special equipment and software, and staff capable of setting up the equipment and extracting the data. Third, eye-tracking data require considerable processing and cleaning before they can be analyzed. Lastly, eye-tracking has been mostly used to test web and paper instruments, making its relevance for interviewer-administered surveys unclear.

## Summary

This chapter discusses three lab-based methods for evaluating survey questions – focus groups, cognitive interviews, and eye-tracking. Focus groups are an effective exploratory tool to be used at the early stages of questionnaire development to learn from a target population how they think of a topic and what language and terms they use to discuss the topic. Cognitive interviews are a great diagnostic tool to be used after items have been developed to learn about the cognitive processes people go through when providing answers to survey questions and to identify issues related mostly to comprehension and retrieval. Both methods are traditionally held in person, in a laboratory setting, where researchers control the environment and the stimuli. However, both methods are increasingly conducted via video-conferencing software. Remote testing has the advantages of reaching more people and getting to diverse geographical locations in a cost-efficient manner. However, researchers cannot control the environmental impact on respondents in remote sessions and are likely in competition for participants' attention with many stimuli. Research is needed to fully understand the amount and quality of information collected remotely versus in person. Eye-tracking provides a direct window to where respondents look and for how long. It is a great tool to identify specific parts of survey questions that are difficult for respondents to understand and to uncover usability issues.

**Exercises**

1 Based on your reading of this chapter, under what circumstances do you think you will want to use focus groups, cognitive interviews, and eye-tracking for question evaluation and testing?
2 Develop four cognitive probes that you can use to evaluate the following yes-no survey question: Do you have a car?

# 12  Expert Methods

## Introduction

As the name implies, expert methods involve experts to review and evaluate survey questions. Since data collection is not needed and actual respondents are not involved, these methods do not directly observe the survey response process. Instead, experts carry out reviews and evaluations drawing on their expertise and prior experience to predict problems with the survey questions. This is the least expensive method and requires the least time (because there is no data collection).

Following Tourangeau et al.'s (2020a) typology, we distinguish between methods involving human experts and methods involving computer systems. For methods involving human experts, we make a further distinction between expert reviews and the Questionnaire Appraisal System (QAS). In particular, we use expert reviews in this book to specifically refer to an informal appraisal process involving the collection of qualitative feedback from human experts about the performance of tested survey items. By contrast, QAS refers to a reviewing process involving expert judgments guided by formal appraisal systems that offer a detailed set of potential problem codes.

> Expert methods using human experts include expert reviews and QAS. Expert methods utilizing computer systems include Question Understanding Aid (QUAID) and Survey Quality Predictor (SQP).

## Expert Reviews

With expert reviews, experts provide qualitative feedback on the performance of survey items. Different types of human experts can be involved in this process and ideally, more than one expert will be involved in the review process. Subject matter experts draw on their specialized background knowledge to provide valuable input on terminology used in tested survey questions and if the type of information collected by those questions captures intended concepts (McCarthy, 2020). Interviewers are effective at identifying questions particularly problematic for interviewer administration. Post-survey processing staff can identify survey questions needing heavy editing and imputation. Bilingual survey methodologists can identify questions that are poorly translated. In this chapter, we discuss expert reviews conducted by survey methodologists with a focus on evaluation of question performance based on the survey response process model, questionnaire

DOI: 10.4324/9781003367826-15

design principles and best practices, empirical survey literature, and our own research experience.

The goal for expert reviews is to ensure that respondents understand the survey questions as intended and are able to recall the needed information and form an answer matching one of the response options. As a result, identifying problems with survey questions is a key outcome. However, actual implementation of expert reviews varies. Expert reviews can be conducted in groups or individually, unstructured or structured by issues to address, yielding open-ended comments or ratings, and so on. For instance, Maitland and Presser (2020) asked three experts to conduct expert reviews independently. The experts were asked to describe problems they found with question wording, response options, and introductions leading to questions. The qualitative feedback resulting from expert reviews was further coded into problem categories for analysis purposes. Yan et al. (2012a) asked four experts to independently judge whether tested survey items had any serious problems, to describe the problems, and to rate each item on a 5-point scale, ranging from "This is a very good item" (= 1) to "This is a very bad item" (= 5). The average of the four ratings was used to rank order the items in their analysis. Olson (2010) instructed six expert reviewers to first code the tested survey items on burden, sensitivity, and social desirability concerns, and then to rate the likelihood of a failure during the survey response process, using a 4-point scale ranging from "Unlikely that a failure of this stage will occur" (= 0) to "Very likely that a failure of this stage will occur" (= 3). Experts were also asked to write about the individual types of problems they thought were likely to occur. Even though the three studies conducted expert reviews very differently, they were able to obtain the desired information with regard to the performance of survey questions being tested. Researchers can decide what works for their particular evaluation task.

The main advantage of expert reviews is that they are quick and relatively inexpensive to do (Tourangeau et al., 2020a). Experts generally detect more problems than other methods (Yan et al., 2012a) and positively predict questions with data quality problems (Maitland & Presser, 2020; Olson, 2010). Furthermore, experts can make good suggestions about how to fix the detected problems or suggest questions that need to undergo additional testing and evaluation (such as cognitive interviewing). Expert reviews are most helpful after questions have been drafted and can be used for questionnaires administered in any mode of data collection. Preferably, experts with different backgrounds (such as subject matter experts, survey methodologists, interviewers, and supervisors) are involved in the process to the extent possible. Key limitations with expert reviews are the low levels of consistency across reviews (Presser & Blair, 1994) and idiosyncratic and inconsistent results across experts (Olson, 2010).

**Questionnaire Appraisal System**

QAS is a systematic and standardized appraisal system that evaluates a survey item for seven classes of problems involving question reading, question instructions, question clarity, assumptions, knowledge or memory, sensitivity or bias, and response categories (Willis & Lessler, 1999). In the 1999 version, each question is evaluated for the presence of 26 potential problems under the seven classes, as shown in Table 12.1. Interested readers are referred to Willis and Lessler (1999) for detailed descriptions of each problem code. Figure 12.1 presents a screenshot of the first page of the QAS-99 form. A subsequent enhancement, the QAS-04, included updates for multilingual and cross-cultural

*Table 12.1* Problem Codes in QAS-99 and QAS-04

| Problem type | Problem codes |
| --- | --- |
| Question reading | What to read; missing information; how to read |
| Question instructions | Conflicting or inaccurate instructions; complicated instructions |
| Question clarity | Wording; technical terms; vague, reference periods |
| Assumptions | Inappropriate assumptions; assumes constant behavior; double-barreled |
| Knowledge or memory | Knowledge may not exist; attitude may not exist; recall failure; computation problem |
| Sensitivity or bias | Sensitive questions (general); sensitive questions (specific); socially acceptable responses implied |
| Response categories | Open-ended question; mismatch; technical terms; vague; overlapping; missing eligible responses; illogical order |
| Cross-cultural considerations (new to QAS-04) | Reference periods; knowledge; measuring units; assumptions; response categories; name format; politeness |
| Translation (new to QAS-4) | Double negatives; idioms; acronyms; term 'you' is not defined; time adverbs; no equivalent term or concept; references applicable only to English; adjectives modifying other adjectives |

instrument development, with updates focusing on concept comparability across languages or cultures (Dean et al., 2007), as shown in the bottom rows of Table 12.1. QAS allows evaluators to use the problem checklist to determine whether the tested item passes or fails each problem type. Question writers then use the feedback to develop recommendations for correcting found issues.

Compared to expert reviews, QAS is a structured and standardized approach yielding feedback with the same content and format. Furthermore, QAS does not require evaluators to be experts in survey methodology or subject matters. As a matter of fact, QAS was developed to be used by non-experts as well and can be used by evaluators with varying degree of knowledge. Another benefit of QAS is its focus on cognitive issues in the survey response process. Empirical literature shows that problems identified by QAS are linked to respondents' problem behaviors (Dykema et al., 2020), accuracy (Maitland & Presser, 2020), and reliability of survey questions (Dykema et al., 2020).

One primary limitation of QAS is that it tends to find problems with almost every tested survey item as reviewers are encouraged to be liberal with the checklist (Rothgeb et al., 2001). Another drawback is the lack of attention to visual design features that are an important part of self-administered questionnaires, question order effects, and the social-cultural context in which the questions will be administered. Finally, QAS can be very time consuming, depending on the questionnaire length, as the checklist has to be applied to every individual question.

## QUESTION APPRAISAL SYSTEM (QAS-99): CODING FORM

*INSTRUCTIONS. Use one form for EACH question to be reviewed. In reviewing each question:*

1) WRITE OR TYPE IN QUESTION NUMBER. ATTACH QUESTION.

> Question number or question here:

2) Proceed through the form - Circle or highlight YES or NO for each Problem Type (1a... 8).
3) Whenever a YES is circled, write detailed notes on this form that describe the problem.

**STEP 1 - READING: Determine if it is difficult for the interviewers to read the question uniformly to all respondents.**

| | | |
|---|---|---|
| 1a. | **WHAT TO READ**: Interviewer may have difficulty determining what *parts* of the question should be read. | YES  NO |

*Figure 12.1* Screenshot of QAS-99 Form.

## Question Understanding AID

The QUAID is a computer tool developed to review survey items for comprehension issues, drawing on models from computer science, computational linguistics, discourse processing, and cognitive science (Graesser et al., 2006). Users of this tool (http://quaid.cohmetrix.com/) are required to manually enter the question stem, response options, and introductions or definitions (when available), as shown on the left side of the screen in Figure 12.2. The tool provides feedback on the survey item (on the right side of the screen in Figure 12.2) on five classes of comprehension problems: unfamiliar technical terms, vague or imprecise predicate or relative terms, vague or imprecise noun phrases, complex syntax, and working memory overload.

QUAID is a computer expert review method and does not require users to have any expertise in survey methodology or subject matter. There are two other benefits of this method. First, the tool is free of charge to the public. Second, the tool provides almost instant feedback on the tested item. In addition, it can detect syntactical problems with the survey questions.

However, similar to QAS, the primary limitation of QUAID lies in its sole focus on question features, ignoring visual design features of self-administered instruments, context effects within the questionnaire, and social-cultural context in which the questions are to be administered. In addition, question writers need to take the results with a grain of salt – as shown in the screen capture, the word "very" is flagged to be an imprecise relative term. However, question writers need to decide whether that problem is worth worrying about. Empirically, QUAID results are *not* consistently associated with reliability

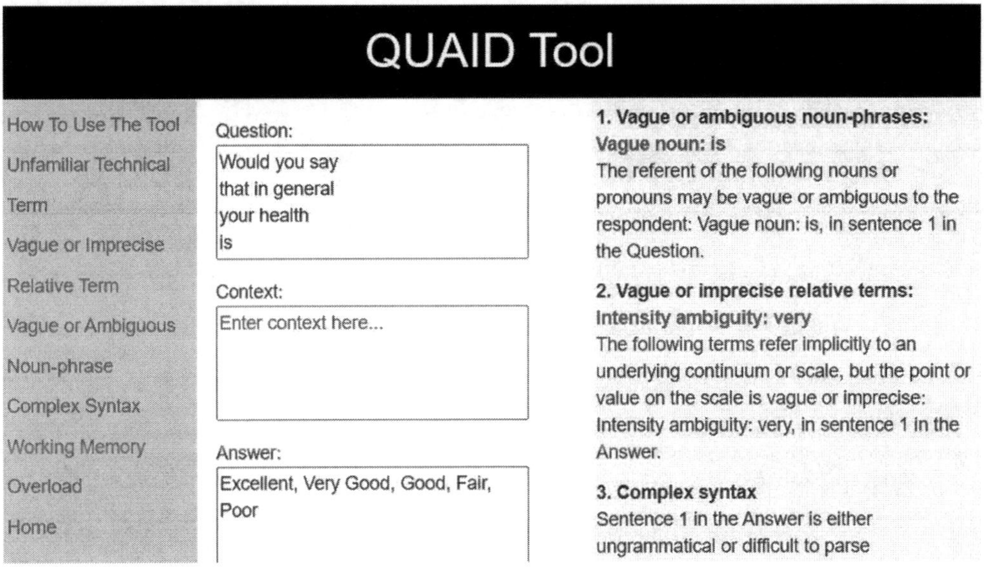

*Figure 12.2* QUAID Tool Interface With Example Test Question.

(Dykema et al., 2020; Tourangeau et al., 2021). Studies have reported that it performs worse than expert reviews and cognitive interviewing with regard to predicting accuracy of survey responses when compared to benchmark value (e.g., Maitland & Presser, 2020; Olson, 2010).

**Survey Quality Predictor**

The SQP is another computer tool developed to predict reliability, validity, and quality (defined as the product of reliability and validity) of survey items based on meta-analyses of a large number of multitrait-multimethod (MTMM) studies (Saris & Gallhofer, 2014).

Users of SQP enter the target survey item to be tested to the SQP (http://sqp.upf.edu/) and begin coding to provide contextual information about the item (e.g., the topic of the survey, the mode, and location of data collection), as shown in Figure 12.3. SQP automatically codes some characteristics such as the number of words in the question, and the user is prompted to code other features such as concept measured by the tested item, the number and type of response categories, perceived saliency and sensitivity of the question, and so on (the right panel of Figure 12.4 displays a list of features coded by the user). After coding is completed, SQP estimates and returns the predicted reliability, validity, and quality of the tested item (Figure 12.5).

Because some features coded by the users are fairly subjective in nature (e.g., perceived sensitivity and saliency), the predicted quality measures are subject to coding errors and coder reliability, which is a limitation of SQP. Another limitation is that survey items included in the MTMM experiments are largely attitudinal rather than factual or behavioral. As a result, quality estimates for factual or behavioral

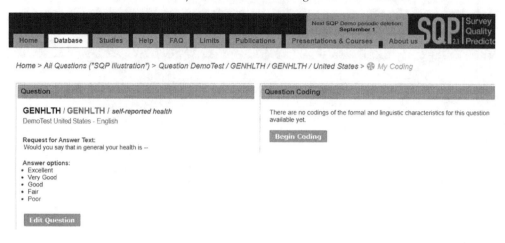

*Figure 12.3* SQP Interface Before Coding Is Started.

items might not be accurate. However, SQP can be very fast and inexpensive to use because no data collection is required. Empirically, SQP performed worse than expert reviews and cognitive interviews in predicting accuracy of survey responses obtained (Maitland & Presser, 2020). Furthermore, SQP was *not* associated with respondents' problem behaviors (Dykema et al., 2020), did *not* predict actual reliability (Dykema et al., 2020; Maitland & Presser, 2016), did *not* agree with question evaluation methods (Yan et al., 2012a), and had a weak correlation with other measures of reliability (Tourangeau et al., 2021).

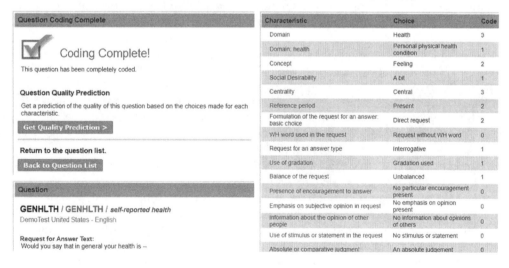

*Figure 12.4* SQP Interface After Coding Is Completed.

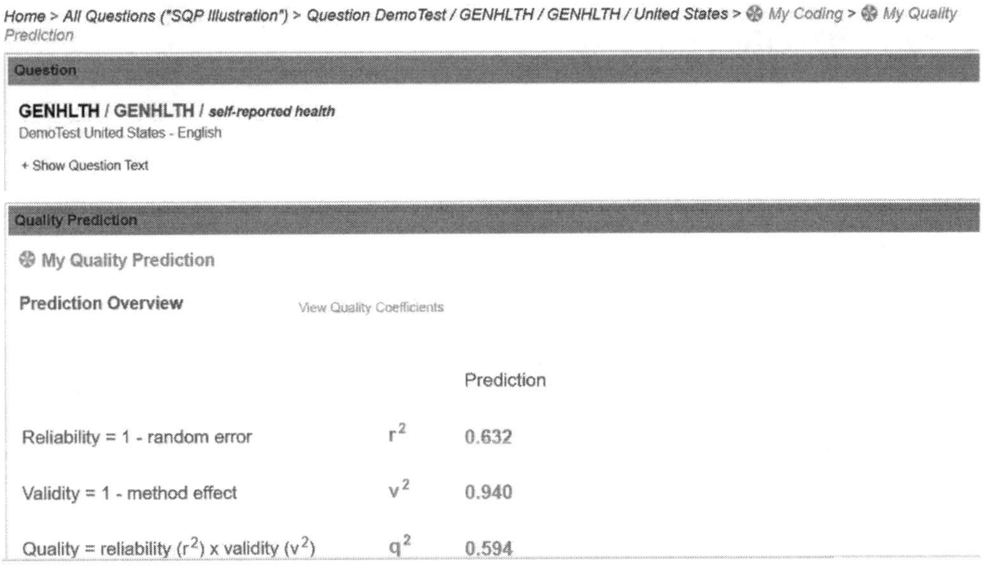

Figure 12.5 Quality Predictions Provided by SQP.

## Summary

This chapter describes four expert methods that can be used to test and evaluate survey questions. A common and defining feature of expert methods is that no data collection is needed, which is both advantageous and disadvantageous. The main strengths of expert methods are low cost and quick feedback. However, the expert methods lack attention to the context in which the tested survey items are administered. The expert methods are appropriate for researchers with a small budget for question evaluation, projects that need quick feedback on question evaluation, and the early stages of the questionnaire evaluation process (for instance, before more expensive methods such as cognitive interviews or a pilot are used). We recommend that question writers take advantage of the strengths of expert methods by using at least one of them to start the question evaluation process, but not rely on these methods as the only pretesting technique.

## Exercise

1 Below is a survey item from the American National Election Studies. Please evaluate this item using the four methods discussed in this chapter.

Some people think that the way people talk needs to change with the times to be more sensitive to people from different backgrounds. Others think that this has already gone too far and many people are just too easily offended. Which is closer to your opinion?

1  *The way people talk needs to change a lot*
2  *The way people talk needs to change a little*
3  *People are a little too easily offended*
4  *People are much too easily offended*

# 13 Field-based Methods

**Introduction**

This chapter describes methods requiring actual data collection to assess survey items. They are the most costly and time-consuming question evaluation techniques because of their data collection component. We start with two methods drawing on additional, qualitative information collected from a larger number of respondents than typically required in lab-based methods to inform question performance (web probing and respondent and interviewer debriefing). We then discuss the use of randomized experiments, response latency, and behavior coding to evaluate the performance of survey questions. We introduce quantitative methods used to evaluate reliability and validity of resultant answers. Finally, we discuss how item response theory (IRT) and pilot tests can be used for question evaluation.

**Web Probing**

Web probing is an approach of embedding cognitive probes typically used in lab-based cognitive interviews in a web survey. Respondents first answer a survey item (i.e., the target item to be tested and probed on) and then answer follow-up probe(s) about the target question. The purpose of follow-up probes is the same as probes used in traditional cognitive interviewing described in Chapter 11 – to collect additional information on how respondents go about answering the target question. Probes are scripted and programmed into a web survey instrument to gather respondents' comprehension of the target question, how and what information they retrieved, the process of generating a judgment or an estimate, and mapping the judgment or estimate to one of the offered response options. Web probing can be employed during the question evaluation and testing stage before target items are fielded. It can also be employed during the fielding of target survey items so that researchers can use the feedback to monitor their performance and to better understand responses by, for instance, respondents from different cultural backgrounds. Of course, more than one target item can be probed on and more than one probe can be embedded for each target item. In addition, probes can be asked immediately after the target item is answered as in concurrent probes in traditional cognitive interviewing or after respondents complete the full questionnaire, analogous to retrospective probes in cognitive interviews. Probes can be general (expansive probes) or specific (directive probes), open-ended or closed.

Because probes are part of a web survey, from respondents' perspective, they are just additional survey questions to answer. As a result, web probing has the advantages of quickly and unobtrusively collecting a large amount of information from a large number of respondents at a low cost. However, the major weakness of this approach is that only scripted anticipatory probes can be programmed into the web survey ahead of time. Spontaneous, reactive probes, typically asked by cognitive interviewers in response to a respondent behavior, cannot be utilized in the context of web probing. Studies comparing web probing to conventional cognitive interviewing demonstrate that the two techniques produce similar results in terms of the types and the number of major issues or problems with the target question uncovered (e.g., Fowler & Willis, 2020; Geisen & Murphy, 2020). Interested readers are referred to Meitinger et al. (2024) for strategies to improve response quality of web probing such as providing clear introduction of web probing to respondents.

**Respondent and Interviewer Debriefings**

Respondent and interviewer debriefings allow researchers to collect additional feedback on their survey experience throughout data collection. Respondents typically answer debriefing questions at the conclusion of the interview, while interviewers are usually convened by phone, virtually, or in person to talk about their experiences after the data collection is concluded. Sometimes, interviewers are asked to provide feedback by responding to debriefing questions at the end of the interview, answering a separate debriefing questionnaire, or completing a special form to track problematic questions.

Common respondent debriefing questions ask respondents about their perceptions of the survey such as perceived burden (e.g., Yan et al., 2020), sensitivity of the survey (e.g., Yan et al., 2020) or specific survey items (e.g., Kreuter et al., 2008a), difficulty of answering particular questions (e.g., Read, 2019; Yan et al., 2020), perceived survey length (Read, 2019; Yan et al., 2020), attitudes toward the survey such as interest (e.g., Yan et al., 2020), importance of the survey (e.g., Sharp & Frankel, 1983), and willingness to be interviewed again (e.g., Sharp & Frankel, 1983).

Common interviewer debriefing questions capture interviewers' observations and assessment of respondents' question-answering process (West et al., 2020). Example interviewer debriefing questions include respondents' understanding of survey questions, difficulty answering survey questions, and whether respondents asked for clarifications or needed help from interviewers (West et al., 2020).

When debriefing questions are added to the end of a survey instrument used in data collection, the cost of implementing respondent or interviewer debriefing is marginal, which is a major advantage of this method. However, the additional debriefing questions do make the actual survey longer, which may affect respondents' attitudes toward the survey. In addition, respondents may not want to spend the extra time on completing the debriefing questions or be unwilling to admit they have had problems with the survey. Similarly, interviewers may not complete a separate interviewer debriefing questionnaire, or their attribution of respondent difficulty may be incorrect.

**Randomized Experiments**

Randomized experiments can be embedded in the actual fielding of the survey or in a field test, to compare different versions of questions. For a between-subject randomized experiment, respondents are randomly assigned to receive different versions of the questions. Because of the randomization, the only thing that is different across experimental conditions is the version of questions respondents are assigned to receive. As a result, observed differences across conditions reflect differences resulting from the different question versions. However, observed differences do not necessarily lead to a conclusion which version of the question produces better data, unless question writers make assumptions or have strong theoretical reasons for deciding that one version of the question is better than another. Tourangeau (2004) describes four design issues with the use of randomized experiments. One pertains to whether the experiment is designed to test packages of variables or to conduct a fully crossed factorial design. The former tends to be used when the purpose of the experiment is to calibrate the impact of replacing an old questionnaire with a new one. By contrast, a fully crossed factorial design, as the name implies, fully crosses different levels of multiple experimental factors. For instance, a design aimed to test hypotheses about the individual and joint impact of the direction and labeling of a response scale should have four experimental conditions that fully cross the two levels of scale direction (e.g., low-to-high vs. high-to-low) with the two levels of the scale labeling (fully labeled vs. end-labeled), resulting in (1) low-to-high, fully labeled, (2) low-to-high, end-labeled, (3) high-to-low, fully labeled, and (4) high-to-low, end-labeled experimental groups.

The major advantage of randomized experiments is that they produce quantitative size of differences observed between experimental conditions (e.g., two versions of question wording). However, a complicated experimental design increases the cost and logistical complexity of implementing the design. For instance, a fully crossed three-by-four factorial design requires the development and preparation of 12 versions of the questionnaire, making it harder to implement if the experiment is embedded in a mail survey. Furthermore, the results may be harder to interpret and difficult to conclude which version or combination should be adopted. In addition to those challenges, experiments are typically expensive because they require large sample sizes to grant enough statistical power to detect differences.

**Response Latency**

Response latency refers to time taken to answer survey questions. It is a type of paradata typically captured automatically by computer-assisted surveys such as web or computer-assisted interviewing. Response latency can be determined for each individual survey item, for groups of survey items (i.e., at the question module or question block level), or at the overall questionnaire level. Response latency information can be captured from servers (server-side paradata) or from respondents' device (client-side paradata). The tradeoffs and comparisons between server-side response latency and client-side response latency are described elsewhere (Yan & Olson, 2013; Yan & Tourangeau, 2008).

Regardless of how response latencies are captured, long response latency is commonly considered indicative of difficulty or challenges respondents have while answering survey item(s) (Tourangeau et al., 2020b; Yan & Tourangeau, 2008). As a result, for question evaluation and testing purposes, survey items incurring long response latency are identified as problematic and candidates for further improvement.

The key advantages of this question evaluation method are that the cost of collecting timing information is marginal for computer-assisted surveys and that the cost of collecting timings for individual items is almost the same as the cost of collecting timings for the full survey once the system is set up. However, there are several disadvantages to this method. First, this method is not feasible for survey questions asked in a mode that does not generate timestamps automatically (such as a paper survey). Second, the raw timing data can be messy and there are always outliers. Data manipulation and data cleaning are needed to derive meaningful measures of response latency. Researchers and analysts have to make assumptions and determine how to treat outliers (Yan & Olson, 2013). Third, analyses of response latencies might indicate which survey item(s) are problematic but they do not indicate what are the problems and do not suggest what are the potential fixes (Yan et al., 2012a). Lastly, the assumption that long response latency is indicative of response difficulty is a strong one and may not apply to everyone or every survey item. As a matter of fact, Yan et al. (2015) have demonstrated empirically that longer time spent answering one survey question measuring subjective well-being is associated with data of lower quality for respondents aged between 50 and 70, but data of higher quality for respondents aged 70 and above. As a result, one cannot rely on response latency data as the only method for question evaluation.

**Behavior Coding**

Behavior coding is a systematic coding of interviewer-respondent interactions typically used to monitor interviewer performance (that is, the extent to which interviewers comply with the prescribed way of asking survey questions) and to identify problems with survey questions. The coding can be done in real time or on recorded interviews after the interview is concluded. When behavior coding is used for the purpose of questionnaire assessment, its goal is to identify interviewer or respondent behaviors indicative of problems with the question-answering process. A paradigmatic sequence of the question-answering process starts with an interviewer asking a question as worded, a respondent providing an adequate answer to that question, and an interviewer recording the answer correctly (Schaeffer & Maynard, 1996). Any deviation from this paradigmatic sequence suggests a breakdown occurring at any of the four stages of the survey response process.

Interviewer behaviors indicating problems with survey items include interviewers not reading questions verbatim and not maintaining the meaning of a survey question (e.g., Fowler & Cannell, 1996; Oksenberg et al., 1991). Respondent behaviors suggesting problems with questions include respondents asking for clarification, requesting interviewers to repeat the question, providing an inadequate answer that needs probing, failing to select from one of the provided response options, qualifying their response, and interrupting or answering before the interviewer finishes reading the question (e.g., Fowler & Cannell, 1996; Oksenberg et al., 1991). All these are indicative of undefined or ambiguous terms, unclear or difficult response tasks, or poor question order. Survey items producing more problematic interviewer or respondent behaviors suggest breakdowns with the question-answering process and are assumed to be candidates for improvement. Two criteria are commonly used to flag whether a survey item is problematic. The 15% rule identifies a problematic item when a problematic interviewer or respondent behavior code is assigned at least 15% of the time the question is asked and answered (e.g., Fowler, 1992), and the standard deviation rule, which identifies questions one or two standard deviations above the mean problematic code assignment.

The coding of interviewer and respondent behaviors is typically conducted by human coders, who can be coders trained specifically for this task, supervisors, or project staff. However, human coding is time-consuming and expensive. As a result, typically only a small proportion of interviews are coded. Generally, 30 interviews are considered sufficient to produce meaningful results. As with some of the already discussed pretesting methods, problematic interviewer and respondent behavior codes do not necessarily point to specific issues and do not necessarily suggest how to fix them, which is a limitation of behavior coding.

## Quantitative Methods Evaluating Reliability and Validity

As mentioned in Chapter 1, reliability and validity are two important measures of data quality. A variety of methods can be used to assess reliability and validity of a survey item. These methods differ in the amount of data needed and required assumptions (Tourangeau et al., 2020b, 2021; Yan & Sun, 2022). In the following sections, we illustrate how quantitative methods are used to assess validity and reliability. However, we do not focus on the mathematics behind each method; instead, we refer readers to additional resources wherever possible.

### Assessing Reliability Using Data from Interviews and Reinterviews

Four methods require two data collection points in the form of interview and reinterview. That is, the same item is administered twice in two interviews, usually about a week apart. All four methods consider consistency of answers provided at the original interview and the reinterview as reliability. **Gross discrepancy rate** (GDR) is calculated as the percentage of respondents providing inconsistent answers to the same item at two-time points. Low GDR means high reliability. **Kappa** also calculates the percentage of consistent answers provided by respondents to the same item administered at two-time points, but it corrects for chance agreement. High kappa indicates high reliability. The third method **correlates** answers to the same item provided at two-time points. Pearson correlations can be calculated on continuous or interval items. Tetrachoric correlations are used on dichotomous items, whereas polychoric correlations are used on ordinal items. High correlations suggest high reliability. The fourth method is **index of inconsistency** (IOI). For continuous items, it is calculated as 1 minus the correlation between answers at time 1 and time 2. For categorical variables, IOI is calculated as 1 minus kappa. Low IOI is indicative of high reliability. All four methods rely on a simple statistical model assuming that a survey answer reflects the underlying true value plus a random error (Tourangeau et al., 2021; Yan & Sun, 2022). Furthermore, all four methods assume that the true value does not change over time, respondents do not memorize their answers at time 1, and the essential survey conditions between time 1 and time 2 are the same, which by itself is a strong assumption (Tourangeau et al., 2021).

Tourangeau et al. have used GDR, kappa, and over-time correlation to evaluate the reliability of hundreds of survey items and found that all three measures of reliability overlap substantially (Tourangeau et al., 2021) and that reliability is higher with factual questions, shorter questions, questions that do not use scales, questions with fewer response options, and questions asking about a noncentral topic (Tourangeau et al., 2020b). Maitland and Presser (2016) used IOI to evaluate reliability and showed that a combination of five methods (Questionnaire Appraisal System, Question Understanding Aid Survey Quality Predictor, and expert reviews described in Chapter 12 and cognitive interviewing described in Chapter 11) was the most predictive of reliability.

## Assessing Reliability through Complex Modeling Approaches

The **quasi-simplex model** requires a longitudinal design with three rounds of data collection that are at least 1 year apart from each other (Alwin, 2007). At each round, answers provided by respondents reflect the true value and a random error component. Furthermore, the true value at a particular round reflects the true value at the previous round plus a change over time. Reliability is estimated as the strength of the relationship between respondent answers and the true value, where high values indicate high reliability. We refer readers to Alwin (2007), Wiley and Wiley (1970), and Heise (1969) for the mathematical assumptions required to make quasi-simplex models identifiable.

Two studies applied this method to estimate reliability. Tourangeau et al. (2020b) applied the quasi-simplex model to 60 survey items and found that reliability estimated using this method strongly correlated with reliability estimated using over-time correlations. Hout and Hastings (2016) evaluated reliability in the General Social Survey using this approach and found that demographic items yielded higher reliability than attitudes about race and immigration.

The **multitrait-multimethod (MTMM)** approach conventionally requires nine survey items to be included in one data collection for the model to be identifiable. The nine items measure three traits (or concepts) using three methods. According to the true-score MTMM proposed by Saris and Gallhofer (2007), reliability is measured by the relationship between answers and the true score, whereas validity is measured by the relationship between the true score and the trait the survey item is supposed to capture. A recent variation allows respondents to answer six questions measuring two of the three traits via a split-ballot design instead of all nine items in the original MTMM design (Saris et al., 2004), but more assumptions are needed to estimate reliability and validity. Interested readers are referred to Saris and Gallhofer (2007) for more information on MTMM.

As an example, Saris et al. (2010) applied this method to evaluate the performance of survey items using an agree/disagree scale and scales specific to survey items. The latter scales are called "item-specific" or construct-specific scales (Chapter 4 also discusses agree/disagree scale and item-specific/construct-specific scales). Table 13.1 displays the wording and scales of three questions and reliability estimated through the MTMM design. The survey item displayed at the first row uses an item-specific scale, whereas the second and third rows use an agree/disagree scale. The second row includes a negative word – "rarely" – in the question wording. As shown in Table 13.1, survey items using an agree/disagree scale yielded less reliable answers than the item using an item-specific scale, especially the one with a negative word in the question wording. Based on their findings, Saris et al. (2010) advocate the use of item-specific scales over agree/disagree scales.

**Latent class analysis (LCA)** models the relationship between survey items and the (categorical) latent concept these items are supposed to measure. LCA is able to assign respondents into one of the latent classes and allows researchers to calculate the prevalence of misclassification; that is, respondents who self-report as a voter but are classified by LCA as a non-voter (false positive) and respondents who self-report as a non-voter but are classified as a voter (false negative). The overall misclassification rate reflecting both false positives and false negatives has been used to assess question performance; survey items producing a lower misclassification rate are assumed to perform better (e.g., Yan et al., 2012a). In addition, reliability of each item used in LCA can be calculated directly using the formula provided in Clogg and Manning (1996)

Table 13.1 Survey Items Examined in Saris et al. (2010)

| Question wording | Response scale | Reliability estimated through MTMM | Validity estimated via MTMM |
|---|---|---|---|
| Please indicate how often you think the following applies to doctors in general… Before doctors decide on a treatment, they discuss it with their patient | • Never or almost never<br>• Some of the time<br>• About half of the time<br>• Most of the time<br>• Always or almost always | 0.74 | 1 |
| Please indicate how much you agree or disagree with each of the following statements about doctors in general… Before doctors decide on a treatment, they *rarely* discuss it with their patient | • Agree strongly<br>• Agree<br>• Neither disagree nor agree<br>• Disagree<br>• Disagree strongly | 0.46 | 0.41 |
| Please indicate how much you agree or disagree with each of the following statements about doctors in general… Before doctors decide on a treatment, they *usually* discuss it with their patient | • Agree strongly<br>• Agree<br>• Neither disagree nor agree<br>• Disagree<br>• Disagree strongly | 0.59 | 0.62 |

(see Tourangeau et al., 2021, as an example). Again, a higher value indicates higher reliability. Mathematically, LCA requires at least three survey items for the model to be identifiable. Additional assumptions are needed if two items are used in LCA (see Yan et al., 2012b; Yan & Tourangeau, 2022 for examples). Other key assumptions for this method include local independence, which requires answers to items to be uncorrelated given the latent class membership. Interested readers are referred to McCutcheon (1987) for more information.

As an example of applying LCA to question evaluation, Kreuter et al. (2008b) used LCA to evaluate the performance of three items. The first item asked respondents directly if they ever received a grade of "D" or "F" for a class, whereas the second item asked them if they received an unsatisfactory or failing grade. The third item asked respondents about the worst grade they ever received in a course. They found that the second item asking about ever received an unsatisfactory or failing grade yielded the highest misclassification rate, making it the worst-performing item of the three.

**Methods to Examine Validity**

Validity refers to the extent that a survey item accurately measures the concept it is intended to measure. A common method to assess validity is to examine the correlation between answers to the target survey item and to other survey items as a measure of construct validity. Ideally, the correlation should be high between answers to the target item and answers to another survey item that ought to be related to the target item at least in theory (i.e., convergent validity), whereas the correlation should be low between answers to the target item and answers to another item that is not conceptually related (i.e., divergent validity).

Tourangeau et al. (2020a) discussed two other methods to assess validity. One is to compare respondents whose answers to the target item ought to be different. For instance, respondents with worse health should answer more negatively to the target item measuring health than those with better health. A second method is to compare answers to a target survey item to those from a comparable sample using alternative question wording or a different data collection mode as in a split-ballot design or to an external benchmark. If the distribution of answers to the target item is similar to the external benchmark or the distribution of answers from the comparable sample, then the target item is considered to have a high face validity. The major weakness of the three methods described above is that the question writer has to make assumptions about what item the target item should be correlated with, which population subgroups ought to answer the target item differently, and how similar the distribution of answers to the target item should be to the external benchmark or the distribution from the comparable sample. As described earlier, both MTMM and SQP (see Chapter 12) also provide estimates of validity.

## Item Response Theory

IRT models the relationship between a respondent's answer to the target survey item in a battery or a scale and their position on the latent construct intended to be measured by scale. The target item could employ a dichotomous response format (e.g., yes/no, true/false) or a response scale with three or more scale points. The latent construct is assumed to be continuous. IRT assumes a monotonic, logistic curve relating a respondent's position on the latent construct to the probability of a respondent providing a particular answer. Interested readers are referred to Van der Linden and Hambleton (1997).

Reeve and Fayers (2005) used IRT to evaluate the Mental Health Summary Scale consisting of 14 survey items. IRT showed that the two items asking whether respondents had a lot of energy and whether respondents felt full of pep were redundant. So were the two items asking respondents whether they felt worn out and felt tired. Little content information was lost if the "pep" and "worn out" items were deleted from the scale.

A major weakness of IRT is the same as other complex models (e.g., LCA, MTMM) – multiple items are needed to use this method. Violations of assumptions needed for model fitting lead to biased estimates and misleading results. Furthermore, staff with specialized statistical expertise are needed to use these methods. More importantly, the quantitative measures do not reveal causes of low reliability or validity, high misclassification, and flatter information curves. They also do not suggest how the survey items should be revised to improve reliability and validity, reduce misclassification, and increase informativeness.

## Pretests

Pretests are small-scale rehearsals of the data collection protocol before the main study launch. They are also called pilot studies. The purpose of a pretest is to carry out the study as planned to detect any problems with the data collection protocol (including question wording, instrument programming, and business rules used in data collection). Question writers using pretests to assess questionnaire performance often examine univariate distributions of the answers with an eye for high missing data rates or problematic answer patterns (e.g., almost all respondents select "no" to a particular question or many respondents provid out-of-range values or inconsistent answers). Question writers tend to build other evaluation methods into a pretest such as randomized experiments, respondent debriefing questions, interviewer assessment questions, collection of response latencies, and additional questions to enable examination of reliability and validity and to make identifiable complex models (such as LCA, MTMM, IRT). Behavior coding can be conducted on recordings of the pilot tests as well.

The key advantage of this method is that survey items are assessed in a realistic setting and in the context of the full questionnaire, whereas the primary disadvantages are the cost and time needed to conduct the pilot (Tourangeau et al., 2020a).

### Summary

This chapter describes question evaluation methods requiring survey data from actual data collection. Some of them (such as **web probing** and **respondent and interviewer debriefings**) provide a window to the causes of breakdowns of the survey response process. **Behavior coding** reveals undesirable interviewer and respondent behaviors accompanying the breakdowns. The rest of the methods – **randomized experiment, response latency**, quantitative methods to estimate **reliability**, methods to evaluate **validity**, **IRT**, and **pilot tests** – do not always reveal what went wrong and do not suggest how to improve the survey items. Researchers have to make assumptions for the models to run and they have to make assumptions when interpreting results.

Literature comparing different question evaluation methods indicates that the methods differ in their ability to identify problematic questions and they do not always converge in their assessment (Maitland & Presser, 2018; Tourangeau et al., 2021; Yan et al., 2012a). The survey field has not come to conclusions as to what method(s) people should use and in what sequence or combination. However, the recommendation is to adopt a decision-tree approach, to use at least one method to test and evaluate survey questions before fielding them, and to use multiple methods when possible (Tourangeau et al., 2020a).

### Exercises

1 Describe when kappa is a better choice to estimate reliability than MTMM.
2 Describe one advantage and one disadvantage of using web probing for question evaluation.

# 14 Usability Testing

**History and Overview of the Usability Testing Process**

Usability testing originates from the Human Factors field, a discipline that studies how humans interact with systems, products, or devices. The field combines knowledge from disciplines such as psychology, sociology, industrial design, visual design, biomechanics, and anthropometry. The term "usability" was first introduced in the late 1970s to describe how people interacted with computers (Bennett, 1979). From a questionnaire design perspective, usability focuses on how the user (survey respondent or interviewer) interacts with the survey instrument (Hansen & Couper, 2004).

The application of usability testing in survey research coincides with the time when the term "usability" was first introduced. During that period, survey researchers began to focus on the layout of their paper-and-pencil surveys and study how respondents interacted with them (e.g., Dillman, 1978). Later, with the introduction of computer-assisted interviewing – computer-assisted personal and telephone interviewing in the 1990s, followed by web and mobile web – the focus expanded to how interviewers and respondents interacted with the programmed questionnaire (e.g., Couper, 2000; Hansen et al., 1997).

Geisen and Romano Bergstrom (2017) identify five key components of the usability testing process, as defined by the International Organization for Standardization (9241-11, 1988), and adapt them for survey usability testing:

- *Product* – The survey itself, whether it is a paper, web, or interviewer-administered instrument. In addition, contact materials, such as letters, brochures, and respondent aid materials (e.g., show cards, life history calendars) can be considered products. We tend to focus on products that involve self-administration, because the interviewer is not present to help respondents with any issues, from question comprehension to ensuring that the provided response is in the right format. However, usability testing is equally important for interviewer-administered surveys, where minimizing interviewers' burden and ensuring that the instrument is intuitive for them is essential to minimizing the perceived survey length by respondents.
- *Specified Users of the Product* – For interviewer-administered surveys, interviewers are the users; for self-administered surveys, respondents are the users.
- *Goals of the Users* – It is critical to make the distinction between users' goals and researchers' goals. Usability testing should focus on understanding the goals of respondents and interviewers related to completing the survey as quickly and smoothly as possible.

DOI: 10.4324/9781003367826-17

- *Context of Use* – The usability test should be completed in the context in which the product will be used (i.e., a self-administered survey should be completed by respondents rather than administered by interviewers and ideally, under the same conditions under which they would take the survey when invited, for example, on their mobile device vs. computer).
- *Metrics of Evaluation* – The most common metrics are effectiveness (whether the users can complete the specific task), efficiency (the number of steps and time on task to completion), and satisfaction (user-volunteered comments or solicited reports on reported satisfaction with the product they are evaluating). These metrics may not be universally used for usability testing but apply for testing surveys in general.

Similar to the survey response process model that hypothesizes how respondents *answer* survey questions (Tourangeau et al., 2000), Geisen and Romano Bergstrom (2017) propose a usability model for how respondents interact with the survey instrument. The model can be applied to both self- and interviewer-administered surveys and consists of three main processes:

1. *Interpreting the design* – Similar to comprehending the written language to understand the survey questions, respondents must comprehend the "visual language" (Christian et al., 2005). Visual language processing (discussed in Chapter 7) is automatic and Tourangeau et al. (2004) propose five heuristics (shortcuts) responds use to understand visual design:

    a  Middle means typical
    b  Left and top means first
    c  Near means related
    d  Up means good
    e  Like means close

2. *Completing actions and navigating* – In most self-administered surveys, respondents provide their responses by clicking on a radio button or check box and submitting it; however, often they need to interact with the instrument in a different way, for example, by typing a response, or resolving an error message that pops on their screen. Design features such as placement of the questions, the various navigation buttons or skip logic arrows, and provision and placement of instructions or definitions determine how well respondents will navigate through the survey.
3. *Processing feedback* – In computer-programmed surveys, the survey instrument provides "feedback" by advancing respondents or interviewers to the next question, prompting them not to leave a question blank, or alerting them of an invalid response. Once an error is identified, the error message should be detailed enough to help users determine what caused the issue and figure out how to correct it.

Ideally, usability testing will focus on all three components of the model to understand each usability process and minimize the potential for measurement error. Often, usability testing and cognitive testing are combined to simultaneously assess issues related to question answering and interacting with a self-administered questionnaire.

## Types of Usability Testing and Methods

Rubin and Chisnell (2008) distinguish among three types of usability testing, depending on the stage of survey development when they are performed:

1 *Exploratory/formative testing* – Guides the design of the survey at the early stages (survey interface, icons, widgets, etc.).
2 *Assessment/summative testing* – Takes place in the early to middle design stages, when a testing prototype exists. Typically takes several rounds, with improvements introduced and evaluated at each stage.
3 *Verification/validation testing* – Takes place at the end of the survey development, when a finished product is ready to be released. The focus is on the overall survey experience, from logging in to survey submission.

Depending on the actors who take part in the usability testing, Hansen and Couper (2004) distinguish between usability inspection methods and end-user evaluation methods:

1 *Usability inspection* – Involves evaluation by three to five human-computer interaction or usability experts, who focus on user's language, memory load, fatigue, needed skill level and guidance, design consistency, visual functionality, ease of navigation, and other factors. Although this type of evaluation is not very reliable (Lansdale & Ormerod, 1994), it is a relatively cheap way to identify problems.
2 *End-user evaluation* – Involves evaluation by the ultimate users of the survey and can take place in the field (during a pretest) or in a laboratory setting. Activities can include analyses of performance data (e.g., time on task, changing a response, leaving a question unanswered, using online help), or observational methods, questioning of users, cognitive think alouds, or a combination of these methods. Typically, laboratory testing involves scripted activities (e.g., respondents might be given instructions to change their response to a particular question to test how easy or difficult it would be to do so), in addition to users' natural interaction with the system. Often, at the end of the tasks, participants are asked to report on their satisfaction, ease of use, or confidence in achieving what they intended. Behavior coding (facial expressions, location of the gaze) can also be utilized to assess the user experience. Similar to cognitive interviews, participants are often asked to "think aloud" while performing their tasks, and researchers may try to understand a particular aspect of the interaction with the survey instrument through series of scripted probes (see Chapters 11 and 13 for more details on these methods).

## Conducting Usability Testing – Practical Considerations

Usability testing is typically qualitative, conducted in a lab setting, with a small number of respondents, which does not render generalizability to the target population, but provides an initial idea of what problems might be encountered once data collection is launched. Similar to cognitive interviewing, usability testing may require several rounds that would allow for implementing changes and testing them. Typically, each round of testing would require 7–10 participants. Similar to lab-based evaluation methods (Chapter 11), participants are members of the target population for which the survey is developed and are recruited through local organizations, newspaper ads, online tools such as Craigslist, various social media groups, or word of mouth. Studies might have quotas for relevant demographic characteristics that should be included in the pretest and potential participants are screened for such characteristics. Usability testing sessions are 30–90 minutes long and similar to cognitive testing (Chapter 11), they utilize a usability testing protocol. The usability testing protocol, a script used with each participant, includes an informed consent section, testing scenarios, tasks with relevant scripted probes to better understand the user experience, and self-reported satisfaction with the experience. In addition, researchers can use unscripted probes to follow up on a particular situation that requires more detail.

Participants typically receive a monetary incentive as a compensation for their time and effort. Incentives are often commensurate with the time needed to perform all tasks and may include compensation for travel (for in-person sessions). Incentives for special populations (e.g., doctors) may be higher than those for the general population.

The testing session can be in person or remote. In fact, studies have reported no difference between the two in usability metrics such as time on task, task completion, and issues discovered (e.g., Brush et al., 2004; Tullis et al., 2002). Remote sessions offer the advantage of reaching out to a larger geographical population, are often completed in situations respondents are likely to be when taking the actual survey (e.g., distracted by family) and on devices that are likely to be used when taking the survey (Bartek & Cheatham, 2003).

We recommend testing the questionnaire in the modes in which it will be administered, especially if it is designed to be optimal for each mode. Even seemingly similar modes such as web and mobile web might present different rendering of the instrument and significantly change the respondent experience. If the usability test reveals problems with only one of the modes when the instrument is optimized for each mode, only the problematic mode needs to be fixed and retested. However, if the questionnaire utilizes the same format, text, and structure across all modes (known as "unimode" design, discussed in Chapter 9), then problems discovered in one mode would require careful consideration of a solution that would work across all modes.

Performance measures in usability studies often include accuracy (how many participants successfully completed the assigned task), efficiency (how many actions and how long it takes to complete the assigned task), satisfaction (self-reported satisfaction upon task completion), ease of use (self-reported perception upon task completion), and others. Overall, usability data can be collected through self-reports, observations (direct measures of participant's behavior, such as time on task, task accuracy), and implicit data, such as eye tracking, pupil dilation, electrodermal activity (Geisen & Romano Bergstrom, 2017).

### Combination with Other Pretesting Techniques

As already noted, usability testing is often used in combination with *cognitive interviewing* techniques (Chapter 11) to get insight into both the question answering process, and the interaction with the survey instrument, which are often intertwined. For example, providing a definition in a help text will affect respondents' question comprehension, or providing check boxes next to the response options will signal that more than one answer can be selected.

Similar to examining the interviewer-respondent interaction through *behavior coding* (see Chapter 13), behavior coding is often used in usability testing to provide a fuller picture of the respondent's interaction with the survey instrument. For example, a behavior coding scheme can be utilized to note a respondent's hesitation while completing a task, changing a previously completed action, failing to complete an action, etc. As with cognitive interviewing probes, the development of a coding scheme and its level of detail will depend on the goals of the pretest. Ongena and Dijkstra (2006) distinguish among five coding strategies, depending on the unit of coding, varying from coding every respondent action or utterance to assigning a single evaluative code at the survey completion level. The development of a coding scheme is also influenced by the type of analyses planned to meet the usability test objectives. Ongena and Dijkstra (2006) identify two main types of quantitative analysis utilizing behavior codes:

- Frequency analysis – Counts the occurrence of a specific behavior (e.g., number of times the respondent failed to provide a response).
- Sequence analysis – Identifies patterns of behavior by examining codes in relation to preceding or subsequent behaviors (e.g., "respondent provides inaccurate response" may be followed by "respondent goes back to previous question").

Finally, whether the interviews are coded live or from a recording will also impact the development of the coding scheme. Live coding allows for fewer codes because of the pace of the testing session and the need to make quick decisions on the spot. Live coding provides immediate data and does not require permission to record the testing session; however, depending on the setup, it may be more obtrusive because the coder must be present during testing. Coding from a recording or transcript allows for a more detailed coding scheme because coders control the time, can revisit the sequence of behaviors as needed, and can consult with others on code assignment. Recordings and transcripts do require permission from respondents and are often more time consuming because of an elaborate coding scheme that provides data for more detailed analyses.

## Summary

Usability tests present an opportunity for researchers to explore how respondents interact with the survey instrument and whether that interaction may induce measurement error. It is important to conduct the usability test in the same mode and if possible, within the same conditions potential respondents will experience when taking the survey. Usability studies interact well with other pretesting techniques, such as cognitive interviewing and behavior coding, and should utilize them when possible, for deeper understanding of the potential issues discovered during testing.

## Exercises

1 Discuss ways to distinguish across usability testing methods.
2 List the advantages and disadvantage of using usability experts.

# 15 Use of Artificial Intelligence (AI) and Generative AI (GAI) for Questionnaire Design and Evaluation

**Introduction**

During the last decade, artificial intelligence (AI) and generative artificial intelligence (GAI) have become well-known terms to both researchers and lay persons. They are increasingly used in social sciences and in survey research (e.g., Jansen et al., 2023; Korkmaz, 2024). The use of AI and GAI for questionnaire design and evaluation is in its infancy. This chapter briefly discusses how both can be used, reviews relevant but limited research, and concludes with recommendations.

Before we dive into the use of these new tools for questionnaire design and evaluation, we start with nontechnical definitions of a couple of terms that will be most relevant to questionnaire design and evaluation. **AI** refers to the development of systems or programs that mimic human behavior and decision-making processes. It enables machines to perform tasks, analyze visual and textual data, and respond or adapt to their environment. **Machine learning (ML)** is a subset or application of AI that uses algorithms trained for a task. The performance of ML increases when more data are available for training. **GAI** refers to a specific application of AI generating new content (including text, images, videos, and music), ideas, or data by learning from vast datasets. A well-known example of GAI for text generation is ChatGPT by OpenAI (https://openai.com/chatgpt/). The DALL·E series by OpenAI is an example of GAI for image creation (https://openai.com/index/dall-e-3/). **Large language models (LLMs)** are a specific application of GAI focusing on natural language generation and comprehension.

**Using AI and GAI for Questionnaire Design**

Because GAI and LLMs are able to generate human-like text, people are starting to use them to write survey questions. A Google search of using AI and LLMs to write survey questions will turn up various vendors and links offering services or best practices of AI-based survey question creation. With a friendly interface, anyone can ask ChatGPT to write survey questions. For instance, we asked ChatGPT 3.5 to generate a survey question about health. As shown in Figure 15.1, ChatGPT returns different question formats and question wordings when given different prompts. The first prompt is general and vague, and ChatGPT returned a question that is typically used in daily conversations, but not exactly in surveys. The second prompt has more specific instructions: asking ChatGPT to write a closed survey question with response options, using survey items from a national health survey as examples, and following best practices discussed in a classic questionnaire design text book. The result is a better phrased and formatted survey question.

DOI: 10.4324/9781003367826-18

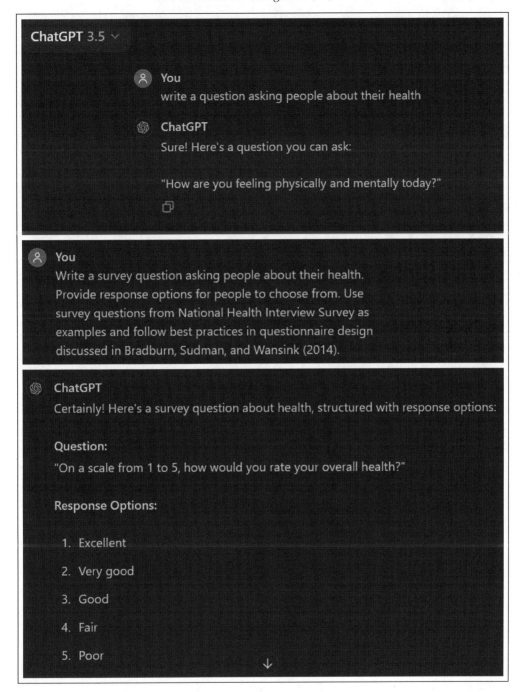

Figure 15.1 An Example of Using ChatGPT to Write Survey Questions.

This example illustrates the importance of having well-written prompts for ChatGPT (and GAI in general) to generate good survey questions. In a way, the task shifts from writing a good question for human beings to writing a good prompt for ChatGPT and GAI. Empirical research evaluating the performance of GAI and LLMs for creating survey questions is scarce and is much needed to establish guidelines for successful use of GAI and LLMs. We believe the key is the quality of prompts. We also believe that best practices for writing good survey questions as discussed in this book are also best practices for writing good prompts for GAI.

**Using AI and GAI for Questionnaire Evaluation and Testing**

Comparatively, there is more research illustrating and evaluating the use of AI and GAI for question evaluation and testing. Sun and Yan (2023) demonstrated a successful use of ML to automatically and efficiently process 100% of recorded interviews to meet both objectives of behavior coding – identifying interviewers at a higher risk of falsification and interviewers not adhering to standardized interviewing protocol. Sun and Yan (2023) showed that, among 142 recordings validated as falsified cases, ML was able to correctly detect 78% as falsified. In addition, the measures generated by ML to examine the extent to which interviewers read questions verbatim and the extent to which interviewers maintained question meaning were in line with human coders' evaluation. Yan et al. (2024) further demonstrated that ML is able to generate measures indicating interaction problems (e.g., number of interviewer turns, number of respondent turns, duration of respondents' first turn, overlapping speech, and presence of positive emotions) and that these measures can successfully detect questions with worse performance as judged by survey experts.

LLMs have also been used to test survey questions. Olivos and Liu (2024) varied the prompts provided to ChatGPT and, not surprisingly, found that prompts affected the results returned by ChatGPT. In particular, ChatGPT provided different suggestions as prompts became more complex and included additional information such as the purpose of the study and the population of the study. Tao et al. (2024) also experimented with different prompts and found that prompts using examples of both flawed questions and flawless questions improve the LLMs' ability to correctly detect problematic questions as judged by survey experts.

**Summary**

The application of AI and GAI for questionnaire development and evaluation is still evolving, and more research is needed to understand the limitations and to identify circumstances where they can be useful and successful. The limited literature suggests that prompts for GAI and LLMs are critical to its performance. Prompts should be specific and should include information about the target population, mode of data collection, and purpose of the survey. Prompts should also include example questions. Given good prompts, GAI and LLMs can be very helpful as initial explorations.

Although we do see the potential of these tools in improving questionnaire design and evaluation, we caution readers to not naively use these tools for their surveys. We believe that human judgment is needed for interpreting and critically evaluating the output returned by AI and GAI. We strongly recommend that researchers using AI and GAI be aware of biases in training data and algorithms and be judicious about outputs from AI and GAI. We also recommend that researchers provide prompts, algorithms, and training data used in their applications to the extent possible for transparency and reproducibility.

**Exercises**

1 Use ChatGPT or Copilot to write a survey question asking about household income. Try different prompts to see what ChatGPT or Copilot returns.
2 Use ChatGPT or Copilot to review the question below and to provide a revision. Again, try different prompts to see what ChatGPT or Copilot returns.

   Some people think that the way people talk needs to change with the times to be more sensitive to people from different backgrounds. Others think that this has already gone too far and many people are just too easily offended. Which is closer to your opinion?

   1  The way people talk needs to change a lot
   2  The way people talk needs to change a little
   3  People are a little too easily offended
   4  People are much too easily offended

# Bibliography

Acquisti, A., John, L. K., & Loewenstein, G. (2012). The impact of relative standards on the propensity to disclose. *Journal of Marketing Research, XLIX*, 160–174.

Allport, G. (1954). *The nature of prejudice*. Addison-Wesley.

Alwin, D. F. (2007). *Margins of error: A study of reliability in survey measurement*. John Wiley.

Alwin, D. F., Baumgartner, E. M., & Beattie, B. A. (2018). Number of response categories and reliability in attitude measurement. *Journal of Survey Statistics and Methodology, 6*, 212–239.

Andreadis, I. (2015). Web surveys optimized for smartphones: Are there differences between computer and smartphone users? *Methods, Data, Analyses, 9*(2), 16. https://doi.org/10.12758/mda.2015.012

Andreenkova, A. V., & Javeline, D. (2019). Sensitive questions in comparative surveys. In T. P. Johnson, B. Pennell, I. A. L. Stoop, & B. Dorer (Eds.), *Advances in comparative survey methods: Multinational, multiregional, and multicultural contexts (3MC)* (pp. 139–160). Wiley.

Andrews, F. M., & Herzog, A. R. (1986). The quality of survey data as related to age of respondent. *Journal of the American Statistical Association, 81*, 403–410.

Antoun, C., & Cernat, A. (2020). Factors affecting completion times: A comparative analysis of smartphone and PC web surveys. *Social Science Computer Review, 38*(4), 477–489. https://doi.org/10.1177/0894439318823703

Antoun, C., Couper, M. P., & Conrad, F. C. (2017). Effects of mobile versus PC web on survey response quality. *Public Opinion Quarterly, 81*(Special Issue), 280–306.

Antoun, C., Katz, J., Argueta, J., & Wang, L. (2018). Design heuristics for effective smartphone surveys. *Social Science Computer Review, 36*(5), 557–574.

Antoun, C., Nichols, E., Olmsted-Hawala, E., & Wang, L. (2020). Using buttons as response options in mobile web surveys. *Survey Practice, 13*(1), 1–10. https://doi.org/10.29115/sp-2020-0002

Axinn, W. G., Barber, J. S., & Ghimire, D. J. (1997). The neighborhood history calendar: A data collection method designed for dynamic multilevel modeling. *Sociological Methodology, 27*, 355–392.

Bachman, J. G., & O'Malley, P. M. (1984). Black–White differences in self-esteem: Are they affected by response styles. *American Journal of Sociology, 90*(3), 624–639. https://doi.org/10.1086/228120

Bailar, B., Bailey, L., & Stevens, J. (1977). Measures of interviewer bias and variance. *Journal of Marketing Research, 14*(3), 337–343.

Bartek, V., & Cheatham, D. (2003). *Experience remote usability testing, Part 1: Examine study results on the benefits and downside of remote usability testing*. Available at http://www.ibm.com/developerworks/library/wa-rmusts1/wa-rmusts1-pdf.pdf

Barton, A. H. (1958). Asking the embarrassing question. *Public Opinion Quarterly, 22*, 67–68.

Bassili, J. N., & Fletcher, J. F. (1991). Response-time measurement in survey research: A method for CATI and a new look at nonattitudes. *Public Opinion Quarterly, 55*, 331–346.

Bauman, K., & Dent, C. (1982). Influence of an objective measure on self-reports of behavior. *Journal of Applied Psychology, 67*, 623–628.

Bearman, N., & Appleton, K. (2012). Using Google Maps to collect spatial responses in a survey environment. *Area, 44*(2), 160–169. http://www.jstor.org/stable/23251530

Beatty, P. C., & Willis, G. B. (2007). Research synthesis: The practice of cognitive interviewing. *Public Opinion Quarterly, 71*, 287–311.

Belak, E., & Vehovar, V. (1995). Interviewers' effects in telephone surveys: The case of international victim survey. In Fargligoj, A. & Kramberger, A. (Eds.), *Contributions to methodology and statistics*. Metodoloski zvezki, 10, Ljubljana.

Belli, R., Shay, W., & Stafford, F. (2001). Event history calendars and question list surveys: A direct comparison of interviewing methods. *Public Opinion Quarterly*, 65(1), 45–74. https://doi.org/10.1086/320037

Belson, W. (1981). *The design and understanding of survey questions*. Gower Publishing.

Bennett, W. F. (1979). The analysis of transient spectral components with the autoregressive spectral estimator. *Journal of the Royal Statistical Society. Series C (Applied Statistics*, 28(1), 1–13. https://doi.org/10.2307/2346804

Berzelak, J. (2014). *Mode effects in web surveys* (doctoral dissertation). University of Ljubljana. Available at http://dk.fdv.uni-lj.si/doktorska_dela/pdfs/dr_berzelakjernej.pdf

Biemer, P., & Brown, G. (2005). Model-based estimation of drug use prevalence using item count data. *Journal of Official Statistics*, 21, 287–308.

Billet, L., & Waterplas, L. (1988). *Response-effecten bij survey-vragen in het Nederlands taalgebied*. Katholieke Universiteit.

Bishop, G. F., Tuchfarber, A. J., & Oldendick, R. W. (1986). Opinions on fictitious issues: The pressure to answer survey questions. *Public Opinion Quarterly*, 50(2), 240–250.

Blair, E., Sudman, S., Bradburn, N. M., & Stocking, C. (1997). How to ask questions about drinking and sex: Response effects in measuring consumer behavior. *Journal of Marketing Research*, 14, 316–321.

Blair, J., & Conrad, F. G. (2011). Sample size for cognitive interview pretesting. *Public Opinion Quarterly*, 75(4), 636–658. https://doi.org/10.1093/poq/nfr035

Borgers, N., de Leeuw, E., & Hox, J. (2000). Children as respondents in survey research: Cognitive development and response quality. *Bulletin de Methodologie Sociologique*, 66, 60–75.

Borgers, N., & Hox, J. (2001). Item nonresponse in questionnaire research with children. *Journal of Official Statistics*, 17(2), 321–335.

Boruch, R. F. (1971). Assuring confidentiality of responses in social research: A note on strategies. *American Sociologist*, 6, 308–311.

Bosch, O. J., Revilla, M., DeCastellarnau, A., & Weber, W. (2019a). Measurement reliability, validity, and quality of slider versus radio button scales in an online probability-based panel in Norway. *Social Science Computer Review*, 37(1), 119–132. https://doi.org/10.1177/0894439317750089

Bosch, O. J., Revilla, M., & Paura, E. (2019b). Answering mobile surveys with images: An exploration using a computer vision API. *Social Science Computer Review*, 37(5), 669–683. https://doi.org/10.1177/0894439318791515

Bosch, O. J., Revilla, M., Qureshi, D. D., & Höhne, J. K. (2022). A new experiment on the use of images to answer web survey questions. *Journal of the Royal Statistical Society Series A: Statistics in Society*, 185(3), 955–980. https://doi.org/10.1111/rssa.12856

Bradburn, N. (1983). Response effects. In P. Rossi, J. Wright, & A. Anderson (Eds.), *Handbook of survey research* (pp. 289–328). Wiley.

Bradburn, N., Sudman, S., & Wansink, B. (2004). *Asking questions: The definitive guide to questionnaire design—For market research, political polls, and social and health questionnaires* (Research Methods for the Social Sciences). Wiley and Sons.

Brener, N. D., Eaton, D. K., Kann, L., Grunbaum, J. A., Gross, L. A., Kyle, T. M., et al. (2006). The association of survey setting and mode with self-reported health risk behaviors among high school students. *Public Opinion Quarterly*, 70, 354–374.

Brewer, W. (1988). Memory for randomly sampled autobiographical events. In U. Neisser, & E. Winograd (Eds.), *Remembering considered: Ecological and traditional approaches to the study of memory* (pp. 21–90). Cambridge University Press.

Brown, J. D., Heggeness, M. L., Dorinski, D. M., Warren, L., & Yi, M. (2019). Predicting the effect of adding a citizenship question to the 2020 Census. *Demography*, 56, 1173–1194.

Brown, N. R. (2002). Encoding, representing, and estimating event frequencies: Multiple strategy perspective. In P. Sedlmeier, & T. Betsch (Eds.), *Frequency processing and cognition* (pp. 37–54). Oxford University Press.

Brüderl, J., Castiglioni, L., Ludwig, V., Pforr, K., & Schmiedeberg, C. (2016). Collecting event history data with a panel survey: Combining an electronic event history calendar and dependent interviewing. *Methods, Data, Analyses*, 11(1). https://doi.org/10.12758/mda.2016.013

Brush, A., Ames, M., & Davis, J. (2004). *A comparison of synchronous remote and local usability studies for an expert interface*. In Extended Abstracts of the 2004 Conference on Human Factors and Computing Systems-CHI '04.
Bugelski, B. R. (1977). Imagery and verbal behavior. *Journal of Mental Imagery, 1*, 39–52.
Burt, C. (1992). Retrieval characteristics of autobiographical memories. *Applied Cognitive Psychology, 6*, 389–404.
Burton, S., & Blair, E. (1991). Task conditions, response formulation processes, and response accuracy for behavioral frequency questions in surveys. *Public Opinion Quarterly, 55*, 50–79.
Cacioppo, J. T., Gardner, W. L., & Berntson, G. G. (1997). Beyond bipolar conceptualizations and measures: The case of attitudes and evaluative space. *Personality and Social Psychology Review, 1*, 3–25.
Cannell, C., & Fowler, F. (1965). *Comparison of hospitalization reporting in three survey procedures*. Vital and Health Statistics. U.S. Public Health Service, Series 2, No. 8.
Cannell, C., Marquis, K., & Laurent, A. (1977). *A summary of studies of interviewing methodology*. Vital and Health Statistics, Series 2, No. 69. U.S. Government Printing Office.
Cannell, C., Miller, P., & Oksenberg, L. (1981). Research on interviewing techniques. In S. Leinhardt (Ed.), *Sociological methodology* (pp. 389–437). Jossey-Bass.
Centers for Disease Control and Prevention (CDC) (2020). *2017-2019 National Survey of Family Growth (NSFG): Summary of design and data collection methods*. Available at https://www.cdc.gov/nchs/data/nsfg/NSFG-2017-2019-Summary-Design-Data-Collection-508.pdf
Cernat, A., Couper, M. P., & Ofstedal, M. B. (2016). Estimation of mode effects in the Health and Retirement Study using measurement models. *Journal of Survey Statistics and Methodology, 4*, 501–524.
Charoenruk, N., & Olson, K. M. (2018). Do listeners perceive interviewers' attributes from their voices and do perceptions differ by question type? *Field Methods, 30*(4), 312–328.
Chassein, B., Strack, F., & Schwarz, N. (1987). *Erinnerungsstrategie und Haufigkeitsskala: Zum unterschiedlichen Einfluss von relationaler versus episodischer Erinnerung aui Haufigkeitsurteile*. 29th Tagung Experimentell Arbeitender Psychologn, FRG.
Chiu, L. H. (1972). A cross-cultural comparison of cognitive styles in Chinese and American children. *International Journal of Psychology, 7*, 235–242.
Christian, L. M., & Dillman, D. A. (2004). The influence of graphical and symbolic language manipulations on responses to self-administered questions. *Public Opinion Quarterly, 68*(1), 57–80.
Christian, L. M., Dillman, D. A., & Smyth, J. D. (2005). *Instructing web and telephone respondents to report date answers in a format desired by the surveyor*. Technical report #05-067. Social & Economic Sciences Research Center Pullman, Washington State University. Retrieved on https://www.sesrc.wsu.edu/dillman/papers/2005/instructingwebandtelephone.pdf.
Christian, L. M., Dillman, D. A., & Smyth, J. D. (2007). Helping respondents get it right the first time: The influence of words, symbols, and graphics in web surveys. *Public Opinion Quarterly, 71*(1), 113–125.
Chun, K. T., Campbell, J. B., & Yoo, J. H. (1974). Extreme response styles in cross-cultural research: A reminder. *Journal of Cross-Cultural Psychology, 5*, 465–480.
Cibelli, K. L. (2017). *The effects of respondent commitment and feedback on response quality in online surveys* (doctoral dissertation). University of Michigan.
Clarke, I. III (2000). Extreme response style in cross-cultural research: An empirical investigation. *Journal of Social Behavior & Personality, 15*(1), 137–152.
Clement, S. L., Severin-Nielsen, M. K., & Shamshiri-Petersen, D. (2020). Device effects on survey response quality. A comparison of smartphone, tablet and PC responses on a cross sectional probability sample. *Survey Methods: Insights from the Field, Special Issue: Advancements in Online and Mobile Survey Methods*. https://doi.org/10.13094/SMIF-2020-00020
Clifford, S., & Jerit, J. (2015). Do attempts to improve respondent attention increase social desirability bias? *Public Opinion Quarterly, 79*, 790–802.
Clogg, C. C., & Manning, W. D. (1996). Assessing reliability of categorical measurements using latent class models. In A. van Eye, & C. C. Clogg (Eds.), *Categorical variables in developmental research: Methods of analysis* (pp. 169–182). Academic Press.
Collins, M., & Butcher, B. (1982). Interviewer and clustering effects in an attitude survey. *Journal of the Marketing Research Society, 25*(1), 39–58.

Conrad, F., Tourangeau, R., Couper, M., & Zhang, C. (2017). Reducing speeding in web surveys by providing immediate feedback. *Survey Research Methods, 11*(1), 45–61. https://doi.org/10.18148/srm/2017.v11i1.6304

Conrad, F. G., Couper, M. P., Tourangeau, R., & Galesic, M. (2005). Interactive feedback can improve quality of responses in web surveys. In *JSM proceedings*, pp. 3835–3840.

Conrad, F. G., Couper, M. P., Tourangeau, R., & Peytchev, A. (2006). Use and non-use of clarification features in web surveys. *Journal of Official Statistics, 22*(2), 245–269.

Conrad, F. G., Schober, M. F., & Coiner, T. (2007). Bringing features of human dialogue to web surveys. *Applied Cognitive Psychology, 21*(2), 165–187.

Conrad, F. G., Schober, M. F., & Schwarz, N. (2014). Pragmatic processes in survey interviewing. In T. M. Holtgraves (Ed.), *The Oxford handbook of language and social psychology* (pp. 420–437). Oxford University Press. https://doi.org/10.1093/oxfordhb/9780199838639.013.005

Converse, P. E. (1964). The nature of belief systems in mass publics. In D. E. Apter (Ed.), *Ideology and discontent* (pp. 206–261). The Free Press.

Converse, P. E. (1970). Attitudes and non-attitudes: Continuation of a dialogue. In E. R. Tufte (Ed.), *The quantitative analysis of social problems*. Addison-Wesley.

Converse, J. M., & Presser, S. (1986). *Survey questions: Handcrafting the standardized questionnaire*. Sage.

Conway, M. A. (1996). Autobiographical knowledge and autobiographical memory. *Memory and Cognition, 15*, 119–132.

Couper, M. (2000). Usability evaluation of computer-assisted survey instruments. *Social Science Computer Review, 18*(4), 384–396.

Couper, M. P. (2008). *Designing effective web surveys*. Cambridge University Press.

Couper, M. P., Conrad, F. G., & Tourangeau, R. (2003). The effect of images on web survey responses. In R. Banks et al. (Eds.), *Survey and statistical computing IV: The impact of technology on the survey response process* (pp. 343–350). Association for Survey Computing.

Couper, M. P., Conrad, F. G., & Tourangeau, R. (2007). Visual context effects in web surveys. *Public Opinion Quarterly, 71*(4), 623–634. https://doi.org/10.1093/poq/nfm044

Couper, M. P., Tourangeau, R., Conrad, F. G., & Crawford, S. D. (2004b). What they see is what we get: Response options for web surveys. *Social Science Computer Review, 22*(1), 111–127. https://doi.org/10.1177/0894439303256555

Couper, M. P., Tourangeau, R., Conrad, F. G., & Singer, E. (2006). Evaluating the effectiveness of visual analog scales. *Social Science Computer Review, 24*, 227–245.

Couper, M. P., Tourangeau, R., & Kenyon, K. (2004a). Picture this! Exploring visual effects in web surveys. *Public Opinion Quarterly, 68*(2), 255–266. https://doi.org/10.1093/poq/nfh013

Couper, M. P., Traugott, M. W., & Lamias, M. J. (2001). Web survey design and administration. *Public Opinion Quarterly, 65*(2), 230–253. https://doi.org/10.1086/322199

Craik, F. I. M. (1999). Memory, aging and survey measurement. In N. Schwarz, D. Park, B. Knäuper, & S. Sudman (Eds.), *Cognition, aging, and self-reports* (pp. 95–115). Taylor & Francis.

d'Ardenne, J., & Collins, D. (2020). Combining multiple question evaluation methods: What does it mean when the data appear to conflict. In P. Beatty, D. Collins, L. Kaye, J. Padilla, G. Willis, & A. Wilmot (Eds.), *Advances in questionnaire design, development, evaluation and testing* (pp. 91–116). Wiley.

Daikeler, J., Bach, R. L., Silber, H., & Eckman, S. (2022). Motivated misreporting in smartphone surveys. *Social Science Computer Review, 40*(1), 95–107. https://doi.org/10.1177/0894439319900936

Dale, T., & Walsoe, H. (2020). Optimizing grid questions for smartphones: A comparison of optimized and non-optimized designs and effects on data quality on different devices. In *Advances in questionnaire design, development, evaluation and testing* (pp. 375–402). John Wiley & Sons.

Dasgupta, S., Vaughan, A. S., Kramer, M. R., Sanchez, T. H., & Sullivan, P. S. (2014). Use of a google map tool embedded in an internet survey instrument: Is it a valid and reliable alternative to geocoded address data? *JMIR Research Protocols, 3*(2), e24. https://doi.org/10.2196/resprot.2946

Davis, P., & Scott, A. (1995). The effect of interviewer variance on domain comparisons. *Survey Methodology, 21*(2), 99–106.

Davis, R. E., Couper, M. P., Janz, N. K., Caldwell, C. H., & Resnicow, K. (2010). Interviewer effects in public health surveys. *Health Education Research, 25*(1), 14–26.

de Leeuw, E., & Berzelak, N. (2016). Survey mode or survey modes. In C. Wolf, D. Joye, T. W. Smith, & Y.-C. Fu (Eds.), *The sage handbook of survey methodology* (pp. 142–156). Sage Publications.

de Leeuw, E., Borgers, N., & Smits, A. (2004). Pretesting questionnaires for children and adolescents. In S. Presser, J. Rothgeb, M. Couper, J. Lessler, E. Martin, J. Martin, & E. Singer (Eds.), *Methods for testing and evaluating* (pp. 409–429). Wiley and Sons.

de Leeuw, E. D. (2005). To mix or not to mix data collection modes in surveys. *Journal of Official Statistics, 21*, 223–255.

de Leeuw, E. D. (2018). Mixed-mode: Past, present, and future. *Survey Research Methods, 12*(2), 75–89. https://doi.org/10.18148/srm/2018.v12i2.7402

de Leeuw, E. D., Hox, J. J., & Boevé, A. (2016). Handling do-not-know answers: Exploring new approaches in online and mixed-mode surveys. *Social Science Computer Review, 34*(1), 116–132. https://doi.org/10.1177/0894439315573744

Dean, E., Caspar, R., McAvinchey, G., Reed, L., & Quiroz, R. (2007). Developing a low-cost technique for parallel cross-cultural instrument development: The Question Appraisal System (QAS-04). *International Journal of Social Research Methodology, 10*(3), 227–241. https://doi.org/10.1080/13645570701401032.

DeLeeuw, E. D. (2018). Mixed-mode: Past, present, and future. *Survey Research Methods, 12*(2), 75–89. https://doi.org/10.18148/srm/2018.v12i2.7402

DeMaio, T., & Bates, N. (1992). Redesigning the Census long form: A review. In C. F. Turner, & E. Martin (Eds.), *Surveying the subjective phenomena* (Vol. 2, pp. 257–282). Russell Sage Foundation.

DeMaio, T., & Landreth, A. (2004). Do different cognitive interview techniques produce different results? In S. Presser et al. (Eds.), *Methods for testing and evaluating survey questionnaires* (pp. 891–908). John Wiley and Sons.

DeMaio, T. J. (1984). Social desirability and survey measurement: A review. In C. F. Turner, & E. Martin (Eds.), *Surveying subjective phenomena* (pp. 257–282). Russell Sage Foundation.

Dillman, D. (1978). *Mail and telephone surveys: The total design method*. Wiley.

Dillman, D. (2000). *Mail and internet surveys* (p. 68). Wiley.

Dillman, D., & Edwards, M. (2016). Designing a mixed-mode survey. In *The SAGE handbook of survey methodology* (pp. 255–268). SAGE Publications Ltd. https://doi.org/10.4135/9781473957893

Dillman, D., Jackson, A., Pavlov, R., & Schaefer, D. (1998). *Results from cognitive tests of 6-person accordion versus bi-fold census forms* (Technical Report N 98-15). Washington State University, Social and Economic Sciences Research Center.

Dillman, D., Sinclair, D., & Clark, J. (1993). Effects of questionnaire length, respondent-friendly design, and a difficult question on response rates for occupant-addressed census mail surveys. *Public Opinion Quarterly, 57*, 289–304.

Dillman, D. A. (2000). *Mail and internet surveys: The tailored design method* (2nd ed.). John Wiley and Sons.

Dillman, D. A., & Christian, L. M. (2005). Survey mode as a source of instability across surveys. *Field Methods, 17*(1), 30–52.

Dillman, D. A., Smith, J. D., & Christian, L. M. (2014). *Internet, phone, mail and mixed-mode surveys: The tailored design method*. Wiley.

Diop, A., Le, K. T., & Traugott, M. (2015). Third-party presence effect with propensity score matching. *Journal of Survey Statistics and Methodology, 3*(2), 193–215.

Droitcour, J., Caspar, R. A., Hubbard, M. L., Parsely, T. L., Visscher, W., & Ezzati, T. M. (1991). The item count technique as a method of indirect questioning: A review of its development and a case study application. In P. P. Biemer, R. M. Groves, L. E. Lyberg, N. A. Mathiowetz, & S. Sudman (Eds.), *Measurement errors in surveys* (pp. 185–210). Wiley.

Dykema, J., Garbarski, D., Wall, I. F., & Edwards, D. F. (2019). Measuring trust in medical researchers: Adding insights from cognitive interviews to examine agree–disagree and construct-specific survey questions. *Journal of Official Statistics, 35*, 353–386.

Dykema, J., Schaeffer, N. C., Garbaski, D., & Hout, M. (2020). The role of question characteristics in designing and evaluating survey questions. In P. Beatty, D. Collins, L. Kaye, J. Padilla, G. Willis, & A. Wilmot (Eds.), *Advances in questionnaire design, development, evaluation and testing* (pp. 119–152). Wiley.

Eckman, S., Kreuter, F., Kirchner, A., Jäckle, A., Tourangeau, R., & Presser, S. (2014). Assessing the mechanisms of misreporting to filter questions in surveys. *Public Opinion Quarterly, 78*(3), 721–733. https://doi.org/10.1093/poq/nfu030

Einstein, A. (1954). *Ideas and opinions*. Crown.

Elevelt, A., Höhne, J. K., & Blom, A. G. (2021). Squats in surveys: Investigating the feasibility of, compliance with, and respondents' performance on fitness tasks in self-administered smartphone surveys using acceleration data. *Frontiers in Public Health, 9*, 627509. https://doi.org/10.3389/fpubh.2021.627509

Ericsson, K. A., & Simon, H. A. (1984). *Protocol analysis: Verbal reports as data*. MIT Press.

Esposito, J. L. (2004). Iterative, multiple-method questionnaire evaluation research: A case study. *Journal of Official Statistics, 20*, 143.

Fellegi, I. P. (1964). Response variance and its estimation. *Journal of the American Statistical Association, 59*, 1016–1041.

Fendrich, M., & Johnson, T. P. (2001). Examining prevalence differences in three national surveys of youth: Impact of consent procedures, mode, and editing rules. *Journal of Drug Issues, 31*(3), 615–642.

Fiske, A., Kitayama, S., Markus, H., & Nisbett, R. (1998). The cultural matrix of social psychology. In D. Gillbert, T. Fiske, & G. Lindzey (Eds.), *Handbook of social psychology* (4th ed., pp. 915–981). McGraw-Hill.

Fowler, F. J. Jr (1992). How unclear terms affect survey data. *Public Opinion Quarterly, 6*, 218–231.

Fowler, F. J. Jr., & Cannell, C. F. (1996). Using behavioral coding to identify cognitive problems with survey questions. In N. Schwarz, & S. Sudman (Eds.), *Answering questions: Methodology for determining cognitive and communicative processes in survey research* (pp. 15–36). Jossey-Bass.

Fowler, S., & Willis, G. B. (2020). The practice of cognitive interviewing through web probing. In P. Beatty, D. Collins, L. Kaye, J. Padilla, G. Willis, & A. Wilmot (Eds.), *Advances in questionnaire design, development, evaluation and testing* (pp. 451–470). Wiley.

Fox, J. A., & Tracy, P. E. (1984). Measuring associations with randomized response. *Social Science Research, 13*, 188–197.

Fox, M. T., Sidani, S., & Streiner, D. (2007). Using standardized survey items with older adults hospitalized for chronic illness. *Research in Nursing & Health, 30*, 468–481.

Freedman, D., Thornton, A., Camburn, D., Alwin, D., & Young-DeMarco, L. (1988). The life-history calendar: A technique for collecting retrospective data. In C. Clogg (Ed.), *Sociological methodology* (pp. 37–68). American Sociological Association.

Fricker, S., Galesic, M., Tourangeau, R., & Yan, T. (2005). An experimental comparison of web and telephone surveys. *Public Opinion Quarterly, 69*, 370–392.

Galesic, M., & Bosnjak, M. (2009). Effects of questionnaire length on participation and indicators of response quality in a web survey. *Public Opinion Quarterly, 73*(2), 349–360. https://doi.org/10.1093/poq/nfp031

Galesic, M., & Tourangeau, R. (2007). What is sexual harassment? It depends on who asks! Framing effects on survey responses. *Applied Cognitive Psychology, 21*, 189–202.

Galesic, M., Tourangeau, R., Couper, M. P., & Conrad, F. G. (2008). Eye-tracking data: New insights on response order effects and other cognitive shortcuts in survey responding. *Public Opinion Quarterly, 72*(5), 892–913.

Galesic, M., & Yan, T. (2011). Use of eye tracking for studying survey response processes. In M. Das, P. Ester, & L. Kaczmirek (Eds.), *Social and behavioral research and the internet: Advances in applied methods and research strategies* (pp. 349–370). Routledge. https://doi.org/10.4324/9780203844922-14

Gannon, K. M., & Ostrom, T. M. (1996). How meaning is given to rating scales: The effects of response language on category activation. *Journal of Experimental Social Psychology, 32*, 337–360.

Gavras, K., Höhne, J. K., Blom, A. G., & Schoen, H. (2022). Innovating the collection of open-ended answers: The linguistic and content characteristics of written and oral answers to political attitude questions. *Journal of the Royal Statistical Society Series A: Statistics in Society, 185*(3), 872–890. https://doi.org/10.1111/rssa.12807

Geisen, E., & Murphy, J. (2020). A compendium of web and mobile survey pretesting methods. In P. Beatty, D. Collins, L. Kaye, J. Padilla, G. Willis, & A. Wilmot (Eds.), *Advances in questionnaire design, development, evaluation and testing* (pp. 289–314). Wiley.

Geisen, E., & Romano Bergstrom, J. (2017). *Usability testing for survey research*. Morgan Kaufmann.

General Social Survey. (2002). Questionnaire. Available at https://gss.norc.org/content/dam/gss/get-documentation/pdf/quex/2002%20GSS%20V1.pdf

Gilbert, E. E. (2015). A comparison of branched versus unbranched rating scales for the measurement of attitudes in surveys. *Public Opinion Quarterly, 79*, 443–470.

Gillund, G., & Shiffrin, R. (1984). A retrieval model for both recognition and recall. *Psychological Review*, *91*, 1–67.

Giroux, S., Tharp, K., & Wietelman, D. (2019). Impacts of implementing an automatic advancement feature in mobile and web surveys. *Survey Practice*, *12*(1). https://doi.org/10.29115/SP-2018-0034

Gohring, N., & Smyth, J. (2013). Using visual design theory to improve skip instructions: An experimental test. Paper presented at the American Association for Public Opinion Research Annual Conference, Boston, MA.

Goldstone, R. L. (1998). Perceptual learning. *Annual Review of Psychology*, *49*, 585–612.

Grady, R. H., Greenspan, R. L., & Liu, M. (2019). What is the best size for matrix-style questions in online surveys? *Social Science Computer Review*, *37*(3), 435–445. https://doi.org/10.1177/0894439318773733

Graesser, A. C., Cai, Z., Louwerse, M. M., & Daniel, F. (2006). Question understanding aid (QUAID): A web facility that tests question comprehensibility. *Public Opinion Quarterly*, *70*(1), 3–22.

Gray, P. G. (1956). Examples of interviewer variability taken from two sample surveys. *Applied Statistics*, *5*, 73–85.

Greenberg, B. G., Abul-Ela, A.-L. A., & Horvitz, D. G. (1969). The unrelated question randomized response model: Theoretical framework. *Journal of the American Statistical Association*, *64*, 520–539.

Grembowski, D. (1985). Survey questionnaire salience. *American Journal of Public Health*, *75*(11), 1350.

Grice, H. P. (1975). Logic and conversation. In P. Cole, & T. Morgan (Eds.), *Syntax and semantics: Speech acts* (Vol. 3, pp. 41–58). Seminar Press.

Groves, R., Fowler, F., Couper, M., Lepkowski, J., Singer, E., & Tourangeau, R. (2004). *Survey methodology*. Wiley and Sons.

Groves, R. M. (1989). *Survey error and survey costs*. John Wiley & Sons.

Groves, R. M., & Magilavy, L. J. (1986). Measuring and explaining interviewer effects in centralized telephone surveys. *Public Opinion Quarterly*, *50*(2), 251–266.

Gummer, T., Höhne, J. K., & Rettig, T., et al. (2023a). Is there a growing use of mobile devices in web surveys? Evidence from 128 web surveys in Germany. *Quality and Quantity*, *57*, 5333–5353. https://doi.org/10.1007/s11135-022-01601-8

Gummer, T., & Kunz, T. (2022). Relying on external information sources when answering knowledge questions in web surveys, *Sociological Methods & Research*, *51*, 816–136, https://doi.org/10.1177/0049124119882470

Gummer, T., Kunz, T., Rettig, R., & Hohne, J. (2023b). How to detect and influence looking up answers to political knowledge questions in web surveys. *Public Opinion Quarterly*, *87*(Special Issue), 507–541.

Haberstroh, S., Oyserman, D., Schwarz, N., Kuhnen, U., & Ji, L. (2002). Is the interdependent self more sensitive to question context than the independent self? Self-construal and the observation of conversational norms. *Journal of Experimental Social Psychology*, *38*, 323–329.

Hall, J., Jao, L., Di Placido, C., & Manikis, R. (2021). "Deep questions for a saturday morning": An investigation of the Australian and Canadian general public's definitions of gender. *Social Science Quarterly*, *102*(4), 1866–1881.

Han, J., Leichtman, M., & Wang, Q. (1998). Autobiographical memory in korean, Chinese and American children. *Developmental Psychology*, *31*, 701–713.

Hanmer, M. J., Banks, A. J., & White, I. K. (2014). Experiments to reduce the over-reporting of voting: A pipeline to the truth. *Political Analysis*, *22*, 130–141.

Hansen, M. H., Hurwitz, W. N., & Bershad, M. A. (1960). Measurement errors in censuses and surveys. *Bulletin of the International Statistical Institute, 32nd Session*, *38*(2), 359–374.

Hanson, R. H., & Marks, E. S. (1958). Influence of the interviewer on the accuracy of survey results. *Journal of the American Statistical Association*, *53*, 635–655.

Hansen, S., & Couper, M. (2004). Usability testing to evaluate computer-assisted instruments. In S. Presser, J. Rothgeb, M. Couper, J. Lessler, E. Martin, J. Martin, & E. Singer (Eds.), *Methods for testing and evaluating survey questionnaires*. Wiley and Sons, Inc.

Hansen, S. E., Fuchs, M., & Couper, M. P. (1997). *CAI instrument and system usability testing*. Paper presented at the annual conference of the American Association for Public Opinion Research, Norfolk, VA.

Hayashi, E. (1992). Belief systems, the way of thinking, and sentiments of five nations. *Behaviormetrica, 19*, 127–170.

Heise, D. R. (1969). Separating reliability and stability in test-retest correlation. *American Sociological Review, 34*, 93–101.

Hill, R. J., & Hall, N. E. (1963). A note on rapport and the quality of interview data. *Southwestern Social Science Quarterly, 44*, 247–255.

HINTS (2023). *HINTS 6 methodology report*. Available at https://hints.cancer.gov/docs/methodologyreports/HINTS_6_MethodologyReport.pdf

Hippler, H. J., & Schwarz, N. (1989). 'No opinion'-filters: A cognitive perspective. *International Journal of Public Opinion Research, 1*(1), 77–87. https://doi.org/10.1093/ijpor/1.1.77

Hoffman, C., Lau, I., & Johnson, D. R. (1986). The linguistic relativity of person cognition: An English-Chinese comparison. *Journal of Personality and Social Psychology, 51*, 1097–1105.

Hofstede, G. (1980). *Culture's consequences*. Sage.

Höhne, J. K., Cornesse, C., Schlosser, S., Couper, M. P., & Blom, A. G. (2020c). Looking up answers to political knowledge questions in web surveys. *Public Opinion Quarterly, 84*, 986–999. https://doi.org/10.1093/poq/nfaa049

Höhne, J. K., Revilla, M., & Schlosser, S. (2020a). Motion instructions in surveys: Compliance, acceleration, and response quality. *International Journal of Market Research, 62*(1), 43–57. https://doi.org/10.1177/1470785319858587

Höhne, J. K., & Schlosser, S. (2019). SurveyMotion: What can we learn from sensor data about respondents' completion and response behavior in mobile web surveys? *International Journal of Social Research Methodology, 22*, 379–391. https://doi.org/10.1080/13645579.2018.1550279

Höhne, J. K., Schlosser, S., Couper, M. P., & Blom, A. G. (2020b). Switching away: On-device media multitasking in web surveys. *Computers in Human Behavior*. https://doi.org/10.1016/j.chb.2020.106417

Höhne, J. K., & Yan, T. (2020). Investigating the impact of violations of the "left and top means first" heuristic on response behavior and data quality. *International Journal of Social Research Methodology, 23*(3), 347–353. https://doi.org/10.1080/13645579.2019.1696087

Holbrook, A. L., Cho, Y. I., & Johnson, T. (2006). The impact of question and respondent characteristics on comprehension and mapping difficulties. *Public Opinion Quarterly, 70*, 565–595.

Holbrook, A. L., & Krosnick, J. A. (2010). Measuring voter turnout by using the randomized response technique: Evidence calling into question the method's validity. *Public Opinion Quarterly, 74*, 328–343.

Holbrook, A. L., Krosnick, J. A., Moore, D., & Tourangeau, R. (2007). Response order effects in dichotomous categorical questions presented orally: The impact of question and respondent attributes. *Public Opinion Quarterly, 71*(3), 325–348.

Holland, J. L., & Christian, L. M. (2009). The influence of topic interest and interactive probing on responses to open-ended questions in web surveys. *Social Science Computer Review, 27*(2), 196–212. https://doi.org/10.1177/0894439308327481

Holtgraves, T. (2004). Social desirability and self-reports: Testing models of socially desirable responding. *Personality and Social Psychology Bulletin, 30*, 161–172.

Holtgraves, T., Eck, J., & Lasky, B. (1997). Face management, question wording, and social desirability. *Journal of Applied Social Psychology, 27*, 1650–1671.

Hout, M. M., & Hastings, O. P. (2016). Reliability of the core items in the general social survey: Estimates from the three-wave panels, 2006–2014. *Sociological Science, 3*, 971–1002.

Hox, J. J., de Leeuw, E. D., & Klausch, T. (2017). Mixed mode research: Issues in design and analysis. In P. Biemer, E. D. de Leeuw, & S. Eckman (Eds.), *Total survey error in practice* (pp. 511–530). Wiley.

Hu, J. (2019). Horizontal or vertical? The effects of visual orientation of categorical response options on survey responses in web surveys. *Social Science Computer Review, 1*, 1–14.

Hughes, A., Chromy, J., Giacoletti, K., & Odom, D. (2002). Impact of interviewer experience on respondent reports of substance use. In J. Gfroerer, J. Eyerman, & J. Chromy (Eds). *Redesigning an ongoing national household survey: Methodological issues*. DHHS Publication No. SMA03-3768. Substance Abuse and Mental Health Services Administration, Office of Applied Studies.

Hui, C. H., & Triandis, H. C. (1989). Effects of culture and response format on extreme response style. *Journal of Cross-Cultural Psychology, 20*, 296–309.

Hunt, E., & Agnoli, F. (1991). The Whorfian hypothesis: A cognitive psychology perspective. *Psychological Review, 98*, 377–389.

Hyman, H. H., & Sheatsley, P. B. (1950). The current status of American public opinion. In J. C. Payne (Ed.), *The teaching of contemporary affairs* (pp. 11–34).

Imai, K. (2011). Multivariate regression analysis for the item count technique. *Journal of American Statistical Association, 106*, 407–416.

Jabine, T. B., Straf, M. L., Tanur, J. M., & Tourangeau, R. (1984). *Cognitive aspects of survey methodology: Building a bridge between disciplines.* National Academy Press.

Jäckle, A., Burton, J., Couper, M. P., & Lessof, C. (2019). Participation in a mobile app survey to collect expenditure data as part of a large-scale probability household panel: Coverage and participation rates and biases. *Survey Research Methods, 13*(1), 23–44. https://doi.org/10.18148/srm/2019.v1i1.7297

Jann, B., Jerke, J., & Krumpal, I. (2012). Asking sensitive questions using the crosswise model: An experimental survey measuring plagiarism. *Public Opinion Quarterly, 76*, 32–49.

Jansen, B. J., Jung, S., & Salminen, J. (2023). Employing large language models in survey research. *Natural Language Processing Journal, 4*. https://doi.org/10.1016/j.nlp.2023.100020

Ji, L., Schwarz, N., & Nisbett, R. (2000). Culture, autobiographical memory and behavioral frequency reports: Measurement issues in cross-cultural studies. *Personality and Social Psychology Bulletin, 26*, 586–594.

Ji, L., Zhang, Z., & Nisbett, R. (2002). *Culture, language and categorization.* Queens University.

Ji, L., Zhang, Z., & Nisbett, R. (2004). Is it culture or is it language? Examination of language effects in cross-cultural research on categorization. *Journal of Personality and Social Psychology, 87*(1), 57–65.

Jobe, J. B., Tourangeau, R., & Smith, A. F. (1993). Contributions of survey research to the understanding of memory. *Applied Cognitive Psychology, 7*, 567–584.

Johnson, M. K. (1983). A multiple-entry, modular memory system. In G. Bower (Ed.), *The psychology of learning and motivation* (Vol. 17, pp. 81–123). Academic Press.

Johnson, T. (1998). Approaches to equivalence in cross-cultural and cross-national survey research. In J. Harkness (Ed.), *Cross-cultural survey equivalence.* Zentrum fur Umfragen, Methoden und Analysen-ZUMA. https://nbn-resolving.org/urn:nbn:de:0168-ssoar-49730-6

Johnson, T. P., & van de Vijver, F. J. R. (2002). Social desirability in cross-cultural research. In J. A. Harkness, F. J. R. van de Vijver, & P. P. H. Mohler (Eds.), *Cross-cultural survey methods* (pp. 193–209). Wiley.

Jones, E. F., & Forrest, J. (1992). Underreporting of abortion in surveys of U.S. Women: 1976 to 1988. *Demography, 29*, 113–126.

Jones, R. K., & Kost, K. (2007). Underreporting of induced and spontaneous abortion in the United States: An analysis of the 2002 national survey of family growth. *Studies in Family Planning, 38*, 187–197.

Judd, C., Drake, R., Downing, J., & Krosnick, J. (1991). Some dynamic properties of attitude structures: Context-induced response facilitation and polarization. *Journal of Personality and Social Psychology, 60*(2).

Just, M. A., & Carpenter, P. A. (1993). The intensity dimension of thought: Pupillometric indices of sentence processing. *Canadian Journal of Experimental Psychology/Revue canadienne de psychologie expérimentale, 47*(2), 310–339. https://doi.org/10.1037/h0078820

Juster, T., & Smith, J. P. (1997). Improving the quality of economic data: Lessons from the HRS and AHEAD. *Journal of the American Statistical Association, 92*, 1268–1278.

Kalton, G., & Schuman, H. (1982). The effect of the question on survey responses: A review. *Journal of the Royal Statistical Society. Series A (General), 145*(1), 1982, 42–73. https://doi.org/10.2307/2981421

Kamoen, N., Holleman, B., Mak, P., Sanders, T., & van den Bergh, H. (2011). Agree or disagree? Cognitive processes in answering contrastive survey questions. *Discourse Processes, 48*(5), 355–385. https://doi.org/10.1080/0163853x.2011.578910

Kamoen, N., Holleman, B., Mak, P., Sanders, T., & Van Den Bergh, H. (2017). Why are negative questions difficult to answer? On the processing of linguistic contrasts in surveys. *Public Opinion Quarterly, 81*, 613–635.

Kaplowitz, M. D., Lupi, F., & Hoehn, J. P. (2004). Multiple methods for developing and evaluating a stated-choice questionnaire to value wetlands. In S. Presser et al. (Eds.), *Methods for testing and evaluating survey questionnaires* (pp. 503–524). John Wiley and Sons.

Kay, P., & Kempton, W. (1984). What is the Sapir-Whorf hypothesis? *American Anthropologist*, *86*, 65–79.

Kern, C., Höhne, J. K., Schlosser, S., & Revilla, M. (2021). Completion conditions and response behavior in smartphone surveys: A prediction approach using acceleration data. *Social Science Computer Review*, *39*(6), 1253–1271. https://doi.org/10.1177/0894439320971233

Keusch, F., & Yan, T. (2017). Web versus mobile web: An experimental study of device effects and self-selection effects. *Social Science Computer Review*, *35*(6), 751–769. https://doi.org/10.1177/0894439316675566

Keusch, F., & Yan, T. (2018). Is satisficing responsible for response order effects in rating scale questions? *Survey Research Methods*, *12*(3), 259–270. https://doi.org/10.18148/srm/2018.v12i3.7263

Keusch, F., & Yan, T. (2019). Impact of response scale features on survey responses to factual/behavioral questions. In P. J. Lavrakas et al. (Eds.), *Experimental methods in survey research: Techniques that combine random sampling with random assignment* (pp.131–150). Wiley and Sons.

Kish, L. (1962). Studies of interviewer variance for attitudinal variables. *Journal of the American Statistical Association*, *57*, 92–115.

Kitayama, S., & Cohen, D. (Eds.). (2007). *Handbook of cultural psychology*. The Guilford Press.

Klausch, T., Hox, J. J., & Schouten, B. (2013). Measurement effects of survey mode on equivalence of attitudinal rating scale questions. *Sociological Methods & Research*, *52*(3), 227–263.

Knäuper, B. (1998). Filter questions and question interpretation: Presuppositions at work. *Public Opinion Quarterly*, *62*(1), 70–78. https://doi.org/10.1086/297832

Knäuper, B. (1999). The impact of age and education on response order effects in attitude measurement. *Public Opinion Quarterly*, *63*, 347–370.

Knäuper, B., Carriere, K., Chamandy, M., Xu, Z., Schwarz, N., & Rosen, N. O. (2016). How aging affects self-reports. *European Journal of Ageing*, *13*, 185–193.

Knäuper, B., Schwarz, N., Park, D., & Fritsch, A. (2007). The perils of interpreting age differences in attitude reports: Question order effects decrease with age. *Journal of Official Statistics*, *23*, 1–14.

Knäuper, B., Schwarz, N., & Park, D. C. (2004). Frequency reports across age groups. *Journal of Official Statistics*, *20*, 91–96.

Kolodner, J. (1985). Memory for experience. In G. H. Bower (Ed.), *The psychology of learning and motivation* (pp. 1–57). Academic Press.

Korkmaz, G. (2024). *Artificial intelligence in the survey process: Use cases and challenges*. Paper presented at the AI Day for Federal Statistics. Slides accessed at: https://www.nationalacademies.org/documents/embed/link/LF2255DA3DD1C41C0A42D3BEF0989ACAECE3053A6A9B/file/DFE78E3415041049B33C7F8AE09E9771F1041163590F?noSaveAs=1

Krestar, M. L., Looman, W., Powers, S., Dawson, N., & Judge, K. S. (2012). Including individuals with memory impairment in the research process: The importance of scales and response categories used in surveys. *Journal of Empirical Research on Human Research Ethics: An International Journal*, *7*(2), 70–79.

Kreuter, F., Presser, S., & Tourangeau, R. (2008a). Social desirability bias in CATI, IVR, and web surveys. *Public Opinion Quarterly*, *72*, 847–865.

Kreuter, F., Yan, T., & Tourangeau, R. (2008b). Good item or bad—can latent class analysis tell? The utility of latent class analysis for the evaluation of survey questions. *Journal of the Royal Statistical Society, Series A*, *171*, 723–738.

Krosnick, J. A. (1991). Response strategies for coping with the cognitive demands of attitude measures in surveys. *Applied Cognitive Psychology*, *5*, 213–236.

Krosnick, J. A. (1999). Survey research. *Annual Review of Psychology*, *50*, 537–567.

Krosnick, J. A., & Alwin, D. F. (1987). An evaluation of a cognitive theory of response-order effects in survey measurement. *Public Opinion Quarterly*, *51*, 201–219.

Krosnick, J. A., & Berent, M. K. (1993). Comparisons of party identification and policy preferences: The impact of survey question format. *American Journal of Political Science*, *37*, 941–964.

Krosnick, J. A., & Presser, S. (2010). Questionnaire design. In J. D. Wright, & P. V. Marsden (Eds.), *Handbook of survey research* (2nd ed., pp. 263–313). Elsevier.

Krueger, R. A. (1994). *Focus groups: A practical guide for applied research* (2nd ed.). Sage.

Krueger, R. A., & Casey, M. A. (2014). *Focus groups: A practical guide for applied research*. SAGE Publications.

Krumpal, I. (2013). Determinants of social desirability bias in sensitive surveys: A literature review. *Quality & Quantity*, *47*, 2025–2047.

Kunz, T. (2015). *Rating scales in web surveys. A test of new drag-and-drop rating procedures* (doctoral dissertation). Darmstadt University of Technology.

Kutschar, P., & Weichbold, M. (2019). Interviewing elderly in nursing homes–Respondent and survey characteristics as predictors of item nonresponse. *Survey Methods: Insights from the Field*. Available at https://surveyinsights.org/?p=11064

Lansdale, M., & Ormerod, T. C. (1994). *Understanding interfaces: A handbook of human-computer dialogue*. Academic Press.

Lau, C. Q. (2018). Rating scale design among Ethiopian entrepreneurs: A split-ballot experiment. *International Journal of Public Opinion Research, 30*, 327–341.

Lee, L., Brittingham, A., Tourangeau, R., Willis, G., Ching, P., Jobe, J., & Black, S. (1999). Are reporting errors due to encoding limitations or retrieval failure? Surveys of child vaccination as a case study. *Applied Cognitive Psychology, 13*(1), 43–63.

Lelkes, Y., & Weiss, R. (2015). Much ado about acquiescence: The relative validity and reliability of construct-specific and agree–disagree questions. *Research and Politics, 2*(3). https://doi.org/10.1177/2053168015604173

Lenzner, T., & Höhne, J. K. (2021). Measuring subjective social stratification: How does the graphical layout of rating scales affect response distributions, response effort, and criterion validity in web surveys? *International Journal of Social Research Methodology, 25*(2), 269–275. https://doi.org/10.1080/13645579.2021.1874607

Lenzner, T., Kaczmirek, L., & Galesic, M. (2011). Seeing through the eyes of the respondent: An eye-tracking study on survey question comprehension. *International Journal of Public Opinion Research, 23*, 361–373.

Levinson, S. (2003). *Space in language and cognition: Explorations of cognitive diversity*. University Press.

Linton, M. (1982). Transformations of memory in everyday life. In U. Neisser (Ed.), *Memory observed* (pp. 77–91). Freeman.

Liu, M., & Conrad, F. G. (2019). Where should i start? On default values for slider questions in web surveys. *Social Science Computer Review, 37*(2), 248–269. https://doi.org/10.1177/0894439318755336

Liu, M., & Keusch, F. (2017). Effects of scale direction on response style of ordinal rating scales. *Journal of Official Statistics, 33*, 137–154.

Liu, M., & Wang, Y. (2014). Data collection mode effects on political knowledge. *Survey Methods: Insights from the Field*. Available at http://surveyinsights.org/?p=5317.

Lobe, B., Morgan, D., & Hoffman, K. A. (2020). Qualitative data collection in an era of social distancing, *International Journal of Qualitative Methods, 19*, 1–8, https://doi.org/10.1177/1609406920937875

Loftus, E. (1984). Protocol analysis of responses to survey recall questions. In T. B. Jabine, M. L. Straf, J. M. Tanur, & R. Tourangeau (Eds.), *Cognitive aspects of survey methodology: Building a bridge between disciplines* (pp. 61–64). National Academy Press.

Loftus, E., & Marburger, W. (1983). Since the eruption of mt. St. Helens, has anyone beaten you up? Improving the accuracy of retrospective reports with landmark events. *Memory and Cognition, 11*, 114–120.

Loftus, E., Smith, K., Klinger, M., & Fiedler, J. (1992). Memory and mismemory for health events. In J. Tanur (Ed.), *Questions about questions: Inquiries into the cognitive basis of surveys* (pp. 102–137). Russell Sage Foundation.

Longacre, R. E. (1956). Review of "Language and Reality" by Wilbur M. Urban and "Four Articles on Metalinguistics" by Benjamin Lee Whorf. *Language, 32*, 298–308.

Maineri, A. M., Bison, I., & Luijkx, R. (2021). Slider bars in multi-device web surveys. *Social Science Computer Review, 39*(4), 573–591. https://doi.org/10.1177/0894439319879132

Maitland, A., & Presser, S. (2016). How accurately do different evaluation methods predict the reliability of survey questions? *Journal of Survey Statistics and Methodology, 4*, 362–381.

Maitland, A., & Presser, S. (2018). How do question evaluation methods compare in predicting problems observed in typical survey conditions? *Journal of Survey Statistics and Methodology, 6*, 465–490.

Maitland, A., & Presser, S. (2020). A comparison of five question evaluation methods in predicting the validity of respondent answers to factual items. In P. Beatty, D. Collins, L. Kaye, J. Padilla, G. Willis, & A. Wilmot (Eds.), *Advances in questionnaire design, development, evaluation and testing* (pp. 75–90). Wiley.

Maitland, A., Sun, H., Bertling, J., & Almonte, D. (2016). *Exploration of grid questions on fourth grade students using eye-tracking*. Paper presented at the annual conference of American Associations of Public Opinion Research.

Malhotra, N., Krosnick, J., & Thomas, R. (2009). Optimal design of branching questions to measure bipolar constructs. *Public Opinion Quarterly, 73*(2), 304–324. https://doi.org/10.1093/poq/nfp023

Mangione, T. W., Fowler, F. J., & Louis, T. A. (1992). Question characteristics and interviewer effects. *Journal of Official Statistics, 8*(3), 293–307.

Marian, V., & Neisser, U. (2000). Language-dependent recall of autobiographical memories. *Journal of Experimental Psychology: General, 129*(3), 361–368.

Marin, G., Gamba, R. J., & Marin, B. V. (1992). Extreme response style and acquiescence among Hispanics. *Journal of Cross-Cultural Psychology, 23*, 498–509.

Marin, G., & Marin, B. V. (1991). *Research with Hispanic populations*. Sage.

Marin, G., Triandis, H. C., Betancourt, H., & Kashima, Y. (1983). Ethnic affirmation versus social desirability: Explaining discrepancies in bilinguals' responses to a questionnaire. *Journal of Cross-Cultural Psychology, 14*(2), 173–186.

Markus, H., & Kitayama, S. (1991). Culture and the self: Implications for cognition, emotion and motivation. *Psychological Review, 98*, 224–253.

Martin, E., Childs, J. H., DeMaio, T., Hill, J., Reiser, C., Gerber, E., Styles, K., & Dillman, D. (2007). *Guidelines for designing questionnaires for administration in different modes*. Research and Methodology Directorate, Center for Behavioral Science Methods Research Report Series (Survey Methodology #2007-42). U.S. Census Bureau. Available at https://www.census.gov/library/workingpapers/2007/adrm/rsm2007-42.html

Mason, R., Carlson, J. E., & Tourangeau, R. (1994). Contrast effects and subtraction in part-whole questions. *Public Opinion Quarterly, 58*, 569–578.

Massey, S. (2022). Using emojis and drawings in surveys to measure children's attitudes to mathematics. *International Journal of Social Research Methodology, 25*(6), 877–889. https://doi.org/10.1080/13645579.2021.1940774

Masuda, T., & Nisbett, R. (2001). Attending holistically vs. analytically: Comparing the context sensitivity of Japanese and Americans. *Journal of Personality and Social Psychology, 81*, 922–934.

Mathiowetz, N., & Duncan, G. (1988). Out of work, out of mind: Response errors in retrospective reports of unemployment. *Journal of Business and Economic Statistics, 6*, 221–229.

Mavletova, A., & Couper, M. P. (2014). Mobile Web survey design: Scrolling versus paging, SMS versus e-mail invitations. *Journal of Survey Statistics and Methodology, 2*, 498–518.

Mazaheri, M., & Theuns, P. (2009). Structural equation modeling (SEM) for satisfaction and dissatisfaction ratings; Multiple group invariance analysis across scales with different response format. *Social Indicators Research, 90*, 203–221.

McCarthy, J. S. (2020). Planning your multimethod questionnaire testing bento box: Complementary methods for a well-balanced test. In P. Beatty, D. Collins, L. Kaye, J. Padilla, G. Willis, & A. Wilmot (Eds.), *Advances in questionnaire design, development, evaluation and testing* (pp. 723–748). Wiley.

McClain, C. A., Couper, M. P., Hupp, A. L., Keusch, F., Peterson, G., Piskorowski, A. D., & West, B. T. (2019). A typology of web survey paradata for assessing total survey error. *Social Science Computer Review, 37*(2), 196–213. https://doi.org/10.1177/0894439318759670

McCutcheon, A. L. (1987). *Latent class analysis*. Sage.

McDonald, J. A., Scott, Z. A., & Hanmer, M. J. (2017). Using self-prophecy to combat vote over-reporting on public opinion surveys. *Electoral Studies, 50*, 137–141.

McGonagle, K. A., Freedman, V., Griffin, J., & Dascola, M. (2017). *Web development in the PSID: Transition and testing of a web version of the 2015 PSID telephone instrument*. Technical Series Paper #17-02, Institute for Social Research, University of Michigan.

Means, B., Nigam, A., Zarrow, M., Loftus, E., & Donaldson, M. (1989). *Autobiographical memory for health-related events*. Vital and Health Statistics Series 6, No. 2. U.S. Government Printing Office.

Meitinger, K., Neuert, C., & Behr, D. (2024). Cross-cultural web probing. In C.U. Krägeloh, M. Alyami, & O.N. Medvedev (Eds.). *International handbook of behavioral health assessment*. Springer. https://doi.org/10.1007/978-3-030-89738-3_3-1

Menon, A. (1994). Judgments of behavioral frequencies: Memory search and retrieval strategies. In N. Schwartz, & S. Sudman (Eds.), *Autobiographical memory and the validity of retrospective reports* (pp. 107–120). Springer-Verlag.

Mensch, B., & Kandel, D. (1988). Underreporting of substance use in a national longitudinal youth cohort. *Public Opinion Quarterly, 52*, 100–124.

Metzler, A., Kunz, T., & Fuchs, M. (2015). The use and positioning of clarification features in web surveys. *Psihologija, 48*(4), 379–408. https://doi.org/10.2298/psi1504379m

Middleton, K. L., & Jones, J. L. (2000). Socially desirable response sets: The impact of country culture. *Psychology & Marketing, 17*, 149–163.

Miller, J. D. (1984). A new survey technique for studying deviant behavior (PhD thesis). The George Washington University.

Miller, H. G., Turner, C. F., & Moses, L. E. (1990). Methodological issues in AIDS surveys. In *AIDS: The second decade*. National Academy Press.

Mockovak, W. (2018). *Horizontal vs. vertical scales vs. use of a grid in online data collection: Which is better?* Bureau of Labor Statistics, Office of Survey Methods Research Papers. https://www.bls.gov/osmr/research-papers/2018/pdf/st180020.pdf

Motta, M. P., Callaghan, T. H., & Smith, B. (2017). Looking for answers: Identifying search behavior and improving knowledge-based data quality in online surveys, *International Journal of Public Opinion Research, 29*, 575–603, https://doi.org/10.1093/ijpor/edw027

Munzert, S., & Selb, P. (2017). Measuring political knowledge in web-based surveys: An experimental validation of visual versus verbal instruments, *Social Science Computer Review, 35*, 167–183, https://doi.org/10.1177/0894439315616325

Nederhof, A. J. (1988). Effects of a final telephone reminder and questionnaire cover design in mail surveys. *Social Science Research, 17*, 353–361.

Neter, J., & Waksberg, J. (1964). A study of response errors in expenditure data from household interviews. *Journal of the American Statistical Association, 59*, 18–55.

Neubarth, W. (2010). Drag & drop: A flexible method for moving objects, implementing rankings, and a wide range of other applications. In S. D. Gosling & J. A. Johnson (Eds.), *Advanced methods for conducting online behavioral research* (pp. 63–74). American Psychological Association. https://doi.org/10.1037/12076-005

Nisbett, R. (2003). *The geography of thought. How Asians and Westerners think differently, and why*. Free Press.

O'Muircheartaigh, C., & Campanelli, P. (1998). The relative impact of interviewer effects and sample design effects on survey precision. *Journal of the Royal Statistical Society, A, 161*, 63–77.

O'Muircheartaigh, C., Gaskell, G., & Wright, D. B. (1995). Weighing anchors: Verbal and numeric labels for response scales. *Journal of Official Statistics, 11*, 295–307.

O'Muircheartaigh, C. A., & Wiggins, R. D. (1981). The impact of interviewer variability in an epidemiological survey. *Psychology & Medicine, 11*, 817–824.

O'Reilly, M., Ronzoni, P., & Dogra, N. (2013). *Research with children*. SAGE Publications, Inc. https://doi.org/10.4135/9781526486653

Oksenberg, L., Cannell, C. F., & Kalton, G. (1991). New strategies for pretesting survey questions. *Journal of Official Statistics, 7*, 349–365.

Olivos, F., & Liu, M. (2024). ChatGPTest: Opportunities and cautionary tales of utilizing AI for questionnaire pretesting. *arXiv*, 2405.06329. https://doi.org/10.13140/RG.2.2.20036.03200

Olson, K. (2010). An examination of questionnaire evaluation by expert reviewers. *Field Methods, 22*, 295–318.

Olson, K., & Peytchev, A. (2007). Effect of interviewer experience on interview pace and interviewer attitudes. *Public Opinion Quarterly, 71*(2), 273–286.

Olson, K., Smyth, J., & Ganshert, A. (2018). The effects of respondent and question characteristics on respondent answering behaviors in telephone interviews. *Journal of Statistics and Methodology, 3*, 361–396. https://doi.org/10.1093/jssam/smy006

Ong, A., & Weiss, D. J. (2000). The impact of anonymity on responses to sensitive questions. *Journal of Applied Social Psychology, 30*, 691–708.

Ongena, Y., & Dijkstra, W. (2006). Methods of behavior coding of survey interviews. *Journal of Official Statistics, 22*(3), 419–451.

Oyserman, D., Coon, H., & Kemmelmeier, M. (2002). Rethinking individualism and collectivism: Evaluation of theoretical assumptions and meta-analyses. *Psychological Bulletin, 128*(1), 3–72.

Paradis, C., Willners, C., & Jones, S. (2009). Good and bad opposites: Using textual and experimental techniques to measure antonym canonicity. *The Mental Lexicon, 4*, 380–429.
Pasek, J., & Krosnick, J. A. (2010). Optimizing survey questionnaire design in political science: Insights from psychology. In J. E. Leighley (Ed.), *Oxford Handbook of American elections and political behavior* (pp. 27–50). Oxford University Press.
Pederson, E., Danziger, E., Wilkins, D., Levinson, S., Kita, S., & Senft, G. (1998). Semantic typology and spatial conceptualization. *Language and Society, 74*, 557–589.
Peter, J., & Valkenburg, P. M. (2011). The impact of "forgiving" introductions on the reporting of sensitive behavior in surveys: The role of social desirability response style and developmental status. *Public Opinion Quarterly, 75*, 779–787.
Petty, R., & Cacioppo, J. (1981). *Attitudes and persuasion: Classic and contemporary approaches.* Wim. C. Brown.
Peytchev, A. (2007). *Participation decisions and measurement error in web surveys.* (doctoral dissertation). University of Michigan. https://hdl.handle.net/2027.42/96497
Peytchev, A., Conrad, F. G., Couper, M. P., & Tourangeau, R. (2010). Increasing respondents' use of definitions in web surveys. *Journal of Official Statistics, 26*(4), 633–650.
Peytchev, A., & Crawford, S. (2005). A typology of real-time validations in web-based surveys. *Social Science Computer Review, 23*(2), 235–249.
Peytcheva, E. (2019). Can the language of a survey interview influence respondent answers. In T. Johnson, B. Pennell, I. Stoop, & B. Dorer (Eds.), *Advances in comparative survey methodology*, 325–337. J. Wiley and Sons, Inc.
Peytcheva, E. (2020). The effect of language of survey administration on the response formation process. In Sha, & Gable (Eds.), *The essential role of language in survey research*, 3–21. RTI Press.
Phillips, J. M. (2021). Using examples to increase recall in self-administered questionnaires. *International Journal of Market Research, 63*(6), 738–753. https://doi.org/10.1177/14707853211052177
Pleis, J. R., Dahlhamer, J. M., & Meyer, P. S. (2006). Unfolding the answers? Income nonresponse and income brackets in the National Health Interview Survey. In *Proceedings of the section on survey research methods*. American Statistical Association.
Presser, S., & Blair, J. (1994). Survey pretesting: Do different methods produce different results? *Sociological Methodology, 24*, 73–104.
Rasinski, K. A., Visser, P. S., Zagatsky, M., & Rickett, E. M. (2004). Using implicit goal priming to improve the quality of self-report data. *Journal of Experimental Social Psychology, 41*(3), 321–327.
Read, B. (2019). Respondent burden in a Mobile App: evidence from a shopping receipt scanning study. Survey Research Methods, 13(1), 45–71. https://doi.org/10.18148/srm/2019.v1i1.7379
Redline, C., Dillman, D., Carley-Baxter, L., & Creecy, R. (2005). Factors that influence reading and comprehension of branching instructions if self-administered questionnaires. *Allgemeines Statistiches Archiv (Journal of the German Statistical Society), 89*(1), 21–28.
Redline, C., Dillman, D., Dajani, A., & Scaggs, M. (2003). Improving navigational performance in U.S. Census 2000 by altering the visual administered languages of branching instructions. *Journal of Official Statistics, 19*, 403–419.
Redline, C. D. (2013). Clarifying categorical concepts in a web survey. *Public Opinion Quarterly, 77*(S1), 89–105.
Redline, C. D., Dillman, D. A., Dajani, A., & Scaggs, M. A. (2003). Improving navigational performance in U.S. Census 2000 by altering the visually administered languages of branching instructions. *Journal of Official Statistics, 19*(4), 403–419.
Reeve, B. B., & Fayers, P. (2005). Applying item response theory modeling for evaluating questionnaire item and scale properties. In P. Fayers, & R. D. Hays (Eds.), *Assessing quality of life in clinical trials: Methods of practice* (2nd ed., pp. 53–73). Oxford University Press.
Reiser, B., Black, J., & Abelson, R. (1985). Knowledge structures in the organization and retrieval of autobiographical memories. *Cognitive Psychology, 17*, 89–137.
Revilla, M., & Couper, M. P. (2018). Comparing grids with vertical and horizontal item-by-item formats for PCs and smartphones. *Social Science Computer Review, 36*, 349–368.
Revilla, M., Couper, M. P., Bosch, O. J., & Asensio, M. (2020). Testing the use of voice input in a smartphone web survey. *Social Science Computer Review, 38*(2), 207–224. https://doi.org/10.1177/0894439318810715
Revilla, M., & Ochoa, C. (2015). Quality of different scales in an online survey in Mexico and Colombia. *Journal of Politics in Latin America, 7*, 157–177.

Revilla, M. A., Saris, W. E., & Krosnick, J. A. (2014). Choosing the number of categories in agree–disagree scales. *Sociological Methods & Research*, *43*, 73–97.

Rice, S. (1929). Contagious bias in the interview: A methodological note. *American Journal of Sociology*, *35*, 420–423.

Roberts, J. K., Pavlakis, A. E., & Richards, M. P. (2021). It's more complicated than it seems: Virtual qualitative research in the COVID-19 era. *International Journal of Qualitative Methods*. https://doi.org/10.1177/16094069211002959

Rosch, E. H. (1978). Principles of categorization. In E. Rosch, & B. Lloyd (Eds.), *Principles of categorization* (pp. b27–48). Erlbaum.

Ross, M. (1989). Relation of implicit theories to the construction of personal histories. *Psychological Review*, *96*(2), 341–357.

Ross, M., Xun, W. Q. E., & Wilson, A. (2002). Language and the bicultural self. *Personality and Social Psychology Bulletin*, *28*(8), 1040–1050.

Rothgeb, J., Willis, G., & Forsyth, B. (2001). Questionnaire pretesting methods: Do different techniques and different organizations produce similar results. In *Proceedings of the section on survey methods*. American Statistical Association.

Rubin, J., & Chisnell, D. (2008). *Handbook of usability testing: How to plan, design, and conduct effective tests*. Wiley.

Rugg, D. (1941). Experiments in wording questions II. *Public Opinion Quarterly*, *5*, 91–92.

Salthouse, T. A., & Babcock, R. L. (1991). Decomposing adult age differences in working memory. *Developmental Psychology*, *27*, 763–776.

Sanbonmatsu, D., & Fazio, R. (1990). The role of attitudes in memory-based decision making. *Journal of Personality and Social Psychology*, *59*(4).

Saris, W., & Gallhofer, I. (2007). *Design, evaluation, and analysis of questionnaires for survey research*. John Wiley.

Saris, W., Revilla, M., Krosnick, J. A., & Shaeffer, E. M. (2010). Comparing questions with agree/disagree response options to questions with item-specific response options. *Survey Research Methods*, *4*(1), 61–79. https://doi.org/10.18148/srm/2010.v4i1.2682

Saris, W., Satorra, A., & Coenders, G. (2004). A new approach to evaluating the quality of measurement instruments: The split-ballot MTMM design. *Sociological Methodology*, *34*, 311–347.

Saris, W. E., & Gallhofer, I. N. (2014). *Design, evaluation, and analysis of questionnaires for survey research* (2nd ed.). John Wiley and Sons, Inc.

Schaeffer, N. C. (1991). Hardly ever or constantly? Group comparisons using vague quantifiers. *Public Opinion Quarterly*, *55*, 395–423.

Schaeffer, N. C., & Dykema, J. (2020). Advances in the science of asking questions. *Annual Review of Sociology*, *46*(1), 37–60. https://doi.org/10.1146/annurev-soc-121919-054544.

Schaeffer, N. C., & Maynard, D. W. (1996). From paradigm to prototype and back again: Interactive aspects of cognitive processing in standardized survey interviews. In N. Schwarz, & S. Sudman (Eds.), *Answering questions: Methodology for determining cognitive and communicative processes in survey research* (pp. 65–88). Jossey-Bass.

Schaeffer, N. C., & Presser, S. (2003). The science of asking questions. *Annual Review of Sociology*, *29*, 65–88.

Schaeffer, N. C., & Thomson, E. (1992). The discovery of grounded uncertainty: Developing standardized questions about strength of fertility motivation. In P. V. Marsden (Ed.), *Sociological methodology* (Vol. 22, pp. 37–82). Basil Blackwell.

Schnell, R. (1997). Nonresponse in bevolkerungsumfragen. Opladen: Leske + Budrich. (In German).

Schnell, R., & Kreuter, F. (2005). Separating interviewer and sampling-point effects. *Journal of Official Statistics*, *21*(3), 389–410.

Schober, M. F., & Conrad, F. G. (1997). Does conversational interviewing reduce survey measurement error? *Public Opinion Quarterly*, *61*, 576–602.

Schober, M. F., Conrad, F. G., & Fricker, S. S. (2004). Misunderstanding standardized language in research interviews. *Applied Cognitive Psychology*, *18*, 169–188.

Schrauf, R. W., & Rubin, D. C. (1998). Bilingual autobiographical memory in older adult immigrants: A test of cognitive explanations of the reminiscence bump and the linguistic encoding of memories. *Journal of Memory and Language*, *39*, 437–457.

Schrauf, R. W., & Rubin, D. C. (2000). Internal languages of retrieval: The bilingual encoding of memories for the personal past. *Memory and Cognition*, *28*, 616–623.

Schudson, Z. C., Beischel, W. J., & van Anders, S. M. (2019). Individual variation in gender/sex category definitions. *Psychology of Sexual Orientation and Gender Diversity, 6*(4), 448–460. https://doi.org/10.1037/sgd0000346.

Schuman, H., & Ludwig, J. (1983). The norm of even-handedness in surveys as in life. *American Sociological Review, 48*(1).

Schuman, H., & Presser, S. (1981). *Questions and answers in attitude surveys: Experiments on question form, wording, and context.* Academic Press.

Schwarz, N. (1990). Assessing frequency reports of mundane behaviors: Contributions of cognitive psychology to questionnaire construction. In C. Hendrick, & M. Clark (Eds.), *Research methods in personality and social psychology* (pp. 98–119). Sage.

Schwarz, N. (2003). Culture-sensitive context effects: A challenge for cross-cultural surveys. In F. Harkness, J. R. Van de Vijver, & P. Mohler (Eds.), *Cross-cultural survey methods.* John Wiley and Sons.

Schwarz, N., & Bienias, J. (1990). What mediates the impact of response alternatives on frequency reports of mundane behaviors? *Applied Cognitive Psychology.*

Schwarz, N., Grayson, C. E., & Knäuper, B. (1998). Formal features of rating scales and the interpretation of question meaning. *International Journal of Public Opinion Research, 10,* 177–183.

Schwarz, N., Hippler, H., Deutsch, B., & Strack, F. (1985). Response categories: Effects on behavior reports and comparative judgement. *Public Opinion Quarterly, 49,* 388–395.

Schwarz, N., Knäuper, B., Hippler, H. J., Noelle-Neumann, E., & Clark, F. (1991a). Rating scales: Numeric values may change the meaning of scale labels. *Public Opinion Quarterly, 55,* 570–582.

Schwarz, N., Munkel, T., & Hippler, H. (1990). What determines a "perspective"? Contrast effects as a function of the dimension tapped by preceding questions. *European Journal of Social Psychology, 20,* 357–361.

Schwarz, N., Oyserman, D., & Peytcheva, E. (2010). Cognition, communication, and culture: Implications for the survey response process. In J. Harkness, et al. (Eds.), *Survey methods in multinational, multiregional, and multicultural contexts.* Wiley and Sons, Inc.

Schwarz, N., Park, D., Knäuper, B., & Sudman, S. (Eds.) (1999). *Cognition, aging, and self-reports.* Psychology Press.

Schwarz, N., Strack, F., & Mai, H. P. (1991b). Assimilation and contrast effects in part–whole question sequences: A conversational logic analysis. *Public Opinion Quarterly, 55,* 3–23.

Scott, J. (1997). Children as respondents: Methods for improving data quality. In L. Lyberg, P. Biemer, M. Collins, E. De Leeuw, C. Dippo, N. Schwarz, & D. Trewin (Eds.), *Survey measurement and process quality.* https://doi.org/10.1002/9781118490013.ch14

Sharp, L. M., & Frankel, J. (1983). Respondent burden: A test of some common assumptions. *Public Opinion Quarterly, 47,* 36–53, https://doi.org/10.1086/268765

Shepperd, J. A., Pogge, G., Hunleth, J. M., Ruiz, S., & Waters, E. A. (2021). Guidelines for conducting virtual cognitive interviews during a pandemic. *Journal of Medical Internet Research, 23*(3), e25173. https://doi.org/10.2196/25173

Sischka, P. E., Décieux, J. P., Mergener, A., Neufang, K. M., & Schmidt, A. F. (2022). The impact of forced answering and reactance on answering behavior in online surveys. *Social Science Computer Review, 40*(2), 405–425. https://doi.org/10.1177/0894439320907067

Sloutsky, V. M. (2003). The role of similarity in the development of categorization. *Trends in Cognitive Sciences, 7,* 246–251.

Smith, A. F., & Jobe, J. B. (1994). Validity of reports of long-term memory of dietary memories: Data and a model. In N. Schwarz, & S. Sudman (Eds.), *Autobiographical memories and the validity of retrospective reports* (pp. 121–140). Springer-Verlag.

Smith, B., Clifford, S., & Jerit, J. (2020). TRENDS: How Internet search undermines the validity of political knowledge measures, *Political Research Quarterly, 73,* 141–155, https://doi.org/10.1177/1065912919882101

Smith, T. W. (1993). *Little things matter: A sampler of how differences in questionnaire format can affect survey responses.* GSS Methodological Report no. 78. National Opinion Research Center.

Smyth, J. D., Christian, L. M., & Dillman, D. A. (2008). Does "yes or no" on the telephone mean the same as "check-all-that-apply" on the web? *Public Opinion Quarterly, 72*(1), 103–113. https://doi.org/10.1093/poq/nfn005

Smyth, J. D., Dillman, D. A., Christian, L. M., & Mcbride, M. (2009). Open-ended questions in web surveys: Can increasing the size of answer boxes and providing extra verbal instructions improve response quality? *Public Opinion Quarterly*, *73*(2), 325–337. https://doi.org/10.1093/poq/nfp029

Smyth, J. D., Dillman, D. A., Christian, L. M., & Stern, M. J. (2006). Comparing check-all and forced-choice question formats in web surveys. *Public Opinion Quarterly*, *70*(1), 66–77. https://doi.org/10.1093/poq/nfj007

Social Science Research Council (1975). *Basic background items for U.S. Household surveys*. Center for Coordination of Research Social Indicators, Social Science Research Council.

Solomon, S. (1978). Measuring dispositional and situational attributions. *Personality and Social Psychology Bulletin*, *4*, 589–594.

Stening, B. W., & Everett, J. E. (1984). Response styles in cross-cultural managerial study. *Journal of Social Psychology*, *122*, 151–156.

Strack, F., Martin, L. L., & Schwarz, N. (1988). Priming and communication: Social determinants of information use in judgments of life satisfaction. *European Journal of Social Psychology*, *18*(5), 429–442. https://doi.org/10.1002/ejsp.2420180505

Strack, F., Schwarz, N., & Wänke, M. (1991). Semantic and pragmatic aspects of context effects in social and psychological research. *Social Cognition*, *9*, 111–125.

Sturgis, P., Roberts, C., & Smith, P. (2014). Middle alternatives revisited: How the neither/nor response acts as a way of saying "I don't know"? *Sociological Methods & Research*, *43*, 15–38.

Sudman, S., & Bradburn, N. (1973). Effects of time and memory factors on response in surveys. *Journal of the American Statistical Association*, *68*, 805–815.

Sudman, S., & Bradburn, N. M. (1982). *Asking questions: A practical guide to questionnaire design* (p. 89). Jossey-Bass.

Sudman, S., Bradburn, N. M., & Schwarz, N. (1996). *Thinking about answers: The application of cognitive processes to survey methodology*. Jossey-Bass.

Sudman, S., Finn, A., & Lannom, L. (1984). The use of bounded recall procedures in single interviews. *Public Opinion Quarterly*, *48*, 520–524.

Suessbrick, A. L., Schober, M. F., & Conrad, F. G. (2000). Different respondents interpret ordinary questions quite differently. *Proceedings of the American Statistical Association, section on survey research methods*. American Statistical Association.

Sun, H., & Yan, T. (2023). Applying machine learning to the evaluation of interviewer performance. *Survey Practice*, *16*(1). https://doi.org/10.29115/SP-2023-0007

Survey Research Center. (2016). *Guidelines for best practice in cross-cultural surveys*. Survey Research Center, Institute for Social Research, University of Michigan. Available at http://www.ccsg.isr.umich.edu/

Tao, R., Yang, R., Walejko, G., Yang, Y., & Groenhout, B. (2024). *Using large language models (LLM) to pretest survey questions*. Paper presented at the Annual Conference of American Association for Public Opinion Research. Atlanta, GA.

Thompson, C. P., Skowronski, J., Larsen, S., & Betz, A. L. (1996). *Autobiographical memory*. Erlbaum.

Toepoel, V., Das, M., & Van Soest, A. (2009). Design of web questionnaires: The effects of the number of items per screen. *Field Methods*, *21*(2), 200–213. https://doi.org/10.1177/1525822x08330261

Toepoel, V., & Dillman, D. A. (2011). Words, numbers, and visual heuristics in web surveys: Is there a hierarchy of importance? *Social Science Computer Review*, *29*(2), 193–207. https://doi.org/10.1177/0894439310370070

Toepoel, V., & Lugtig, P. (2014). What happens if you offer a mobile option to your web panel? Evidence for a probability-based panel of internet users. *Social Science Computer Review*, *32*, 544–560.

Toepoel, V., & Lugtig, P. (2022). Modularization in an era of mobile web: Investigating the effects of cutting a survey into smaller pieces on data quality. *Social Science Computer Review*, *40*(1), 150–164. https://doi.org/10.1177/0894439318784882

Toninelli, D., & Revilla, M. (2020). How mobile device screen size affects data collected in web surveys. In P. Beatty, D. Collins, L. Kaye, J.L. Padilla, G. Willis, & A. Wilmot (Eds.), *Advances in questionnaire design, development, evaluation and testing*. https://doi.org/10.1002/9781119263685.ch14

Tourangeau, R. (1984). Cognitive science and survey methods: A cognitive perspective. In T. B. Jabine, M. L. Straf, J. M. Tanur, & R. Tourangeau (Eds.), *Cognitive aspects of survey methodology: Building a bridge between disciplines* (pp. 73–100). National Academy Press.

Tourangeau, R. (2004). Experimental design considerations for testing and evaluating questionnaires. In S. Presser, J.M. Rothgeb, M.P. Couper, et al. (Eds.), *Methods for testing and evaluating survey questionnaires* (pp. 209–224). Wiley.

Tourangeau, R. (2017). Mixing modes: Tradeoffs among coverage, nonresponse, and measurement error. In P. Biemer, E. D. de Leeuw, & S. Eckman (Eds.), *Total survey error in practice* (pp. 115–132). John Wiley & Sons.

Tourangeau, R. (2018). The survey response process from a cognitive viewpoint. *Quality Assurance in Education, 26*, 169–181.

Tourangeau, R. (2021). Survey reliability: Models, methods, and findings. *Journal of Survey Statistics and Methodology, 9*(5), 961–991.

Tourangeau, R., & Bradburn, N. (2010). The psychology of survey response. In J. D. Wright, & P. V. Marsden (Eds.), *Handbook of survey research* (2nd ed., pp. 315–346). Elsevier.

Tourangeau, R., Conrad, F. G., & Couper, M. P. (2013). *The science of web surveys*. Oxford University Press.

Tourangeau, R., Conrad, F. G., Couper, M. P., & Ye, C. (2014). The effects of providing examples in survey questions. *Public Opinion Quarterly, 78*(1), 100–125.

Tourangeau, R., Couper, M. P., & Conrad, F. (2004). Spacing, position, and order. Interpretive heuristics for visual features of survey questions. *Public Opinion Quarterly, 68*, 368–393.

Tourangeau, R., Couper, M. P., & Conrad, F. (2007). Color, labels, and interpretive heuristics for response scales. *Public Opinion Quarterly, 71*(1), 91–112. https://doi.org/10.1093/poq/nfl046

Tourangeau, R., Couper, M. P., & Steiger, D. M. (2003). Humanizing self-administered surveys: Experiments on social presence in web and IVR surveys. *Computers in Human Behavior, 19*, 1–24.

Tourangeau, R., Maitland, A., Rivero, G., Sun, H., Williams, D., & Yan, T. (2017). Web surveys by smartphone and tablets: Effects on survey responses. *Public Opinion Quarterly, 81*, 896–929. https://doi.org/10.1093/poq/nfx035

Tourangeau, R., Maitland, A., Steiger, D., & Yan, T. (2020a). A framework for making decisions about question evaluation methods. In P. Beatty, D. Collins, L. Kaye, J. Padilla, G. Willis, & A. Wilmot (Eds.), *Advances in questionnaire design, development, evaluation and testing* (pp. 47–73). Wiley.

Tourangeau, R., Rasinski, K., Bradburn, N., & D'Andrade, R. (1989a). Carry-over effects in attitude surveys. *Public Opinion Quarterly, 53*, 495–524.

Tourangeau, R., Rasinski, K., Bradburn, N., & D'Andrade, R. (1989b). Belief accessibility and context effects in attitude measures. *Journal of Experimental Psychology, 25*, 401–421.

Tourangeau, R., & Rasinski, K. A. (1988). Cognitive processes underlying context effects in attitude measurement. *Psychological Bulletin, 103*(3), 299–314.

Tourangeau, R., Rasinski, K. A., & Bradburn, N. (1991a). Measuring happiness in surveys: A test of the subtraction hypothesis. *Public Opinion Quarterly, 55*, 255–266.

Tourangeau, R., Rasinski, K. A., & D'Andrade, R. (1991b). Attitude structure and belief accessibility. *Journal of Experimental Social Psychology, 27*(1), 48–75.

Tourangeau, R., Rips, L., & Rasinski, K. (2000). *The psychology of survey response*. Cambridge University Press.

Tourangeau, R., & Smith, T. W. (1996). Asking sensitive questions: The impact of data collection mode, question format, and question context. *Public Opinion Quarterly, 60*(2), 275–304. https://doi.org/10.1086/297751

Tourangeau, R., Smith, T. W., & Rasinski, K. (1997). Motivation to report sensitive behaviors in surveys: Evidence from a bogus pipeline experiment. *Journal of Applied Social Psychology, 27*, 209–222.

Tourangeau, R., Sun, H., & Yan, T. (2021). Comparing methods for assessing reliability. *Journal of Survey Statistics and Methodology, 9*, 651–673. https://doi.org/10.1093/jssam/smaa018

Tourangeau, R., Sun, H., Yan, T., Maitland, A., Rivero, G., & Williams, D. (2018). Web surveys by smartphones and tablets: Effects on data quality. *Social Science Computer Review, 36*(5), 542–556. https://doi.org/10.1177/0894439317719438

Tourangeau, R., & Yan, T. (2007). Sensitive questions in surveys. *Psychological Bulletin, 133*, 859–883.

Tourangeau, R., Yan, T., & Sun, H. (2020b). Who can you count on? Understanding the determinants of reliability. *Journal of Survey Statistics and Methodology, 8*, 903–931. https://doi.org/10.1093/jssam/smz034

Tourangeau, R., Yan, T., Sun, H., Hyland, A., & Santon, C. A. (2019). The population assessment of tobacco and health (PATH) reliability and validitiy study: Selected reliability and validity estimates. *Tobacco Control, 28*, 663–668. https://doi.org/10.1136/tobaccocontrol-2018-054561

Trafimow, D., Silverman, E. S., Fan, R. M. T., & Law, J. S. F. (1997). The effect of language and priming on the relative accessibility of the private self and the collective self. *Journal of Cross-Cultural Psychology, 28*, 107–123.

Trappmann, M., Krumpal, I., Kirchner, A., & Jann, B. (2014). Item sum: A new technique for asking quantitative sensitive questions. *Journal of Survey Statistics and Methodology, 2*, 58–77.

Triandis, H. C., Davis, E. E., Vassiliou, V., & Nassiakou, M. (1965). *Some methodological problems concerning research on negotiations between monolinguals*. University of Illinois.

Tucker, C. (1983). Interviewer effects in telephone surveys. *Public Opinion Quarterly, 47*, 84–95.

Tullis, T., Flieschman, S., McNulty, M., Cianchette, C., & Bergel, M. (2002). *An empirical comparison of lab and remote usability testing of web sites*. In Proceedings of the usability professionals' association conference. Orlando, FL.

Tulving, E. (1983). *Elements of episodic memory*. Oxford University Press.

Turner, C. F., Lessler, J., & Devore, J. (1992). Effects of mode of administration and wording on reporting of drug use. In C. Turner, J. Lesser, & J. Gfroerer (Eds.), *Survey measurement of drug use: Methodological studies*. DHHS Publication (ADM) 92-1929. Government Printing Office.

Van der Linden, W., & Hambleton, R. (1997). *Handbook of modern item response theory*. Springer-Verlag.

Van Vaerenbergh, Y., & Thomas, T. D. (2013). Response styles in survey research: A literature review of antecedents, consequences, and remedies. *International Journal of Public Opinion Research, 25*(2), 195–217.

Vehovar, V., Couper, M. P., & Čehovin, G. (2022). Alternative layouts for grid questions in PC and mobile web surveys: An experimental evaluation using response quality indicators and survey estimates. *Social Science Computer Review*. https://doi.org/10.1177/08944393221132644

Villar, A., Callegaro, M., & Yang, Y. (2013). Where am i? A meta-analysis of experiments on the effects of progress indicators for web surveys. *Social Science Computer Review, 31*(6), 744–762. https://doi.org/10.1177/0894439313497468

Wagenaar, W. A. (1986). My memory: A study of autobiographical memory over six years. *Cognitive Psychology, 18*, 225–252.

Wang, K. (2010). Effects of unfolding brackets on the quality of income data in a telephone survey. *Survey Practice, 3*(3).

Wang, R., & Krosnick, J. A. (2019). Middle alternatives and measurement validity: A recommendation for survey researchers. *International Journal of Social Research Methodology, 23*, 169–184.

Warner, S. (1965). Randomized response: A survey technique for eliminating evasive answer bias. *Journal of the American Statistical Association, 60*, 63–69.

Wassmann, J., & Dasen, P. R. (1998). Balinese spatial orientation: Some empirical evidence of moderate linguistic relativity. *Journal of the Royal Anthropological Institute, 4*, 689–711.

Watson, J. B. (1925). *Behaviorism*. W.W. Norton.

Weiss, C. (1968). Validity of welfare mothers' interview responses. *Public Opinion Quarterly, 32*, 622–633.

Wells, T., & DiSogra, C. (2011). How the order of response options in a running tally can affect online survey estimates. *Survey Practice, 4*(5). https://doi.org/10.29115/SP-2011-0025.

West, B. T., & Blom, A. G. (2017). Explaining interviewer effects: A research synthesis. *Journal of Survey Statistics and Methodology, 5*, 175–211.

West, B. T., & Peytcheva, E. (2014). Can interviewer behaviors during ACASI affect data quality? *Survey Practice, 7*(5). https://doi.org/10.29115/SP-2014-0023

West, B. T., Yan, T., Kreuter, F., Josten, M., & Schroeder, H. (2020). Examining the utility of interviewer observations on the survey response process. In K. Olson, J. Smyth, J. Dykema, A. Holbrook, F. Kreuter, & B. T. West (Eds.), *Interviewer effects from a total survey error perspective* (pp. 106–119). CRC Press.

Whorf, B. L. (1956). *Language, thought, and reality: Selected writings of Benjamin Lee Whorf*. Wiley.
Wiley, D. E., & Wiley, J. A. (1970). The estimation of measurement error in panel data. *American Sociological Review, 35*, 112–117.
Williams, D., & Brick, J. M. (2018). Trends in U.S. Face-to-Face household survey nonresponse and level of effort. *Journal of Survey Statistics and Methodology, 6*(2), 186–211. https://doi.org/10.1093/jssam/smx019
Williams, M. D., & Hollan, J. D. (1981). The process of retrieval from very long-term memory. *Cognitive Science, 5*, 87–119.
Willis, G. B. (2005). *Cognitive interviewing: A tool for improving questionnaire design*. Sage.
Willis, G. B. (2015). *Analysis of the cognitive interview in questionnaire design*. Sage.
Willis, G. B., & Lessler, J. (1999). *The BRFSS-QAS: A guide for systematically evaluating survey question wording*. Research Triangle Institute.
Willis, G. B., Schechter, S., & Whitaker, K. (1999). A comparison of cognitive interviewing, expert review, and behavior coding: What do they tell us? In *Proceedings of the ASA section on survey research methods*. American Statistical Association.
Wilson, T. D., & Hodges, S. D. (1992). Attitudes as temporary constructions. In L. L. Martin, & A. Tesser (Eds.), *The construction of social judgments* (pp. 37–65). Lawrence Erlbaum Associates, Inc.
Yan, T. (2006). How successful i am depends on what number i get: The effects of numerical scale labels and the need for cognition on survey responses. In *JSM, proceedings of the survey research methods section*. American Statistical Association, pp. 4262–4269.
Yan, T. (2021). Consequences of asking sensitive questions. *Annual Review of Statistics and Its Application, 8*, 109–127. https://doi.org/10.1146/annurev-statistics-040720-033353
Yan, T. (2023). Which scale direction is more difficult for respondents to use? An eye-tracking study. *Survey Practice, 16*(1). https://doi.org/10.29115/SP-2023-0015
Yan, T., & Cantor, D. (2019). Asking survey questions about criminal justice involvement. *Public Health Reports, 134*, 46s–56s. https://doi.org/10.1177/0033354919826566
Yan, T., Conrad, F., Tourangeau, R., & Couper, M. (2011). Should I stay or should I go: The effects of progress feedback, promised task duration, and length of questionnaire on completing web surveys. *International Journal of Public Opinion Research, 23*, 131–147. https://doi.org/10.1093/ijpor/edq046
Yan, T., Curtin, R., & Jans, M. (2010). Trends in income nonresponse over two decades. *Journal of Official Statistics, 26*, 145–164.
Yan, T., Fricker, S., & Tsai, S. (2020). Response burden: What is it and what predicts it? In P. Beatty, D. Collins, L. Kaye, J. Padilla, G. Willis, & A. Wilmot (Eds.), *Advances in questionnaire design, development, evaluation and testing* (pp. 193–212). Wiley.
Yan, T., & Keusch, F. (2015). The effects of the direction of rating scales on survey responses in a telephone survey. *Public Opinion Quarterly, 79*, 145–165. https://doi.org/10.1093/poq/nfu062
Yan, T., Keusch, F., & He, L. (2018). The impact of question and scale characteristics on scale direction effects. *Survey Practice*. https://doi.org/10.29115/SP-2018-0008
Yan, T., Kreuter, F., & Tourangeau, R. (2012a). Evaluating survey questions: A comparison of methods. *Journal of Official Statistics, 28*, 503–529.
Yan, T., Kreuter, F., & Tourangeau, R. (2012b). Latent class analysis of response inconsistencies across modes of data collection. *Social Science Research, 41*, 1017–1027.
Yan, T., & Machado, J. (2023). Review of food diaries used to collect food acquisition data. *Survey Methods: Insights from the Field. Special issue: Food Acquisition Research and Methods*. https://surveyinsights.org/?p=17458
Yan, T., Machado, J., Heller, A., Bonilla, E., Maitland, A., & Kirlin, J. (2017). *The feasibility of using smartphones to record food purchase and acquisition*. Paper presented at the Annual Conference of the American Association for Public Opinion Research.
Yan, T., & Olson, K. (2013). Analyzing paradata to investigate measurement error. In F. Kreuter (Ed.), *Improving surveys with paradata: Analytic use of process information* (pp. 73–96). Wiley and Sons.
Yan, T., Ryan, L., Becker, S., & Smith, J. (2015). Assessing quality of answers to a global subjective well-being question through response times. *Survey Research Methods, 9*, 101–109.
Yan, T., Simas, M., & Page, E. (2024). *Did you use our app diary? The experience of FoodAPS field test*. Paper presented at the 5th Mobile Apps and Sensors in Surveys (MASS) Workshop. Washington, DC.
Yan, T., & Sun, H. (2022). *Comparing methods for assessing reliability*. Short course for annual conference of American Association of Public Opinion Research. Virtual short course.

Yan, T., Sun, H., & Battalahalli, A. (2024). Applying machine learning to survey question assessment. *Survey Practice, 17*(May). https://doi.org/10.29115/SP-2024-0006.

Yan, T., & Tourangeau, R. (2008). Fast times and easy questions: The effects of age, experience, and question complexity on web survey response times. *Applied Cognitive Psychology, 22*, 51–68. https://doi.org/10.1002/acp.1331

Yan, T., & Tourangeau, R. (2022). Detecting underreporters of abortions and miscarriages in the national study of family growth, 2011–2015. *PLoS One, 17*, e0271288.

Yang, M., & Yu, Y. (2011). Effects of identifiers in mail surveys. *Field Methods, 23*, 224–265.

Yang, X., Yan, T., Steiger, D., Caporaso, A., & Kokoska, A. (2021). *Lessons learnt from conducting online one-on-more qualitative interviews during the pandemic*. Paper presented at the annual conference of American Associations of Public Opinion Research.

Zaller, J. R. (1992). *The nature and origins of mass opinion*. Cambridge University Press.

Zax, M., & Takahashi, S. (1967). Cultural influences on response style: Comparison of Japanese and American college students. *Journal of Social Psychology, 71*, 3–10.

Zeglovitis, E., & Kritzinger, S. (2014). New attempts to reduce overreporting of voter turnout and their effects. *International Journal of Public Opinion Research, 26*, 224–234.

# Index

acquiescence 8, 17, 32, 34, 35, 82, 86, 99, 102n2
adapting 101–102
adjustment error 6
adopting 99, 101–102
Alwin, Duane 16, 33, 125
American Community Survey (ACS) 36, 66, 67, 85
American National Election Study (ANES) 36
anonymity 49–50, 54, 57
Antoun, Christopher 82–83
artificial intelligence (AI) 9, 134
assimilation effect 29, 35, 74
attitude(s) 10, 15–16, 26–33, 35, 48, 53, 105, 115, 121, 125
attitudinal questions 4, 19, 42; see also attitude
audio computer-assisted self-interviewing (ACASI) 7, 49, 85
auto-advancing 72
autobiographical events 19

backward telescoping see telescoping
behavior coding 9, 101, 120, 123–124, 128, 131, 133, 136
behavioral questions 4, 13, 19, 24–26
belief sampling model 27–28, 31, 35
Belson, William 12, 31
bias 7–8, 24, 31, 34, 49–50, 52, 86, 91, 100, 107, 114, 115, 127, 137
bipolar scale(s) 31–33, 56
bogus pipeline 52, 57
Bosch, Orio 78, 83
bottom-up strategy 15, 24–25, 27, 60
bounded recall 23
Bradburn, Norman 7, 11, 15, 17, 20, 23, 43, 48, 49, 50, 52
branching 33, 70
breakoff(s) 52, 78–79, 81–82, 88

Cannell, Charles 20, 23, 50, 51, 123
Cantor, David 16, 47, 49, 54
check box(es) 62, 71, 74–76, 130, 132
check-all-that-apply 72, 76, 89

choice design 85–86
choice+ 86
Christian, Leah 70, 76, 81, 89, 130
closed questions 4–5, 16, 43, 74, 90
closing screen 81
codability 97, 99
cognitive interview 9, 48, 101, 106–112, 114, 117–121, 124, 131–133
cognitive probe 108, 112, 120
collectivist culture 94, 99
combo box 76
committee approach 101
comprehension 10–12, 28, 31, 54, 59, 64, 92, 96–97, 102, 107–109, 111, 116, 120, 129, 132, 134; see also survey response model
computerization 69, 87
concurrent approach 107–108
Conrad, Frederick 13, 73, 78, 80, 108
construct validity 126
construct-specific question 35
Consumer Expenditure Surveys (CE) 10
contact mode 87
context effect(s) 7–8, 14, 28–29, 31, 35, 59, 65, 74, 95, 116
contrast effect(s) 16, 29–30, 35, 74
convenience sample 108–109
Cooperative Principle 13
coverage 9, 35, 110
coverage error 6, 85
Couper, Mick 16, 70, 73, 74, 76, 78, 79, 82, 83, 87, 89, 129, 131
cross-wise model 55
cultural frame switching 97
culture(s) 8–9, 37, 48, 59–60, 94–102, 115

data quality 33, 35, 69, 72–73, 79–80, 110, 114, 124
decennial census 36–37, 48, 66
decomposition 20–21
de Leeuw, Edith 56, 57, 59, 79, 80, 85, 86, 87, 88, 92
DeMaio, Theresa 47, 59, 107
demographic question(s) 36–37, 43, 57, 64

diary 20, 22, 49–50, 57, 83
Dillman, Don 21, 59, 60, 61, 62, 64, 66, 70, 78, 79, 81, 83, 85, 87, 88, 89, 90, 91, 92, 93
disclosure 5, 16, 48–50, 52, 57
Don't Know 4, 33, 37–38, 43, 56, 61, 78–79, 87–88
double-barreled 11–12, 18, 115
double-negative 11–12
drag-and-drop 77–78
drop box 74, 76
Dykema, Jennifer 33, 73, 89, 115, 117, 118

episodic memory 19
error of commission 59, 62
error of omission 59, 62
estimation 8, 10, 15–17, 24–25, 97, 108–109
estimation strategy 24–25; *see also* estimation
ethnicity 4, 36–37, 38–39, 106
event history calendar 21, 78
expert methods 113, 119
expert review 9, 113–118, 124
extreme response style 17
eye-tracking 11, 70, 105, 111–112

face-to-face 49, 51, 85–86, 89, 92–93
factual questions 4, 26, 36, 87, 117, 124
field-coded question(s) 5, 89–90
fixation count 111
fixation duration 111
focus group 9, 101, 105–112
forgetting 13, 22–23
forgiving introductions 53
forward telescoping *see* telescoping
Fowler, Floyd 20, 121, 123
full filter 34, 42

Galesic, Mirta 13, 16, 24
Geisen, Emily 70, 121, 129, 132
gender 4, 7, 36–38, 86, 101
General Social Survey (GSS) 35–36, 125
Gestalt grouping priciples 60
Grice, H. P. 13
grid 9n3, 56, 65, 72–73, 78, 82, 88, 91
gross discrepancy rate 124
Groves, Robert 3, 5, 7
Gummer, Tobias 42, 82

Health Information National Trends Survey (HINTS) 67, 86
heuristics 70, 83, 130
Hippler, Hans-Jürgen 34
Höhne, Jan 17, 70, 79, 83
Holbrook, Allyson 16, 54, 56
Holtgraves, Thomas 47, 53
honesty pledge 50
Hox, Joop 56, 86, 87, 92

image 16, 74, 134
impression-based 15, 24, 27
income 36, 41–42, 47–48, 54, 58, 92, 106, 137
index of inconsistency 124
indirect questions 54
individualist culture 94, 102
input field 71, 74–75, 76,78–79
instructions 24, 50–51, 53, 57, 60–62, 65, 69, 76, 81, 87, 89–91, 114–115, 130–131
interactive feature 69–70, 80, 84
intervention 42, 69
interviewer debriefing 9, 120–121, 127
interviewer-respondent interaction 123, 133
intrusive 5, 36, 47, 52, 57
item count technique (ICT) 55
item nonresponse 48, 57, 59, 82, 87–88
item response theory 8, 101, 121, 127–128
item sum techniqiue 55

Jäckle, Annette 83
Ji, Li-Jun 94, 95, 97
Johnson, Timothy 48, 57, 99
judgment 10–11, 14–17, 22, 27, 29, 31, 56, 59, 92, 95, 97–98, 102, 108–109, 114, 120, 136

kappa 8, 124, 128
Keusch, Florian 17, 34, 82
Knäuper, Bärbel 29, 55, 56
knowledge questions 4, 34, 36, 42–43, 86
Kreuter, Frauke 7, 48, 121, 126
Krosnick, Jon 11, 16, 17, 33, 54
Kunz, Tanja 42, 78

landmark events 14, 20–21, 23
language-dependent recall 97
large language models (LLMs) 134
latent class analysis 125
layout 7, 14, 16–17, 60–61, 68, 70, 79, 129
Lenzner, Timothy 17, 79
linguistic determinism 95–96
linguistic relativity 95
Liu, Mingnan 34, 78, 86
Loftus, Elizabeth 23, 107
long-term memory 10, 13–15, 19

machine learning (ML) 9, 135
mail survey 49, 59, 61, 87–88, 122
Maitland, Aaron 56, 105, 114, 115, 117, 118, 124, 128
mapping 13, 16, 30–31, 56, 92, 99, 120
Marlowe-Crowne social desirability scale 99
Marin, Gerardo 8, 99
matrix 72, 88
measurement error 4, 6–8, 34, 41, 59, 72, 84, 86–87, 130, 133

midpoint 32–33
missing data 41, 48, 54, 56, 70, 72, 78–80, 88, 127
mixed-mode survey 61, 85, 92; see also multimode survey
mobile web survey 7, 69, 83–84
mode effects 86, 92, 99
motivated misreporting 16
multimode survey 9, 85–92
multitrait-multimethod (MTMM) 117, 125

National Survey of College Graduates 61, 63
National Survey of Family Growth (NSFG) 47, 86
National Survey on Drug Use and health (NSDUH) 47
Nisbett, Richard 94
nonresponse error 6, 68, 87
numerical labels 79

Office of Management and Budget (OMB) 36
O'Muircheartaigh, Colm 7, 31
Olson, Kristen 7, 56, 86, 114, 117, 122
on-the-fly translation 100
open-ended questions 4, 25, 28, 43, 62, 72, 76, 78
optimizing 9, 82
overreporting 7, 24
over-time correlations 125
Oyserman, Daphna 94

page layout 60, 70
paging design 71–72
paper survey 7, 9, 17, 59, 69–70, 78, 123
paper-and-pencil 49, 129; see also paper survey
paradata 42, 81–82, 92, 122
Peytchev, Andy 7, 24, 69, 73
Peytcheva, Emilia 7, 8, 49
pilot test 120, 128
Population Assessment of Tobacco and Heatlh (PATH) 49, 52
processing error 6
positivity bias 31
pragmatic 11, 13, 96
presupposition 11–12
Presser, Stanely 17, 27, 29, 32, 33, 34, 90, 105, 107, 114, 115, 117, 118, 124, 128
pretest/pretested 9, 79, 96, 99, 101–102, 119, 124, 127–128, 131–133
primacy effects 16, 59, 79, 80
priming 14, 51, 52, 57, 96
privacy 47, 49, 51–52
probing 80, 107–109, 120–121, 123, 128
procedural memory 19
progress indicator 80
prompt 14, 69–70, 80, 89, 117, 130, 134, 136–137

pulldown menu 76
pupil dilation 111, 132

QR code 82
qualitative 36, 43, 100, 106, 109, 113–114, 120, 131
quality 5–6, 8, 13, 25, 33, 35, 56, 68, 70, 72–73, 79–80, 82–83, 101–102, 107, 110, 112–114, 117, 119, 121, 123–124, 136
quantitative 92, 100, 120, 122, 124, 127–128, 133
quasi filter 34
quasi-factual 37
quasi-simplex model 125
question balancing 31–32
question order 14, 27–31, 53, 56, 64–65, 69, 96, 115, 123
Question Understanding Aid (QUAID) 113, 116, 124
Questionnaire Appraisal System (QAS) 9, 113–114, 124
questionnaire evaluation and testing 136
quota 106, 132

race 7, 36–39, 86, 106, 125
radio button 60, 62, 71, 74–78, 130
randomized response technique (RRT) 54
randomized experiment 120–122, 128
range of response options 16–17, 56
Rasinski, Kenneth 27, 51
rate-based estimation 24
recency effects 16, 34
Redline, Cleo 62, 70, 73
reference period 10, 14, 22–25, 59, 62, 115
reliability 8, 16, 33, 35, 56, 79, 105, 115–118, 120, 124–128
remote testing 110–111
respondent debriefing 101, 121, 128
response format 74, 78, 97, 127
response latency 120, 122–123, 128
response mode 85–88, 90, 92
response option alignment 79
response order 16, 33, 69, 82
response rate 48, 85, 88
response style 17
response time 11, 24, 29, 79
retrieval 10–11, 13–15, 19–20, 23–26, 28–29, 73, 97, 102, 109, 111
reverse coding 34
Revilla, Melanie 33, 35, 79, 82, 83
running tally 15, 69, 80–81

sampling error 6
Sapir-Whorf hypothesis 95
Saris, Willem 35, 117, 125
satisficing 11, 59, 82
scale direction effects 17

scale unfolding 33; *see also* branching
Schaeffer, Nora Cate 12, 17, 33, 73, 89, 123
Schnell, Rainer 7
Schober, Michael 13, 73
Schuman, Howard 7, 27, 29, 32, 33, 34, 90
Schwarz, Norbert 7, 14, 17, 24, 25, 29, 31, 34, 55, 79, 96
scrolling design 70–71, 82
select list 76
self-report 14–16, 25, 42, 50–51, 90, 125, 132
semantic memory 19
sensitive question(s) 5, 9, 16, 47–49, 52–57, 86, 115
sequential design 85, 101
sex 36–37, 43, 106
simultaneous design 102
slider bars 77–78; *see also* visual analog scales
Smith, Tom 17, 54, 79
Smyth, Jolene 62, 89
social desirability 5, 7–8, 16, 47, 49–50, 52, 58, 86, 99, 102, 114
socially desirable responding 48–49, 51, 57, 99; *see also* social desirability
spatial frames of reference 98
speeding 69, 80
straightlining 8, 17, 59, 69, 79, 82, 88
Sudman, Seymour 10, 15, 20, 23, 27, 43
Survey Quality Predictor (SQP) 113, 117, 124
survey response model 4, 9–11, 18
Sun, Hanyu 124, 136

target population 3, 6, 9, 36, 48, 55, 106, 108–109, 111, 131–132, 136
telescoping 14, 23, 25
text area 74
text field 74, 76, 78
The National Academies of Science 37
The National Crime Victimization Survey (NCVS) 3, 21, 42

think aloud 107–108, 131
time frame 22, 52–53, 57
Toepoel, Vera 70, 72, 79, 82
top-down estimation 25
Total Survey Error 48
Tourangeau, Roger 8, 10–11, 13–17, 27–29, 47–49, 52–54, 57, 70, 72–74, 79, 82, 85–88, 105, 107, 111–114, 117–118, 122, 124–128, 130
type-ahead 76

underreporting 7, 13, 24
unfolding brackets 41, 54, 58
unified mode 87, 92
unimode 87; *see also* unified mode
unipolar scale 31–33
usability 8–9, 92, 111–112, 129–133

vague quantifier 12, 25
validity 6, 8, 16, 33, 35, 56, 105, 117, 120, 124–128
variance 7
verbal labels 17, 31, 33, 35, 77, 79
visual analog scales 77, 83; *see also* slider bars
visual design 59, 64, 68, 70, 79, 83–84, 89, 92, 115–116, 129–130
voice input 83

web probing 109, 120–121, 128
welcome screen 81
West, Brady 7, 49, 86, 121
Willis, Gordon 48, 107, 108, 109, 114, 121
working memory 10, 13–14, 28–29, 31, 35, 55–56, 116

Yan, Ting 11, 16–17, 47–50, 53–54, 56, 70, 76, 80–83, 86, 106–107, 109, 111, 114, 118, 121–126, 128, 136

Printed in the United States
by Baker & Taylor Publisher Services